Building Smart Cities

Analytics, ICT, and Design Thinking

Building Smart Cities

Analytics, ICT, and Design Thinking

Carol L. Stimmel

CRC Press
Taylor & Francis Group
Boca Raton   London   New York

CRC Press is an imprint of the
Taylor & Francis Group, an **informa** business

AN AUERBACH BOOK

CRC Press
Taylor & Francis Group
6000 Broken Sound Parkway NW, Suite 300
Boca Raton, FL 33487-2742

Printed on acid-free paper
Version Date: 20150716

International Standard Book Number-13: 978-1-4987-0276-8 (Hardback)

Visit the Taylor & Francis Web site at
http://www.taylorandfrancis.com

and the CRC Press Web site at
http://www.crcpress.com

Dedication

When I imagined this book, I thought I'd be writing it for those engineers, designers, artists, architects, city planners, and political appointees whose goal is to ensure that our urban environments are vital, serve all of us well and with justice, and are beautifully livable for generations to come.

That's still true, but there are so many other people who make *my* world a more beautifully livable place. Each of these people not only prevents my life from becoming a catalogue of fatigue and drudgery but also (either willingly or unwillingly) has become woven into the fabric of my imagination, providing me hours of delight and inspiration. Telling their stories is the way I count my blessings.

I'm crazy about all of you.

Contents

Foreword

Over twenty five years ago, when I first met and hired Carol Stimmel to work with me at the National Center for Atmospheric Research, I knew she had a gift for applying humanistic thinking to scientific problems and seeing the world in a different way. This book on designing smart cities proves that this remains true even today. Carol effectively examines the concepts of design thinking to describe a variety of human-centered processes to solve complex problems in the development of our cities as the fastest growing centers of population worldwide.

Her work highlights the fact that urban population is growing at a rapid pace and forcing our city centers to absorb the majority of this population growth. Therefore, we are at a critical juncture where we need to think about ways to create urban environments that are "productive, socially connected and economically successful." This book is appropriate for anyone who is seeking a holistic framework for applying principled thinking to some of the world's more complicated smarter cities challenges. The way Carol lays out the framework for how to think about and address these issues is compelling and fully supported by the facts that she references throughout the book.

In 2013, I had the distinct pleasure of participating in a Smarter Cities Challenge for the city of Cape Town South Africa with the Executive Mayor Alderman Patricia de Lille, as part of IBM's Executive Service Corp. The challenge was "How can the City of Cape Town effectively use and manage its social assets to optimize service delivery?" In the course of this work, I witnessed first hand how applying the design principles that Carol clearly outlines throughout the book helps address some of our most challenging smarter cities challenges. Cape Town itself is a very complex city, being home to citizens from all walks of life who are multi-cultural, multilingual, geographically dispersed, and socioeconomically diverse. I found that adopting the design thinking method that Carol describes for solving such complex city problems truly tested this often misunderstood method and helped us deliver creative solutions to the smarter city challenges with which we were grappling.

As a Distinguished Engineer and Chief Technology Office for IBM, I am a strong believer in using technology to help us solve some of our most challenging problems; but, much like Carol presents throughout this book, I also strongly believe that we need to consider the human element, and not technology alone, in order to be successful. Throughout my over twenty-five year professional IT career, I have been very successful in rely-ing heavily on design thinking principles, including show don't tell, focus on human values, embrace experimentation, craft clarity, be mindful of process, and a tendency to bias towards action and radical collaboration. Most recently I have had the distinct pleasure of leveraging the concepts inherent in the discipline of human-plus-machine by being among the first to bring cognitive computing technologies and innovation to Africa in my current role as the Watson Africa Territory Leader, where my team and I work to prove that technology carefully and thoughtfully applied will continue to bring enduring and profound benefits to humanity.

Carol has set out to carry forward many of the lessons in early smart cities efforts. She lays out her thinking in a rigorous and methodical man-ner that serves to teach the reader design-thinking principles for solving challenging complex smarter cities problems. She also provides an inno-vative framework within which to consider appropriate solutions. But, perhaps the most compelling thing about this book is the demonstra-tion of the fact that the vision for human-centric smart cities is entirely achievable and wholesomely probable – this is not some idyllic future, this is a reality that we are quickly coming to face and for which we have tools to address.

– Sherry Comes
IBM Distinguished Engineer & CTO/Entrepreneur

Preface

The buildings that I build very often have a dreamlike reality. I don't mean by that they have a fantasy quality at all, in fact quite the reverse. They contain in some degree the ingredients that give dreams their power.[1]

Smart cities are a hot topic. They're launched and maximized, emboldened by technology, and designed to perform. But let's get real. Your digital platform might just be another man's privacy nightmare; your sensors and actuators are likely generating noisy distraction to solving the problems of poverty and quality of life in our urban environments. And further, do we really have any confidence that we are indeed improving economic, societal, and environmental outcomes in our cities? Are we making a difference?

We are fascinated with order, efficiency, and optimization. We desire facts, evidence of progress, and colorful charts and graphs that purport to fully predict and prescribe our measurable activities in the *real* world. And yet, for every detailed examination of the structure of our lives; each identification of every urban specimen; every survey, scrutiny, and study, we have greater potential to drown in the perfect data that fails to deeply and meaningfully account for the way we as human beings exist as part of the fabric of the landscape. Our vitality cannot be easily harnessed or applied, nor can our spirit and consciousness be manifested in our plans for the massive investments of time and money in our so-called smart cities. In fact, nowhere in our documents, defined processes,

[1] http://www.brainyquote.com/quotes/authors/c/christopher_alexander.html #Qw2UX7w4fsL5iJhb.99

or project plans are we likely to see a serious treatment of ideas that are not somehow demonstrated through the scientific method. After all, we are often more comfortable with the winnowed truth, over those of cosmologists, artists, teachers, philosophers, and theocrats. We find it difficult to include these voices in our assembly of the components within our material world. We are drawn to the idea that if something counts, then we must account for it.

But for all the value that the emerging smart city can bring to us from its sensors, advanced models, and actuators, there are many things that become so much less by their deconstruction. Left to the pressures of social media today, *Moby-Dick* might have been written in bursts of 140 characters with the hashtag #whitewhalerevenge, and related videos and still shots tagged #blubber #oil #leviathan showing Pip sobbing and beating on his tambourine. With so many of our hours spent tagging and posting every moment of our human voyage, we are in danger of failing to comprehend the full story of our lives in our natural and physical environments.

In our cities, where our buildings stand tall; our streets roll long; and our movements create an urban buzz composed of busker music from the subways, slamming car doors, engine brakes, the whirring of vending machines, the murmur of TVs, the cries and goo-goo-ga-gas of babies, and the whoosh of the revolving door—the things that make up the vital spirit of our urban lives. Simply, it is the buildings we reside in, sleep in, work in, and so often are born and die in that have personal properties that will either support our greatest capacities as human beings, or tear them down. It is all these things, coupled with global transportation, telecommunications, infrastructure, and climate constraints, that drive extremely complex conditions to emerge where we dump massive amounts of money and resources to build smart cities.

Yet, our population centers are far from intelligent or coordinated, and despite many pockets of innovation, our cities have had little net-positive impact on carbon control. Moreover, an uncertain relationship between the shifting demographics from rural to low-income urban remains. It's time to acknowledge that the problem with many smart city efforts is the tendency to oversimplify the issues that cities face and to dangerously assume that those problems can be solved by technology alone. It seems clear that the florid vision of smarter cities as gleaming, efficient towers bursting from the sands, where a one-size-fits-all technology approach creates a sustainable living environment is misguided at best and a cultural failure at worst. But I sincerely believe that it is indeed technology that may play the most important role in helping us improve our urban environments. We just need to find a better way to engage technology for the benefit of people.

And so a paradox emerges: that technology can take away from our experience of living as much as it can add to it.

What's needed now is an approach to building smarter cities that not only incorporates the issues of building technologically advanced smart cities, but also comprehends the shifts in human living within these environments. We need a plan for smart cities that leverages our best learning about technology but that fully acknowledges the importance of creating and sustaining vital communities. This book can help build and fulfill those plans by affording us an opportunity to look more closely at how our profound capabilities to do almost anything with technology can solve real problems that improve lives. All lives.

It's true that human beings are messy and fickle, and when it comes to technology, we can become supremely conflicted and confused. Every day, we fall further out of touch with advanced technologies, befuddled by how they work and what they're doing. Even software engineers and app designers don't know anymore. So when we hear about smart cities or efficiency, carbon controls, safety, and the Internet of Things, many of us are relieved to know that someone else must surely know what's happening. But who are these technology designers? What is the technology doing? Why are certain technology implementations done the way they're done? And why does it even matter anymore? I argue in this book that we must take charge of our urban destiny, that design thinking offers us a path forward, and that we must care more than ever about technology:

We can use the principles of design thinking to reframe the problems of the smart city to capture the real needs of people living in a highly efficient urban environment. In this light, this book presents the relevant technologies required for coordinated, efficient cities; explore the latent needs of community stakeholders in a culturally appropriate context; discuss the tested approaches to ideation, design, prototyping, and building or retrofitting smart cities; and propose a model for a viable smart city project.

The smart city vision that expresses perfection through technology is hypothetical at best and reflects the failed repetition through the ages of equating scientific progress with positive social change. Up until now, despite our best hopes and efforts, technology has yet to bring an end to scarcity or suffering. Technical innovation, instead, can and should be directed in the service of our shared cultural values, especially within the rapidly growing urban milieu.

It is the current and future possibilities of innovation that concern me most. With the ever-growing pools of data that are leaking into our daily lives, and to which we ourselves contribute grandly, we cannot just do anything and everything. Instead, we must focus on creating human-centered approaches to our cities that integrate our human needs and technology to drive us to meet our economic, environmental, and existential needs. You won't find this philosophy in even the best technical specification. We must discover a way to cocreate with the urban dwellers themselves, developing an approach that transforms the complex forces inherent in an urban environment with inspiration and rationality. We must do more than solve problems; we must solve the right problems.

– Carol L. Stimmel, Canaan, New York

About the Author

Carol L. Stimmel is the founder and CEO of Manifest Mind, a collaborative research and consulting organization, working to ensure that companies and investors have the information they need to make enduring investment decisions in the complex world of sustainability. Stimmel is recognized for her integrity, years of experience, independent spirit, and ability to create expert teams on-demand, which have rapidly made Manifest Mind a trusted source of insight for assessing opportunities in developing human economies, the built environment, and natural ecosystems.

With 25 years of experience in emerging technology markets, including operations, research and analysis, and product design, she is a frequent speaker and co-author of *The Manager Pool* (2001), author of *Big Data Analytics Strategies for the Smart Grid* (2014), and her current work on *Building Smart Cities: Analytics, ICT, and Design Thinking* (2015). Stimmel holds several key technology patents and pending applications with myriad co-inventors, including those related to virtual communication, broadcasting, autonomic computing, and energy benchmarking.

During the course of her career, she has founded two companies, worked on investigating digital crime, created software systems for landing aircraft in adverse weather, flown with NASA on data-collection flights, and helped commercialize a few big ideas, such as real-time search and energy management. Stimmel's professional journey has brought her up close and personal with a few big wins and some difficult losses, but most importantly, the opportunity to participate in innovative markets that increasingly impact our lives as human beings—telecommunications and distributed energy resources.

Today, Stimmel's sole focus is on technology-enabled sustainability projects that help propel companies and investors to invest in an inclusive and clean economy, where both positive social change and financial returns can be achieved. As the leader of Manifest Mind, she personally contributes to research and consulting projects that provide strategic insight into the sustainable and efficient delivery of energy, food, and water, especially in urban and emerging environments.

Acknowledgments

A book doesn't happen because one has a great idea. At least mine don't, and I'm somewhat relieved that some of my best thinking never went anywhere. My longtime friends Sherry Comes (the technologist) and Lyn Bain (the user experience strategist) told me at lunch one day that this book had to happen. It was a conversation that simultaneously excited and sickened me as I thought about the possibilities of a well-designed smart city and the potential impacts of one that went completely wrong. A book about smart cities that talks about the role of design had to happen.

That said, this book didn't have a chance without the shepherding of Theron Shreve of DerryField Publishing, the patience and vast skills of production editor Marje Pollack, the beautiful cover art by my dear friend Rob Camarata, and most importantly, the love, care, and concern that my good friend Argot has for ensuring that my grammar is acceptable and that my sometimes very confused ideas become crystallized, readable, and memorable for the reader. Reading books of a technical and complex nature should not be a struggle, especially in a text where the author hopes to bring the ideas of beauty and love for both the built and natural worlds to its proper role in the technology sphere. Trust me, no good book emerges without an editor who also cares about the dreams of the author and the credibility of the content. Argot does that for me. She makes me better, and you are the beneficiary.

While writing this book, I blindly moved across the country from the Rockies to the Berkshires, crushed a few fingers on my right hand a week before Chapter One was due, lost a cat, and started an incredible new life nestled in the hills. I have been welcomed warmly since the night I stayed with my Airbnb hosts The Real Billy Keane and Waterfall Perry. The Blueberry Hill gang in New Lebanon, New York, makes sure I have a plate of unbelievably tasty and healthful food nearly every morning, and the Shaker Dam Coffeehouse in West Stockbridge, Massachusetts, combines the power of art and coffee in a setting that can only be described as "liquid illumination." All have been important waypoints for me on this journey.

With great food and coffee, warm people, uplifting music, and a transcendental world of natural beauty around me, I have nothing but gratitude. I have loved writing this book; it was toil at some stages, but I am hopeful that it makes a difference. Thus, perhaps no one should be more acknowledged than you, the reader.

Section One

Designing Smart Cities for Human Needs

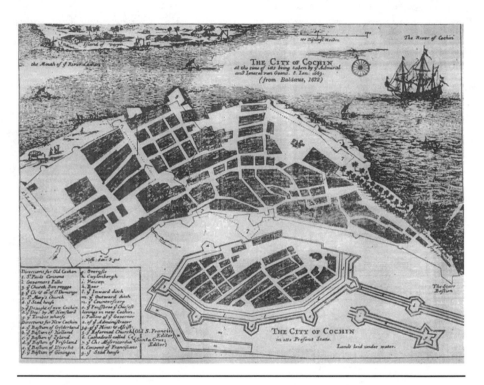

A map of the Dutch-occupied Fort Kochi municipality in 1672.[*]

[*] Image retrieved from the public domain at http://en.wikipedia.org/wiki/File:Fort_Kochi_City_Map_1672.png.

Chapter One

The Imperative for Smart Cities

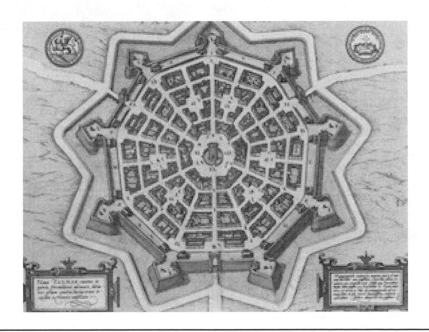

Map of the revolutionary Venetian town of Palmanova, 1572–1680.[1]

---

[1] Author unknown, image retrieved from the public doman at http://commons.wikimedia.org/wiki/File:Palmanova1600.jpg.

1.1 A New Vision

The term "smart city" defines the new urban environment, one that's designed for performance through information and communication technologies (ICTs) and other forms of physical capital. With the effective management of resources through intelligent management, visionaries hope that cities will drive a higher quality of life for citizens, drive down waste, and improve economic conditions. Given that the majority of people across the world will live in urban environments within the next few decades—coupled with the imperative to bring carbon emissions under control—it's not surprising that massive effort and investment are being investing developing strategies and plans for achieving "smart" urban growth.

Unfortunately, it's solely the availability of the ICT infrastructure that has come to define the intelligent city. A focus on the technology of the cities and not the people who are intended to live there has caused expensive missteps, resulting in the creation of ecocities built from scratch that are far from bustling. These failed showcases may serve as laboratories for innovation that will shape the urban future, but they stray far from representing the real work that needs to be done to build smart cities. The

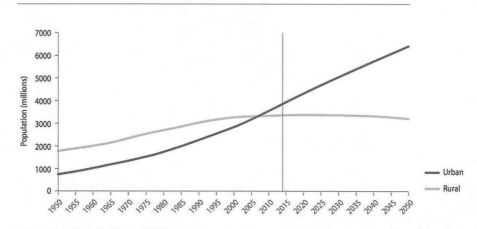

Figure 1.1   Urban and rural populations of the world, 1950–2050. (*Source:* "World Urbanization Prospects: The 2014 Revision," United Nations Department of Economic and Social Affairs/Population Division)

fact is, we already live in these cities—New York, London, Mumbai, and the many other cities that, according to the United Nations, will house two-thirds of the world's population in the next 25 years (Figure 1.1).

These population centers are far from intelligent or coordinated, and despite many pockets of innovation, these cities have had little net positive impact on carbon control. Moreover, an uncertain relationship between the shifting demographics from rural to urban poor remains. It's time to acknowledge that the problem with many smart city efforts is a tendency to oversimplify the problems that conventional cities face and to assume that those problems can be solved with technology alone. It seems clear that the florid vision of smarter cities as gleaming, efficient towers bursting from the sands, where a one-size-fits-all technology approach creates a sustainable living environment, is misguided at best and a cultural failure at worst. Yet, those who sincerely believe that technology has an important role to play in the betterment of our urban environments should not be disheartened.

Steve Jobs, progenitor of Apple, said, "As you evolve that great idea, it changes and grows. It never comes out like it starts because you learn a lot more as you get into the subtleties of it. And you also find there are tremendous tradeoffs that you have to make."[2] The forces driving the imperative for smarter cities—including economic health, poverty mitigation, improved healthcare, better uses of our natural resources, crime reduction, and stewardship of our planet—are quite real, and the ability of technology to empower leaders to transform their cities for vibrancy and health is equally promising. Technology improves our roadways, transportation systems, and the modernized infrastructure with improved analytic functions which contribute to resiliency; it can also improve our educational and healthcare systems and make our cities safer and more streamlined in their operations. However, these changes don't and won't happen just because we connect people and buildings to sensors and digital services. Data collection through ICT is simply an enabler of smarter cities. Ultimately, positive change will only happen if both policy and technological innovation are directed in a unified framework that ensures that human beings are supported in leading healthy and productive lives

[2] Elmer-DeWitt, Philip (2011), "Steve Jobs: The parable of the Stones," *Fortune*. Retrieved November 23, 2014, from http://fortune.com/2011/11/11/steve-jobs-the-parable-of-the-stones.

that don't impinge on our natural resources. The innovative and ethical use of ICT accelerates and catalyzes the sustainable vision that our digital age enables.

1.2 What Is Smart?

"Smart" is an adjective, used informally to describe someone who is clever, intelligent, or generally quick-witted. It's clear, though, that the way we use the word today to describe sensor-based devices is as much a result of our tendency to anthropomorphize nonhuman systems as it is our need to choose the best modifier for a noun. Redefining our culture and our society, smart technology is profoundly altering the way we interact with our friends, communities, transportation modalities, homes, offices, and even our bodies.

Smart technologies mark the convergence between very cheap devices that collect parametric data to detect a state change of some physical entity and a computational system of recording and even further, response. There are myriad classifications of sensors, including acoustic, electric, flow, position, pressure, thermal and proximity. And the sensing technology is just as various, including chemoreceptive, image, inductive, radar, sonar, transduction, ultrasonic, and wireless. Indeed, "sensing" is a very simple proposition. When we clap, we can hear the sound and feel the vibration. A dolphin echolocates by slapping it nostrils together. A cat uses its whiskers as touch receptors. But in all truth, the excitement about smart technologies is the ability to create a system that can seemingly comprehend and create a real-time reaction or even a consequence.

Many of us have some sort of smart device near us at all times. Perhaps you're reading this text on an electronic reader. You likely have a smartphone. You may have smart glasses perched on your nose, a smart thermostat may be controlling the temperature in your home, and you may even live in a city with smart parking, smart streetlights, or smart meters that are measuring your electricity consumption, minute by minute. Our lives are constantly touched by ICT to provide some level of intelligence and coordination to the fire hose of information disgorging all around us. Almost overnight, the common objects in our lives have become nodes in a complex (though sometimes irritatingly dysfunctional) network, often a discordant blend of science fact and science fiction that would have made

Isaac Asimov nod with recognition. Indeed, we are entering a world where the demarcation between human and machine is quickly dissolving; a world that is coming close to fulfilling the promise (or threat) of "singularity." Singularity is a notion attributed to John von Neumann, who described it as the "ever accelerating progress of technology and changes in the mode of human life, which gives the appearance of approaching some essential singularity in the history of the race beyond which human affairs, as we know them, could not continue."[3] Truly, how we choose to cope with this impending dissolution is exactly what will guide how smart cities are designed, built, and ultimately accepted by their communities.

The implications for the built environment, especially our urban environments, are quite staggering. With sensor technologies and the emergence of the Internet of Things, advanced algorithms and orchestration of these things, and data analytics, we now have the unprecedented ability to not only describe our cities in granular detail but to also discover new, creative ways to design and maintain our cities in the most sustainable, innovative, and efficient way possible. These new designs promise to decrease our consumption of natural resources, better control pollution, and more efficiently manage all sorts of network flows. Yet there is danger too, as policy protections lag way behind these capabilities. In 2013, the Edward Snowden leaks about U.S. National Security Administration (NSA) data collection and analysis tactics shocked many; others felt their suspicions confirmed. The NSA had indeed been collecting massive amounts of data—each with a digital fingerprint—that could be used as what Noam Chomsky and Barton Gellman have described as potential "instruments of abuse, surveillance and asymmetrical control."[4]

These issues of weak data governance are reflected globally. Germany learned that its chancellor's cell phone conversations were being intercepted by the US government, resulting in the expulsion of the CIA's station chief from Berlin. The ill-informed use and dissemination of data gathered within urban populations will only grow more consequential, where social sharing can ignite significant backlash, perhaps even

---

[3] Ulam, Stanislaw (1958), "Tribute to John von Neumann," *Bulletin of the American Mathematical Society*, vol. 64, no. 3, part 2, p. 5.

[4] Engaging Data 2013 Conference (2013), "MIT SENSEable City Lab" conference session. Retrieved September 1, 2014, from http://senseable.mit. edu/engagingdata2013.

widespread violence. Consider the case of Michael Brown in Ferguson, Missouri: Security camera footage was strategically released after Brown had been shot and killed, even though early reports indicated he wasn't suspected of any crime when the fatal shooting occurred. The release of the video was deemed "character assassination" among protestors and was arguably the root of escalated protests, another shooting, and the governor's declaration of emergency.[5] As a society, we clearly have not fully comprehended how to contextualize and manage data appropriately.

Any data that's collected must be tested for its accuracy and quality, and interpreted properly by those who are competent to clarify and give meaning to the data and appropriately measure its usefulness. Careless use of data in our cities will result in a lack of confidence and undermine much of the good that can be accomplished through advanced informatics for urban planning and through efficient operations that can improve the quality of our lives. Presciently, New Zealander statesman James Allen is thought to have said, "Evil is not power; it is ignorance and misuse of good." Similarly, while data is morally neutral, how we us it is not. As we move further toward a society that is deeply reliant on data-driven systems for its core functions, academics, researchers, industry, and privacy advocates must find agreement about the principles of data privacy and security. We are shockingly late in addressing the topic, given the accelerating pace of sensor-based technology deployment and the activities of international companies like Google, Facebook, Twitter, and Yahoo. If the promises of a data-driven infrastructure are to develop, it's urgent that a universal data governance contract of some sort emerge.

1.3 A Sensitive Relationship

For sensors to have any purpose, they must rely on engineered algorithms so that the sensors can distinguish between in-bounds and out-of-bounds monitored activities and can then either simply record that information or respond with some sort of action. When an intelligent device's associated sensor or system of sensors detects some sort of specific

[5] Mejia, Paula (2014), "Missouri Gov. Nixon Upset with Michael Brown Video Release," *Newsweek*. Retrieved September 1, 2014, from http://www.newsweek.com/missouri-gov-nixon-distraught-michael-brown-video-release-265114.

condition, something happens—a valve might open, power delivery may shut down, or a variable-speed motor may be adjusted. A sensor action may actuate a safety shutdown on the electricity grid, preventing a larger-scale cascading blackout. In your car, sensors may attempt to provoke some human response by triggering a flashing light, buzz, or audio alert when the fuel level is low. In your house, sensors may simply turn off the living room light when you leave the space. It's easy to see how fear crops up when engineers talk excitedly about the potential of smart systems. Depending on your perspective, smart technology is either the wave of the future or a euphemism for social engineering.

Most often, when the topic of the smart city comes up, it's in the context of a particular vision of technology infrastructure. Thus, many smart cities have emerged as converted commercial and industrial "innovation districts" or superefficient and highly regulated new buildings and roads that are instrumented for two primary purposes: asset management and automation. The oft-stated goal of these efforts is to reduce operational costs, manage power consumption, and drive down the excessive use of natural resources. Unfortunately, this technology-centric approach has not only driven a schism between civil engineers, city planners, policy-makers, and information management experts, it has also alienated service functionaries who are focused on improving schools, hospitals, and public services in general. Like many complex projects, the most difficult part of designing a smart city is getting started by defining the problem in a way that helps solve real problems.

The myopic view that building a smart city is like developing an operating system overlooks the relationships between the many forces within the urban environment, especially those related to poverty and health. Technology plans that implicitly deny the inconvenient fact that people live in cities is strangely perverse. Further, while many cities are working to incrementally improve their human services and infrastructure, the most high-profile smart city projects have demanded billions of dollars and have been nothing more than playgrounds for real-estate speculators, urban planners, master architects, global purveyors of technology and analytic systems, futurists, and governments with the excess cash to make major investments in urban experimentation. Most of these efforts have fallen well short of their lofty goals, many have become political nightmares, and in one case, the project simply disappeared. Create-your-own ecocities like Masdar City in the United Arab Emirates, Songdo in South Korea, and Dongtan in China are examples of high-profile projects that have resulted in disappointment. Despite their creators' well-intentioned visions of massive-scale sustainability, these cities have suffered from a lack of commercial viability (Masdar City), the loss of major investment dollars (Songdo), and charges of corruption (Dongtan).

From a pure technology perspective, much has been learned about developing carbon-neutral cities. It's clear, though, that these efforts require rethinking about the replicability of the solutions that these model cities have spawned. Ecocities are developed as "closed systems," islands of smartness that are isolated from their surrounding environment and often smack of the solitary pleasures of highly analytical, oft-isolated engineers. The words of Friedrich A. Hayek, economist and philosopher, come to mind when he wrote so unflinchingly about the temperament of the engineer: "All the 'data' on which the work is based have explicitly entered his preliminary calculations and been condensed into the 'blueprint' that governs the execution of the whole scheme" and so, "[the engineer] has complete control of the particular little world with which he is concerned."[6]

Smart city observer Richard Sennett has called these cities "stupefying," noting that the problem with the closed-system approach is the desire for equilibrium. Engineers are looking to create a system that maintains a predictable balance, resolves conflicts, and is programmed to cope with "noise" through the use of command and control.[7] Though Sennett doesn't go so far as to say so, his analysis of the failure of the top-billed ecocities seems clear: They assume human behavior is rational. There is much evidence to the contrary. Knock on wood? Avoid a black cat? Never walk under ladders? Wear your favorite shirt before every cricket match? Enraged when cut off in traffic? Israeli behavioral economist Dan Ariely simply states what so many of us would like to deny: "We are fallible, easily confused, not that smart, and often irrational. We are more like Homer Simpson than Superman." Yet, does this mean that

[6]   Hayek, Friedrich A. (1980), "Engineers and Planners," *Mises Daily*, excerpted from *The Counter-Revolution of Science*. Retrieved August 31, 2014, from http://mises.org/daily/2782.

[7]   Sennett, Richard (2012), "The Stupefying Smart City," LSE Cities. Retrieved September 1, 2014, from http://lsecities.net/media/objects/articles/the-stupefying-smart-city/en-gb.

building systems based on logic can have no enduring or meaningful impact on our lives? That's equally as absurd. Ariely views his potentially depressing analysis as an opportunity for optimism. Our systems can help us continually learn from patterns of human behavior (especially our mistakes), and design better policies and tools that accommodate our human designs—and that would likely create a better world.[8]

Sennett also says that alternatively, in an open system, "balance is not so much the aim: the system is programmed to evolve, being open to the unforeseen, changing its very structure as it absorbs new data."[9] As an example, he describes Rio de Janeiro's attempts to better forecast potential physical disasters, coordinate traffic systems, and increase the organization of the police. The city has seen great success in installing various technologies throughout the area. Instead of begging for forgiveness when it set up its ICT network, Rio de Janeiro asked for permission from its citizens, engaging them in the process and educating them about the drivers of the initiative. Utopians have scoffed at Rio's efforts and its command center, which isn't smart enough for purists; however, the teenagers who uploaded global positioning system data to identify disease-ridden trash piles and mitigate them, might disagree. And certainly not all the citizens of Rio de Janeiro are supportive of the multitude of webcams sucking images of residents throughout the city, nor are they pleased with the city's blind eye toward initiatives to increase ecological housing or revitalize natural resources. But as an example of real-world urban transformation, Rio de Janeiro's project has much more to teach us from its successes and failures than any glitzy, half-empty eco-heaven in the desert.

1.3.1 We Can't Turn Back Now

According to the United Nations, by 2050, 66 percent of the world's population is poised to live in urban environments. Similarly, the World Bank estimates a doubling of urban population by 2030, tripling the global

---

[8] Ariely, Dan (n.d.), "Three Questions on Behavioral Economics," Dan Ariely Rationality blog post. Retrieved September 1, 2014, from http://danariely.com/tag/rationality.

[9] Sennett [6].

urban land area from just 2000.[10,11] Remarkably, today's cities are already producing 80 percent of the global gross domestic product (GDP), but they're also consuming nearly two-thirds of the world's energy and spewing over 70 percent of global greenhouse gas emissions.[12] As urbanization increases over the next generation, most growth will likely be concentrated in just several hundred areas in China, India, and Latin America (out of the 1,000-plus cities with current populations of at least 500,000 people) and experience dramatic rises in population, total GDP, per-capita GDP, and—by way of effect—resource consumption.

And yet, poverty, crime, and desperation are rife in many urban settings around the world. We've largely become inured to pictures of despair from fragile regions such as Harare, Zimbabwe, Karachi, and Lagos. Even developed cities like Glasgow, Scotland; Marseilles, France; Detroit, Michigan; Miami, Florida; and Stockton, California, face scarcity, high crime rates, and ethnic tension. Touted "livable" cities such as Toronto and Vancouver, Canada; Melbourne, Australia; Paris, France; and Vienna, Austria, have beautiful built environments and a high quality of life for even the most economically and socially marginalized citizens, but they also have grim urban areas with large pockets of impoverishment and elevated rates of violence. Among these, some also maintain poor access to healthcare, operate under insufficient sanitation standards, and spend little on city services.

Yet, there's something disturbingly subjective to this rather gross analysis. One can certainly have a pitiable life yet still inhabit what many might feel is a glorious city, and further, the whole subject of what brings joy, beauty, and laughter to the people of the world is well beyond the scope of this book. However, even for those who maintain a world view of der Wille zur Macht, we can easily agree on a couple things: Urban environments will continue to affect the majority of the world population in terms of basic health and safety as well as the wellness that comes from those things that make life meaningful for each of us, including

[10] United Nations (2014), "World Urbanization Prospects: 2014 Revision." Retrieved August 31, 2014, from http://esa.un.org/unpd/wup/Highlights/WUP2014-Highlights.pdf.

[11] World Bank (2013), "Urban Development Overview." Retrieved August 31, 2014, from http://www.worldbank.org/en/topic/urbandevelopment/overview.

[12] World Bank [11].

family, friends, neighbors, and our daily work. And the configuration and management of our cities will persist in playing a direct role in our safety, economies, and depth of community relationships. The better we plan, build, operate, and maintain our cities, the more competitive, resilient, healthy, and sustainable our urban communities will be.

1.4 What Do We Really Want from the Smart City?

Many of the earliest smart city proponents declared that their coordinated systems are capable of perfectly knowing all that is knowable in the urban environment, of capturing that knowledge through sensors and monitors, measuring the information, and making infallible decisions that will autonomously optimize and regulate all the critical resources of the city.

Unfortunately, this marketing hyperbole is a distraction for meeting real-world problems and subsumes the critically important issues of urbanization. The amount of money spent on these buzzy visions is quite staggering. At a price tag of US$35 billion, Songdo set out to create the ultimate lifestyle by defining itself as:

> an international city that offers every conceivable amenity, attracting multinational and domestic corporations . . . all the advantages of a master planned environment . . . parks, an advanced technology infrastructure, . . . fine hotels, international schools, museums, a luxury retail mall.[13]

After over a decade of effort, Songdo struggles to achieve its vision, which may not be ideal at all. The city that has "every conceivable amenity" struggles to attract tenants to its shimmering skyscrapers. Half-finished at its targeted completion date, Songdo has evidently not yet earned any profit for 12 years of work.[14] After all, what is really ideal to a city dweller is likely relative to his or her current living conditions. Utopia for some

---

[13] Songdo IBD (n.d.), "Why Songdo: Global Business Hub." Retrieved August 30, 2014, from http://www.songdo.com/songdo-international-business-district/why-songdo/global-business-hub.aspx.

[14] Nam, In-Soo (2013), "South Korea's $35 Billion 'Labor of Love,'" *The Wall Street Journal.* Retrieved August 31, 2014, from http://online.wsj.com/news/articles/SB10001424052702304579404579236150341041182.

may just be a warm meal, a safe place to sleep, and a clean cup of water. When many urban environments are facing fundamental challenges from issues such as mountains of solid waste, lack of universal access to potable water, open sewage systems, and horrific crime and violence, what is there to gain from "every conceivable amenity"?

Of course cities are more than just places to survive; they're diverse, often have significant historical depth, great beauty, and jobs as well as deep community, religious, and ethnic significance. How can we learn anything from a pop-up Shangri-la? From the perspective of maintaining and enhancing community, probably not much; it may in fact be counterproductive. But we can learn from these technology experiments to help us better plan transportation infrastructure, improve streetlighting, establish clean-water supplies, integrate distributed and renewable sources of energy, and install sewage networks. Indeed, city planners and architects can benefit greatly from the systems and tools that technologists have been able to develop in these well-funded eco-projects. After all, even the ancient city-state of Ur in Mesopotamia was built with the logic to maximize the wealth that passed through it. Rejecting what we've learned about the functioning of certain technologies in a lab environment seems foolhardy.

1.5 Managing the Shift

It's paramount that sovereign nations and the global development community alike manage this impending shift to urbanization in a manner that's sustainable, both in terms of economic productivity and our natural resources. Rapid urbanization brings momentous challenges, including a shift of the issues of poverty from rural communities to cities, and a higher demand for basic services, jobs, and affordable housing. Smart technologies will certainly play a role in that shift, and it's up to our city leaders to accommodate those technologies in meaningful and principled manner.

Technology can help in many ways to make a city more livable. It can help usher in a sense of safety, a well-functioning infrastructure, economic health, affordability, green space, and natural and cultural assets. But it can also foment pollution, sprawl, and—good or bad—connectivity. What it cannot do is take the place of the vital relationships that people have with one another, their communities, and their built environment. The quest for an ideal city is not new. Remember Palmanova, the Renaissance settlement founded in 1593? It took decades to construct based on cosmological ideals, and despite its elegance and sustainable design, it was horribly unpopular. According to historians of the period, the town was so unpalatable that criminals were offered pardons if they would just move in.

Building cities that monitor and police our every move, analyze all human and mechanical actions, take note every time a refrigerator door is open, sense and record when showers have run too long or lights have been left on for too many hours sounds fitting for a research environment, but they're likely just tomorrow's high-tech Palmanovas. This implementation of "utopia" violates our most basic sense of liberty and brings to mind the words of US Supreme Court Justice Louis D. Brandeis in his dissenting opinion of the wiretapping case *Olmstead v. United States* (1928): "Time works changes, brings into existence new conditions and purposes." Subtler and more-far-reaching methods of invading privacy have become available to the government. Discovery and invention have made it possible for the government, by means far more effective than stretching upon the rack, to obtain disclosure in court of what is whispered in the closet. But now the prospect of intrusion is even greater. It's true that we need to change our habits and stop presupposing an endless supply of resources, but do we really want smarter cities that exercise presumptive policing through sensor technology?

1.6 Designing for People

What's needed now is an approach to building smarter cities that not only incorporates the issues of building technologically advanced smart cities but also comprehends the shifts in human living within these environments. We need a plan for smart cities that incorporates our best learning about technology but that fully acknowledges the importance of creating and sustaining vital communities.

A largely unexplored approach for developing smart cities is design thinking. A human-centered approach to innovation, design thinking integrates human needs and technology while driving economic success. This method of problem solving doesn't begin with technical specification—which is commonly where the design of smart cities has begun—

but with empathy for the people who live within these environments. In fact, it's really a co-creation process with the urban dwellers themselves that transforms the complex forces inherent in an urban environment with inspiration and rationality. This process of design unlocks innovation because it doesn't just solve problems, it solves the right problems.

We can use the principles of design thinking to reframe the problems of the smart city to capture the real needs of people living in a highly efficient urban environment. Based on the problems defined in this chapter, this book will present the relevant technologies required for coordinated, efficient cities; explore about the latent needs of community stakeholders in a culturally appropriate context; discuss the tested approaches to ideation, design, prototyping, and building or retrofitting smart cities; and propose a model for a viable smart city project.

The smart city vision that expresses perfection through technology is hypothetical at best and reflects the failed repetition through the ages of equating scientific progress with positive social change. Up until now, despite our best hopes and efforts, technology has yet to bring an end to scarcity or suffering. Technical innovation, instead, can and should be directed in the service of our shared cultural values, especially within the rapidly growing urban milieu.

Chapter Two

Technology, Innovation, and the Problem with People

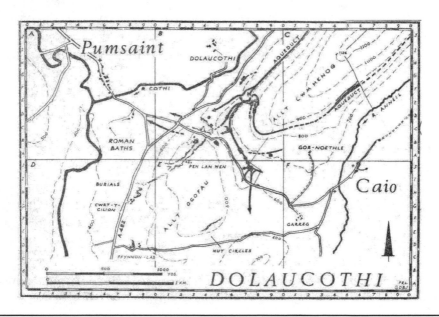

Map of the gold mine at Dolaucothi, showing its aqueducts.[1]

1 Image retrieved from the public domain at http://commons.wikimedia.org/
   wiki/File:Dolaucothimap2.jpg.

2.1 Chapter Goal

This chapter discusses the various problems that occur at the intersection of people and technology in the smart city. In response to the accelerating impulse to look toward technology solutions to solve the challenging problem of how human beings interact with their environment, especially in urban settings, there has been both overly optimistic and pessimistic thinking about the role of technology in smart cities. The reader will learn about some of these philosophical questions and concerns as well as be introduced to a foundational model for designing smart cities that stresses the use of technology for the best benefit of urban dwellers.

2.2 Are We Really Ready for Technology Advancement?

Currently, in developed cities, we have quite disparate systems of control. For example, while crime-prone areas may use closed-circuit television (CCTV) to transmit data captured from monitoring cameras on a private transmission channel, we still have parking enforcement officers shuttling around handing out parking violations. Still, in the context of the city, the use of rudimentary technology has grown, as in the case of CCTV. Known to be used as early as the 1940s by the German military to monitor V-2 rocket launches, CCTV is familiar to many of us for its use in surveillance in high-risk areas, such as banks, airports, casinos, and even convenience stores. More recently, cities have deployed these monitoring systems to deter crime by taking advantage of digital multiplexing (or "muxing"), where many cameras can record at once but transmit in one single data stream. They can also optimize this monitoring by using time-lapse and motion-sensitive recording techniques.

Although its usefulness for deterring crime has been widely questioned (but its value in apprehending criminals is mostly unchallenged), CCTV is popular across the world. In many jurisdictions, it's used for monitoring public spaces, schools, and parks. In fact, the preponderance of CCTV units available through digital media has become so universal that in October 2009 in the United Kingdom, a company called Internet Eyes initiated a new business program that rewarded points to people who spotted criminal acts on CCTV streams. Not surprisingly, the company—which quietly shut down in 2013—received widespread applause for its efforts to "crowdsource surveillance," but it also earned criticism for encouraging a modern-day campaign of neighborhood-style denunciation.

But look at where CCTV has taken us: It's not that CCTV is technologically better than traditional photographic approaches (though it is touted to be); it's that the same fundamental technology is being used in ever-novel ways, achieved by integrating various tools for a new, common purpose. As we know, cameras are used frequently the world over to manage all sorts of events beyond criminal activity. Traffic issues, including red light, speed limit, stop sign, toll booth, flow, and high-occupancy lane enforcement are extremely popular. To prosecute violators in some jurisdictions, the camera will take a picture of the driver for positive identification; other jurisdictions will slap a fine on the registered owner of the vehicle, regardless of whether he was driving when the violation was committed. Once CCTV units could zoom and take a snapshot of a vehicle entering an intersection after the light had gone red, or combine the video technology with radar capabilities to sense speed, then jurisdictions could police speeders and red-light bombers through automatically generated tickets. These require no human intervention; that is, until a ticket recipient shows up in court claiming the illegality of the whole procedure.

Of course, analog CCTV technology is affordable, but as the costs for digital components continue to plummet, Internet Protocol (IP)-based devices are proliferating, despite their being challenged by transmission and other complications. Better compression, use of bandwidth, and even on-board processing of images will continue to make megapixel camera technology more popular in the field, and allow an even greater confluence of capabilities to converge. An obvious example is the use of facial recognition or even behavior-sensitive monitoring. A person identified as Carol Stimmel has walked away from her bag at the airport and left it for more than three minutes. Two hundred fifty people have walked into a theater that is fire safety rated for 175. All things can be monitored, and even today, video analytics are powerful and accurate enough to watch and record people entering stores, exiting subways, standing in lines, and walking the streets.

2.2.1 A Better Vision

A quick look at the humble CCTV camera and we see how the merging of technologies and analytics creates an entirely new specter of system capabilities. It's even more dramatically illustrated when we extend that example to incorporate our abilities to interact with the natural environment (things like our water, our minerals, and the weather) through our built environment (the world created by humans within which we live, work, and play), which is now sensed, measured, and delivered as source of information that can be used to improve our living conditions and facilitate the most efficient use of our ever-scarcer resources.

The fact that we can measure incredibly complex phenomena with great precision does not in and of itself mean much of consequence about our ability to predict, anticipate, or modify even obviously destructive human behavior. For example, we are now able to measure the temperature of any of the Earth's oceans with cross-verifiable accuracy. Many measurements are made using a variety of sensing technologies, including thermometers, satellite remote sensing equipment, acoustic tomography measurements of sound transmission speed and distance parameters, and microwave technology to determine ocean surface topography. Knowing the trending temperatures of the ocean allows us to better predict hurricanes and storm severity, and it allows us to collect key indicators that provide data about the changing climate.

Over time, we have learned that the oceans have absorbed much of the increased heat that the planet has been putting out since the 1880s. In fact, ocean temperature trends are a key piece of evidence that led the Intergovernmental Panel on Climate Change to state that the "[s]cientific evidence for warming of the climate system is unequivocal."[2] Further, there is scientific consensus on the fact that climate-warming trends over the past 100 years are due to human activities. And yet, the existence of this fact has led to very little in the way of global consensus, political commitment, or legally binding agreements to reduce CO_2 emissions that prevent the continuing acceleration of changes to the planet's natural ecosystems.

We see a variety of responses to the issue: international summits, nonbinding protocols, climate-change bills, local action, climate-change marches, reluctant developing economies that are still driven by industrialization, and the developed economies that consume the majority of the world's resources. Still others have changed their eating habits, installed solar panels on their rooftops, and changed out their lightbulbs. While certainly a topic of discussion, climate change won't become an

[2] NASA (n.d.), "Climate Change: Evidence," NASA.gov. Retrieved September 27, 2014, from http://climate.nasa.gov/evidence/.

urgent initiative until policies change to create new economic constructs or the normative judgments in our lives become impactful enough that we develop new beliefs, values, and attitudes toward the environment.

We continue to produce more convincing climate models with an ever-growing amount of data, and while the discussions of the magnitude and rate of future climate change progresses, another important fact becomes quite clear. We are reminded that, when it comes to human activity, the acquisition of data is not the sole determinant in human decision-making. Social factors, biological influences, community drivers, and our most individual of behavioral characteristics also affect our standards of behavior. In short, data means different things to us based on our world view and myriad factors that influence our collective behavior. However, it's also true that without data, we would have no insight into the role that cause and effect plays in choosing our future actions, and indeed consequences are profound effectors of behavior. It's just this reality that many technologists find puzzling, frustrating, and downright irritating.

2.2.2 The Era of the Posthuman?

When we contemplate how we want to design our urban environments, it's perhaps the merging of technology with our humanity that raises even more powerful and important questions. A rather dubious discourse on CCTV doesn't offer anything of a truly desirable picture of what we might want from technology in our smarter cities. It's likely a better demonstration of the deep trepidation many have that technology will do something *to* us rather than do something *for* us.

Wired magazine founder Kevin Kelly would probably find this question to be irrelevant. To immunize ourselves against irrational fears of technology, we only need to understand how it increases the likelihood of a better life. Technology is waiting, not like a spirit, but as a force, like gravity. He says, "Technology's imperative is not a tyrant ordering our lives in lock-step. Its inevitabilities are not scheduled prophesies. They are more like water behind a wall, and incredibly strong urge pent up and waiting to be released."[3] Technology is simply obeying the natural laws of evolution, even when held back by the dam of human postponement;

---

[3] Kelly, Kevin (2010), *What Technology Wants* (p. 416), Penguin Group US. Retrieved from http://books.google.com/books?id=_ToftPd4R8UC&pgis=1.

technology is waiting to replicate and evolve. In fact, technology itself will be subject to a form of natural selection, where it develops more-favorable qualities to ensure its very survivability.

If Kelly is correct, then as humans we need only to shepherd technology to align with its own inherent good. After all, technology just wants to do the right thing. Perhaps the earlier example of the vague disappearance of Internet Eyes demonstrates poor human volition applied to technology capability. It must be said that this view of technology as a natural system is deeply paradoxical, since it implies a vision of utopia that subsumes the human experience. Science fiction writer Vernor Vinge called this condition the "posthuman era"—a shift in evolutionary process where biological evolution gives way to technological evolution (a zealous viewpoint of the philosophy of Singularity). And even if it sounds extreme and implausible, it's impossible to deny the incredible rate of social change visited upon us by the Internet and the complex of the worldwide connectivity of all things great and small.[4]

To demonstrate an alternative perspective, Columbia Law School professor and author of *The Master Switch* Tim Wu provides us a very interesting scenario. He writes, "Imagine that two people are carving a six-foot slab of wood at the same time. One is using a hand-chisel, the other, a chainsaw. If you are interested in the future of that slab, whom would you watch?"[5] Wu goes on to argue that the chainsaw is technology, the chisel is biology, and we're just the block of wood. His view? Biological evolution is an adaptive process that lends itself to our very survival, but technology evolution is founded within what we want. Or what we think we want. We want pretty much anything that allows us to be more "optimal" and "efficient" (so we can be extraordinarily lazy, of course). For example, we want to have a robot do our vacuuming and an iPhone narrate our e-mails even if it grossly misspells our words us at every turn.

Clearly, our human problems are significant enough that we should ponder, consider, and explore developing a vision for the urban

[4] Vance, Ashlee (2010), "Merely Human? That's So Yesterday," NYTimes.com. Retrieved September 14, 2014, from http://www.nytimes.com/2010/06/13/business/13sing.html?pagewanted=all&_r=0.

[5] Wu, Tim (2014), "As Technology Gets Better, Will Society Get Worse?" *The New Yorker*. Retrieved September 14, 2014, from http://www.newyorker.com/tech/elements/as-technology-gets-better-will-society-get-worse.

environment that aligns with a very agreeable mandate to make cities that work for people who want safe, healthy, and vibrant lives. Whether you believe that technology will evolve as a matter of course or that we will effect its evolution to meet our picayune needs, this kind of thinking will take us no further than Raymond M. Smullyan's experimental epistemologist could travel. He found that "According to the machine, my current intentions are in complete conflict. And I can see why! I am caught in a terrible paradox! If the machine is trustworthy, then I had better accept its suggestion to distrust it. But if I distrust it, then I also distrust its suggestion to distrust it, so I am really in a total quandary."[6]

The smart city will result from smart investments in technology, from our responses to the technology itself, and from what we build with the benefit of better sensing, measuring, and actuations. And frankly, much of the problem with building authentically intelligent and beneficial communities is specious arguments and word games. They come from our academics, our technology purveyors, and our futurists. As such, the arguments for or against the smart city tend toward extreme viewpoints, and—with enough study—nearly always expose a neatly tucked-in motivation such as selling technology, selling software, selling a position, gaining or exploiting tenure, or just selling science fiction. While being sensible and realistic is not nearly as entertaining as the theoretical and abstract considerations, it surely does not preclude creativity and innovation. In fact, it may require it in order to give place and value to novel ways of solving social issues, which is the most compelling motivation for urban transformation.

2.3 People and Technology: Collision or Cooperation?

Of course, the smart city is broadly and convincingly appealing. Why wouldn't it be? Only a Luddite wouldn't welcome sensors and cameras attached to a common city network that will provide better services to all citizens, cut costs, optimize operations, and bring efficiencies. Every

[6] Smullyan, Raymond (1982), "An Epistemological Nightmare," Massachusetts Institute of Technology. Retrieved September 15, 2014, from http://www.mit.edu/people/dpolicar/writing/prose/text/epistemologicalNightmare.html.

taxpayer will surely appreciate reduced city expenses and an upswing in safety and a reliable level of service. We stand in long lines for smarter phones and watches. We welcome smart bus stops and parking meters, Wi-Fi across the city collecting and reporting real-time information, lights that adjust to the perfect levels, and even trash cans that are automatically cleaned out when they become excessively odiferous. We support all this smart stuff until we begin to wonder, "Can these same systems that respond to my every need and desire be employed for surveillance and control? Surely, they will be well-governed."

But, consider that a system of sensors and computational intelligence comprises simply a body of data and its interpretations that's dispassionately making decisions, setting parameters, and self-adjusting without the trappings of human idiosyncrasies. If you are a proponent of algorithmic city planning, you will be first in line to have a sensor installed in your driver's license. However, a mass surrender of highly complex city-planning design principles to the ideals of the powerful, technical elite is just the reemergence of the wishful thinkers who believe that the best economic system may be based on energy standards. During the Great Depression in the Unites States, Howard Scott said, "It is the fact that all forms of energy, of whatever sort, may be measured in units of ergs, joules or calories that is of the utmost importance. The solution of the social problems of our time depends upon the recognition of this fact. A dollar may be worth—in buying power—so much today and more or less tomorrow, but a unit of work or heat is the same in 1900, 1929, 1933 or the year 2000." The same discussion reemerged in the 1980s at the Massachusetts Institute of Technology with Ernst Berndt in work funded by the US Department of Energy. Berndt noted that such theories will rise and re-arise whenever the current market pricing system is perceived as unfair and a technology solution is sought to eliminate human turmoil.[7]

And thus it goes today with technocrats who believe that a perfectly instrumented city can heal the wrongs of the urban environment in disarray, forgetting the fact that technology heals nothing; it's just technology. But like a microsurgeon who guides her laser across the eye and restores

[7] Berndt, Ernst R. (1982), "From Technocracy to Net Energy Analysis: Engineers, Economists and Recurring Energy Theories of Value," Massachusetts Institute of Technology. Retrieved September 22, 2014, from http://dspace.mit.edu/bitstream/handle/1721.1/2023/SWP-1353-09057784.pdf?sequence=1.

sight, powerful technology capabilities in the hands of those who wish to serve the betterment of humankind certainly can—and often do—improve society.

Shake off the hyperbole of the technocrats, the distracting obsessions with the superhuman mind, and the Luddites. We need technologies that will work for us, and in order for that to be accomplished, solutions must be designed into a system that meets the unique challenges and desires of the cultures they're deployed into. No human is the same, and communities have evolved with different mores, needs, and problems. These cultures are complex and long-developing systems that have flexed and changed over time, and will continue to do so.

Instead, think of the smart city as a system of services that, like a body in good health and given attentive care, can offer us unique benefits and trials. In the smart city, the skeletal form is the built environment, the spaces where we live, work, and play; the nervous system is the sensing nodes and communications infrastructure; the interstitial tissue is the data flow that holds the smart system together; and the brain is the system center, where the network learns and adapts to produce better outcomes. But most importantly, the heart is the people who breathe life into our communities, who bring vibrancy, relationships, creativity, and innovation. And for the engineering planner, it is often the people—with their unpredictability and individualism—who create the real challenges. Because it is just untrue that if we could just find the right technology, we would solve our problems. The value of the smart city is not in the perfection of the technology; it is in the benefits provided by the adequate provision of services in what is often a very inadequate world.

2.4 Sensors to Services

Perhaps even worse than technocentrism fully realized is the tendency to treat urgent situations and challenges such as transportation, wastage, and water, with poorly designed and inadequately governed systems that are incapable of adapting to meet diverse city needs in the long term. Despite the risk of long-term failure, many of these point solutions are increasingly more expensive to build and maintain, and they're insecure in their lack of interoperability and openness.

Figure 2.1 describes a vision for not just the technical foundation of a smart city—which is where many market players stop in their

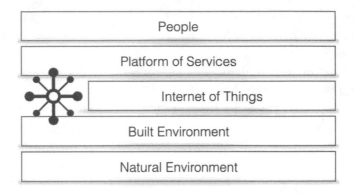

Figure 2.1   A smart city technology stack that synchronizes the natural environment with people.

descriptions—but also for the interplay of this foundation with the natural environment and the people who live in the city. This approach considers that human behavior either virtuously or viciously impacts the natural environment. We will reference this diagram throughout this book as we dive deeper into how we instrument our environment, process the data to make it useful to improve our lives, and teach the system to adapt to the changing needs of the urban environment.

This "sensors-to-services" vision rests on the evolutionary assumptions of the distributed network. A distributed network environment is simply a web of computers where the processing tasks and the data exist across many types of devices, from regional servers to smartphones. The system includes the tiniest sensor that rests at the edge of the networked web to the natural-language processing capabilities of the IBM Watson. The inevitable extension of the distributed network, cloud-based networking allows the ever-growing complex network to be managed at its many levels, from communications and security to advanced applications that can be combined in context-appropriate ways. These applications become a natural extension rather than masters of our lives, as some future-think proposes.

Further to what is described in Figure 2.1, there are three major parts to the technology model. They are an intelligent sensor architecture, a services platform, and an analytics layer. The intelligent sensor architecture includes the sensing devices that contain microprocessor capabilities linked to other sensing devices; the ability to communicate with other sensors to validate, compare, process, and interpret data; and the system response of either machine-based instruction execution or human interpretation and action. The services platform maintains data communication and control, data management, data exchange, and application support services. And the analytics layer contains support for statistical analysis, simulation, operational support, and decision analysis for strategic optimization and urban planning.

2.4.1 What If My World Goes Down?

Would you be more willing to give up your Starbucks latte or your Wi-Fi? What if you were guaranteed that your favorite hockey team would walk away with the Stanley Cup if you gave up your Internet for a week? It's all fun and games until your city needs to be rebooted.

Wireless technology is familiar to nearly everyone. According to various analyst estimates, more than 50 billion devices will be connected globally within the next few years. Many optimistic technologists consider our cities to be "Internet-of-Things (IoT)-ready." But it takes more than a few silos of technology in the urban environment to demonstrate the benefits of a sensor-based city delivered in the context of services. Yes, we know about sensors for home security, radio frequency identification (RFID) shipping tags, automotive sensors, wireless audio technology, remote controls, smart meters, and tablet devices and cell phones with accelerometers, and we know that Bluetooth and Wi-Fi come standard with nearly every new laptop. It's likely, even, that you may have already heard of ZigBee, 6LoWPAN, ANT, and, of course, GPS.

But before we dip into the issues of range, throughput, and power requirements for wireless devices, what exactly is meant by IoT, or what a ubiquitous network vendor would call the Internet of Everything (IoE)? Essentially, the things are the things, and they're either inside of other things doing things or on people, helping people understand themselves better in a world of things. Right? That makes sense.

2.5 The Surprisingly Familiar Sensor

In any discussion of designing a smart anything, especially a city, it's important first to understand the sensing process. At the highest level, a sensor is something that, when stimulated, detects some aspect of physical phenomena (called *input*). By way of a *transducer*, the sensor turns the measurement into a signal so it can be electronically processed and then measured or recorded as *output*. The output is used as input to a further system or process that triggers some responsive action. This is called *actuation* and may require yet another transducer to convert the output to yet another signal type. Some sensors are active, which usually means they require some sort of excitation signal (read: external power source) to actually produce the desired output. Passive sensors, on the other hand, do not require an additional energy source because it's the very act of sensing that will generate an electric signal. Typically, in the course of measurement, passive sensors will actually change in terms of their physical properties.

There is also the important difference between analog and digital signaling. Theoretically, an analog signal is infinite in its resolution (limited only by the accuracy of the device), yet sensor technology is trending toward fewer analog and more digital applications, which can only produce a logical representation of the input data (such as a "0" or a "1"). Digital signals tend to be of higher quality and more reliable for precise measurement (that is, less "noisy"), but there are still many analog signaling devices in operation, including pneumatic, hydraulic, and mechanical systems. And despite the fact that retrofits are often slow to pay back, innovative sensor designers have worked to create digital bolt-ons and other methods for collecting data from analog sources, especially in buildings.

Figure 2.2 describes a very familiar signal-processing system: talking. A microphone amplifies a sound; it then allows other technology—say, an audio speaker—to pick up that amplified signal. This diagram shows how a microphone can collect your voice (as a sensor) and convert the analog signal (through transduction) to a stream of pulses that fairly represents it. The signal can then be amplified (as well as processed and transmitted) and then converted back (through another transduction) to an analog signal that's acceptable by audio speakers, which our analog ears can hear.

Figure 2.2 Talking and hearing using a process of sensors and transducers.

We rely on our own processing system—the human body—all the time. And in much the same way that the body is made up of sensors, the Internet of Things will make up our cities.

2.6 The Internet of Things

We like to count "things" and Internet things are certainly no exception. Because of the increased maturity of standards (especially connectivity) and the dropping costs related to sensor technology (not just sensory hardware but also communication-related technology), analysts now are counting and forecasting how many sensors are embedded in products that send the activities of the world to the cloud. Remember, analysts like to count things. But the number of things really tells us a very uninteresting story. Despite the fact that the sensors, the connectivity capabilities, and even the applications are becoming very cheap to build and deploy, the real IoT game is not in the layers of technology but in the delivery of services that capitalize on that cheap stack of goods. Especially in the smart city.

But, as is often the case in the buzzword world of technology marketeering, we still don't know what the IoT really is. This can be a source of frustration for those who wish to size, forecast, and understand the scope of opportunity related to the IoT, and it's surely vexing for the investors and companies that are working to drive use cases that promote their products and services. Without the shared value of a cohesive message, marketing IoT wares is a lot like selling your own brand of pizza: every place is "The Original Ray's."

Perhaps it will be easier to just dispose of the terminology, because after all, not just about object, it's more about a technology stack. IoT simply doesn't describe the future, and it's certainly not the arms and legs of HAL from *2001: A Space Odyssey*. Maybe it's a little of all of these things, but truthfully, the IoT isn't about things at all. It's a model. And depending on the capabilities of the modeler, it may be a good one or a ludicrous one.

Remember that a model may often represent nothing more than the embodiment of a theory. In this case, the theory is that the devices that make up the connected world will one day deliver applications that will optimize our homes; reduce traffic; watch over our health, the car, and our pets; streamline our manufacturing processes, care for our safety and security, and fine-tune our systems of transportation. In the real world, this model is really about helping us change the way we experience the world—and at some level how the world experiences us. This new experience is about the interactions of the city at both the human and machine-to-machine levels; in fact, it's about the entire ecosystem that's created by connecting all the appropriate available devices, and filtering that data through applications and services that will allow humans and systems to invoke the highest value action in any moment.

2.6.1 The Smart City as Mediator

While we consider the IoT as our conceptual ideal for connecting any device to the Internet, there are many more factors that will allow the "system" of the smart city to mediate between entities—whether that mediation occurs between people, things, or people and things. Approaches to implementing this system have failed in the past because they've been so technocentric. In the hurry to capitalize on smartphones, smart appliances, smart wearable devices, and whatever else you can imagine from smart trains, planes, and automobiles, market makers have had to behave as if the efficient and optimal world were right on top of us and its reality were just a matter of money and will. But, while pieces of it may exist here and there, the smart city will only be fully realized when we are we—as humans in our natural and built environment—are provided services that can only exist when we can connect billions of devices and people, process the data rapidly, and make productive and collectively good decisions. This tendency to dummy down the smart city to simply a collection of things that can and should be counted and enumerated undermines its real value of improving societal and environmental outcomes. And today, that's an ambiguity that's largely theory and politics. It is this very ambiguity that has led some pundits to claim that the real winner in the technology race to the world of IoT will be the inventor of the virtual "god platform," the person who constructs "the highest, most generalized layer of intelligence and user interface that ties together connected devices and web services."[8]

[8] Bruner, J. (2014), "Who Will Build the 'God Platform' for the Internet of Things?" *Forbes.* Retrieved September 27, 2014, from http://www.forbes.com/sites/oreillymedia/2014/09/23/who-will-build-the-god-platform-for-the-internet-of-things.

We need to get comfortable with where we are quite early in the process today, while simultaneously acknowledging the imperative to rapidly invest in and improve our urban environments. Though our early concepts may never be built, they're important exercises of the imagination that enhance our abilities to understand what we must ultimately embody. Conceptual efforts facilitate our abilities to specify and detail the reference models that will be necessary to improve and revitalize our cities. It's certainly true that many components required to revolutionize our cities already exist as sensors, devices, communication standards, and applications, but we have yet to fully cope with the complexities inherent in describing systems that are so driven by the human will.

It's necessary to begin in the world of concept and symbol as we work to push our untranslated ideas and theories of how our cities might behave in a world of sensors and analytics. But as the early efforts of Masdar City and Songdo demonstrated, we pushed too quickly from understanding the behaviors of our smart cities to creating iconic representations. While not without some learning, building cities before we even begin to really put boundaries around our concepts has led to expensive missteps. First, we must take the first step of understanding the behaviors we wish to achieve, and then we must define the systems that will drive those outcomes in a real-world system.

Chapter Three

A New Perspective on Smart Cities

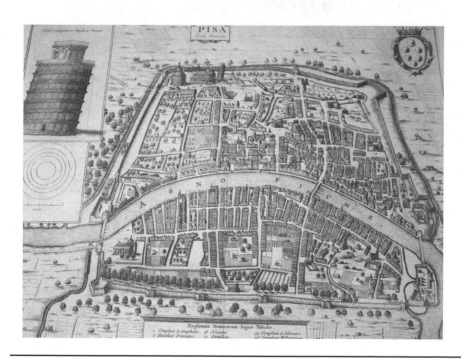

Eighteenth-century map of historical center of Pisa.[1]

---

[1] Image retrieved from the public domain at http://commons.wikimedia.org/wiki/File:Pisa_ancient_map.jpg.

3.1 Chapter Goal

Smart cities are the topic of hot debate. Billions are spent on developing them, yet there seems to be little middle ground between the extremes of viewpoint on them. In fact, up until now, discussions about technology advancement in smart cities have been scuttled by poorly constructed marketing messages and the loose use of terminology and the vitriolic backlash to those messages. In this chapter, we'll relieve the discussion of hyperbole, propose a common terminology and approach to the smart city, and show how well-known models and examples can help establish a useful framework for thinking about smart cities.

3.2 The Position for Moving Forward

Often, in the debate about the relationship between ubiquitous computing and human society, one must either be cast as a technology zealot with a double-shot, extra-foamy soy latte in your right hand, an iPad in your left, and a Google Glass device perched on your face, or a complete Luddite, peering out from a dusty closet, clutching a copy of *Dark Mission: The Secret History of NASA*. There is an unbelievable array of reading material available on the topic of the smart city, rendering any hope for a clear definition murky and too often self-serving.

Urban champions speak of the mounting prowess of the smart city, a settlement that's optimized by sensors and technologies that integrate our very bodies with the built environment and the cloud. More-skeptical prognosticators see a rising dysfunction that will bury humanity as we know it. Occasionally, these strange and useless dialogues will self-destruct into the social media sphere, creating difficult conditions for city planners and technologists alike. Yet, many of these complaints are attached only to the most fantastic scenarios, and in many ways they're completely irrelevant to the topic at hand. The transformative power of advanced technology applications for the smart city comes from the mundane: water monitoring, chemical leakage detection, air quality monitoring, traffic management, resource integration, financial engineering, and load control schemes for balancing the electric grid.

This certainly doesn't make the topic irrelevant to our lives, quite the contrary. In fact, if the predominant vision for the smart city is to be successful, the enabling technology will become simultaneously more transparent and more useful, until it ultimately fades away. And even if the data is completely democratized through widely available services, digital dissidents such as Julian Assange and Edward Snowden will likely be uninterested.

Here's why.

In 1974, the US military launched its first global positioning services (GPS) satellite, called NAVSTAR, after learning that it could use its 1950s-era satellites for continuous signaling applications. Then, partially in response to the Soviets shooting down KAL Flight 007 in 1978 after the plane wandered into USSR airspace, US President Reagan released the GPS technology to be installed in civilian commercial aircraft. The technology continued to dramatically improve and expand; by 1989, Magellan was first to market, with a handheld GPS navigation device for civilian use. However, the US government also feared malfeasant use of the systems, and the Department of Defense (DoD) purposely decreased the accuracy of the system. By 2000, the DoD had ended this policy, and overnight, the average citizen had the ability to navigate with a high degree of precision using GPS products. The floodgates of innovation were open.

By 2004, MapQuest had created a "find me" service that worked on GPS-enabled mobile phones and helped users not only pinpoint their location automatically but also access maps and directions, as well as find nearby places of interest such as airports and restaurants. As open systems and the abilities of interconnected data began to take hold, many mapping applications emerged—including Google Maps and MapQuest—that today offer satellite imagery and street-view perspectives, while also providing data to external users through the apps' web mapping service. Today, owing to the more than 30 active satellites in the GPS system, cross-platform data availability, and the mixing and mashing of technologies and presentation schemas, we now have dozens of navigation applications and in-dash route finders. We can make our own maps, research weather phenomena at our desired vacation destinations, and play geocaching games, and we can do all of this without one single thought of a satellite. We can forget all about the GPS. Why? Because now we just have location services that we turn on and off, depending on our mood. These services employ GPS and data from crowdsourced Wi-Fi hotspots and cell towers to deliver contextual accuracy. Knowing where we are at any time and pumping that information into the social sphere in association with our activities is one of the most integral features of the smartphone phenomenon.

If we deconstruct this narrative to explore its usefulness as a model, we can see that four key things occurred between the 1950s and today:

1. *Technology transfer drives innovation.* When the military allowed its intelligence application from past decades be released into the civilian sphere, it returned our investment in government technology and gave it back in spades. Taking what already existed and giving it to anyone who could get their hands on a GPS receiver, the government enabled new and creative uses for the GPS service that are still being imagined and developed today.
2. *Open data creates economic benefits.* This free provision of GPS technology for the unrestricted development of civilian applications encouraged further investments in technology, including driving the shared gains of jobs, taxes, and tariffs, as well as the movement toward open data paradigms.
3. *Context-based services support many needs.* GPS technology has evolved in myriad ways, and its data is now used in multiple markets and countless ways. From guiding civilian aircraft to siting new infrastructure like cell towers to supporting civil engineering projects to enabling the ubiquitous social media applications, GPS-based technology has transformed society.
4. *Applications are the primary focus.* And finally, because the data was and still is openly available to all (now through several providers), the focus of innovation is always on making better, highly usable tools that leverage raw data. GPS-based information is as accessible as the nearest connected device that can do something with it.

This approach is what we hope to see with many of the advanced technologies that are being designed to serve the urban environment. Even while we discuss the most appropriate and interesting uses of the microchip, it—like the pipes and asphalt of yesteryear—will one day disappear from the human consciousness and into the fabric of our everyday lives. This ubiquity will demand that, as a society, we meet the same standards that any critical infrastructure demands, including, standard approaches that foster the most ethical, forward-looking, robust, and resilient architectural designs.

Similar to the GPS as it traveled from a top-secret military application to a technology that's enabled in smartphones and car dashboards, the smart city will also be successful if the following criteria are pursued:

- New revenue streams are created through the optimal use of resources, such as electricity and water, through conservation and efficiency services.
- New investments in technology are encouraged by providing access to data that can be used in innovative and unimagined ways and that can be paid for creatively.
- The ability to create new services flexibly allows the technologies that form the underlying layer of the smart city to be installed once and used variously and continuously.
- Improved livability is the focus, not how and where the technology is installed.

3.3 What's the Holdup?

So why has this been so difficult? As mentioned previously, there seems to be a lot of agreement that cities should be "better," but there's little consensus on what that means. It's also uncertain whether technology can be folded into the mix to add security, trust, and transparency in how the systems are working, assuaging concerns about data mismanagement and spying.

More and more frequently, technology companies work to set the agenda, but they do so in a way that does more to confuse than clarify. Consider one vision of the smart city (which is quite similar to dozens of other definitions of the concept):

> Smart cities use technology to offer better civic services, maximize energy efficiency by reducing waste and greenhouse gas emissions, enhance public security, manage urban congestion and optimize overall operational efficiency.[2]

---

[2] The MER Group: Telecom Division (n.d.), "Smart City Solution: Enabling Smart Cities by Delivering the Fiber Infrastructure Edge." Retrieved from http://www.mer-group.com/wp-content/uploads/2014/06/smart-city.pdf.

At first blush, this is an innovative and worthy visionary goal for the use of technology in our urban environments. But it turns out that these messages don't mean as much as we'd like, and they feel vague and over-broad in a manner that doesn't inspire confidence. It's worth exploring why this is often the case.

3.3.1 The Efficient, Effective, and Optimal City?

There are several terms that we see repeatedly whenever smart management of any type is discussed. We've already used these terms multiple times in this very book: *efficient*, *effective*, and *optimal*.

Efficient. Being efficient means doing something to achieve maximum productivity with a minimum of waste. Most people use "efficiency" to refer to something that is probably less convenient, more annoying, and less pleasant than what they're used to. They likely think, however, that it might save them money. This is, by definition, not the case. For example, an incandescent lightbulb uses more energy than a light-emitting diode (LED) bulb, but they both can produce the equivalent light output. However, the LED requires less power for the same amount of lumens, making it more efficient. Consider that in order to produce 800 lumens, you would need a 60-watt incandescent bulb or a lower-draw LED that consumes somewhere between 8 and 12 watts. The LED is approximately five times more efficient.

Effective. Efficiency and effectiveness are often confused. In keeping with the lighting theme, consider that an efficient lightbulb produces the same amount of light as an inefficient bulb but at a lower energy cost. An effective lightbulb, on the other hand, produces desirable or intended results. If you want to use less energy under any circumstances, an LED is the right choice for you. But if you want to use LEDs to replace the incandescent bulbs in your art gallery's wall-wash installations, you will soon realize that the color consistency of LED lighting can be highly variable and none of the lights look quite the same. Despite your good intentions to install very efficient lighting, your plan was totally ineffective for your needs.

Optimal. The definition of *optimal* is much more context-sensitive. It means finding the best solution in the face of constraint. When I perform a search on the Internet, information about my interests and locations typically gets included in the algorithm (in part, because of location services), and I get a result that optimally fits my need. For example, if I search for "coffee," and the algorithm is any good, I'll get a few hits for coffee shops near me rather than a coffee bean farm in Guatemala (though that could be just as reasonable a result if no other information is considered). The mathematical definition of *optimal* is a bit cumbersome for our purposes, but essentially, it's some sort of process that allows a system to become as perfect as possible, or, in other words, most effective.

3.4 Smart City Design Goals

Striving for an efficient city means that effort is expended to drive down resource costs whenever possible. Unfortunately, that goal can become quickly all encompassing and may not produce desired outcomes. In fact, some things are better left inefficient. Do you want your doctor to be measured on her effectiveness at getting patients in and out as quickly as possible? Probably not. Misdiagnosis by a festinate doctor can have major consequences.

Instead of asking how to run a city more efficiently, it's more useful to ask how to run it more effectively, that is, how do we want our resources used in the context of desired outcomes? Once the most optimal solution has been determined for a particular issue or urban problem, it's possible to see how that problem can be solved most efficiently. It's a focus on the *what* of the situation rather than the *how*. To confuse efficiency with effectiveness muddies our best understanding of how to achieve our goals with the resources we have available.

The real danger is in re-creating our cities with the same problems we're trying to solve. Do we want to build cities with the same infestations, trash, and smog but run pest control and garbage trucks on a tighter schedule? A more auspicious goal is to leverage advanced technologies to make the most efficient use of all our resources—financial, built, and natural—to improve livability.

It's dangerous to be inaccurate in our statements about the smart city, given the tremendous need to improve our urban environment. Recently, the EU Platform for Intelligent Cities posited, "The current economic crisis, combined with growing citizen expectations, is placing increasing pressure on European cities to provide better and more efficient infrastructures and services, often for less cost."[3] The statement is nebulous at best, but these ideas will likely become more clear as we begin to see real-world technology implementations in existing cities and can develop better theories about what works and what doesn't, and why. For now, it's best to avoid platitudes until we have more evidence about the role of new technology and what other resources will be optimized in our quest for creating smart cities.

3.4.1 Engineering New Models for Investing in the Smart City

One of the things that made the journey from GPS to location services so interesting is the creativity that has gone into developing viable financial models for monetizing free data from the government. Not only have many jobs been created by this phenomenon, but a lot of taxes have been collected too. And theoretically those funds fix our roads, educate our kids, and finance new technologies that will one day loop back into the civil domain.

For an interesting example, imagine that you own a microbrewery. You blend, mash, boil, and refrigerate the finest brew. You also clean and fill bottles to be packaged for delivery. Your energy consumption is through the roof. There are many systems you could invest in that would allow you to recognize substantial energy savings, including more-efficient boilers, motors, packaging systems, and refrigerators. Apart from the equipment you use for brewing, you suspect that the building itself carries opportunities that could yield straightforward payback opportunities. You're an expert in beer, though, not energy efficiency. You don't know where to start: How do you assess equipment; plan your upgrades, replacements, and retrofits; and make sense of it all financially? You already have investors to please, debt to pay, and profits to grow.

Here's a proposition for you. I'm going to come into your brewery and check out your operation, your building, and even your finances. After I learn about your goals, how things are running today, and how you're hoping to not only improve your cost savings but also enhance your green

[3] EU Platform for Intelligent Cities (n.d.), "Smart Cities." Retrieved October 19, 2014, from http://www.epic-cities.eu/content/smart-cities.

image, I'm going to do the remarkable. I'm going to pay for 70 percent of all the changes I think you need to make in order to reach your energy-efficiency goals, and you're going to put in 30 percent. Then, for the next 12 years, any money you save from the baseline I've calculated, I'm going to take 50 percent and you get to keep the rest.

Payback periods are widely variable depending on geographic factors, how equipment is used, building envelope characteristics, and numerous other influences. For breweries, most energy-saving strategies offer a payback period that ranges from a few months to nearly four years. So together we make a US$75,000 investment in your business and obtain 25 percent cost savings from these energy expenditures. Thus, even if I'm just taking half the leftovers, my gross profit margin at the end of the 12 years would easily be over 80 percent on my 70 percent portion of the investment.

It doesn't stop there. Let's look at how I can even do better than that as an investor, help out my most-favored vendors along the way, and encourage more innovation.

- As an investor, I can protect my investment by doing regular credit checks on your company and perhaps help you obtain financing for your 30 percent, assuming it's even easier to obtain with my backing.
- I likely have my favorite energy-efficiency equipment suppliers, so I can give them better deal flow, allow them to integrate their own financing into their sales offerings, and ultimately loosen the financial constraints on suppliers.
- I can also offer you, the business, the ability to make payments to me, enabling you to go cash-flow-positive on day one, if the savings exceed your monthly payments to me.
- Your business recognizes savings, reduces the carbon footprint, and improves your marketing capital with no cash outlay.
- If I'm smart, and have lots of properties under my management, I may add other services and analytics functions to further tune and optimize the premises under my purview.

Financial engineering is a fascinating topic and will play an increasingly important role in funding the development of the smart city. In no way do governments have the money to make straightforward investments of this scope. However, there is plenty of good incentive for other investors to move into sustainability, for reasons much more profound than green-washing and brand management. Tricky regulatory questions are emerging that will need to be directly addressed, such as the ownership of water rights and the scope of the social contract to provide a basic supply of clean water, electricity, and other infrastructure services as well as health-care to citizens.

3.4.2 Context-Sensitive Technology Services

Technology companies with a combination of traditional government and private investment have done much to set the smart city agenda, so it's not surprising that many of the early efforts have been heavily focused on risk management for their investments. Yet, the so-called greenfield cities of Masdar City and Songdo, among others, have managed their financial exposure with limited success and their lessons are not terribly useful for the cities that we already inhabit, and have for many years. The same strategies that are used to build a city from the ground up are hardly well suited to most other developed or developing cities because urban environments have evolved their own character, sometimes over hundreds of years. These settlements are varied, chaotic, and sometimes fraught with political and economic challenges and require flexibility in their approach.

Some purveyors have taken a diversification approach to selling smart technologies. Not unlike other large-scale industries, smart technology businesses have set up sales offices around the world in both well-developed and underdeveloped markets in the hopes that some of these emerging markets will find success, along with more-predictable wins. Unfortunately, this approach ties itself to a strategy that depends on certain characteristics, including well-managed capital markets, a stable government, a somewhat familiar system of jurisprudence, and basic property rights. In some cases, it's essential to have a reliable infrastructure that provides electricity, water, and transportation. John D. Macomber, in his work on sustainable cities, describes these difficult markets as "unsettled," noting that they're "less politically stable, their public services are unreliable, contracts are hard to enforce in them, and so on. Poorly regulated low-rise urban sprawl is the norm. Cities such as Rio de Janeiro [Brazil], Lagos [Portugal], Karachi [Pakistan], Dhaka [Bangladesh], and Jakarta

[Indonesia] are prime examples."[4] In his work, he develops a "hygiene" list that he feels describes the basic requirements of any company wanting to work on smart city efforts in these regions. His approach is helpful, though it's perhaps even more helpful with a certain level of abstraction that broadens its applicability to a wider range of situations.

In an attempt to do just that, there are several important characteristics for technology providers that wish to enter the smart city market. The inclusion of these characteristics will help avoid some of the earlier missteps around the world, especially when it comes to the management of terrifically complex projects.

Here are standard criteria for any company that wants to have a good shot at participating in the smart city sphere for the long haul. These requirements are also represented in Figure 3.1.

- Ability to **run projects in multifaceted environments** with many stakeholders with divergent interests
- **Strong company leadership** that's able to work with politicians, regulators, and special interest groups
- Ability to bring technology into the urban environment comfortably based on a variety of **financial-engineering strategies**, unexpected slowdowns, election cycles, and strategy changes
- Positive and proven partnerships and relationships with other key market participants
- A trusted, principled, and **transparent** approach to brand management

Figure 3.1   Bringing products and services to the urban environment.

[4] Macomber, John D. (2013), "Building Sustainable Cities," *Harvard Business Review*. Retrieved from http://hbr.org/2013/07/building-sustainable-cities/ar/pr.

3.4.3 What About the Start-Up?

In the developed world where we will cumulatively spend months of our lifetime checking e-mails, we have come to believe that the web is the great normalizer. If anyone can build a solid product, then they have an equal chance of becoming wildly successful. That may be partially true, but in working with smart cities, we're dealing with the deep and dark forces that manage the built environment. Even the computer systems within these environments may be decades old and frustratingly arcane. Jakob Nielsen, the renowned web content architect, said in his book, *Designing Excellent Websites: Secrets of an Information Architect*, "Only 10 percent of the current Fortune 500 companies will survive the next 10 years. The rest will shrivel to a fraction of their former selves, because they won't make a successful transition to the customer-centric web economy." He was correct in many ways, but he sure wasn't talking about the government or any quasigovernmental institutions like water or energy providers. Instead, the truth is likely much closer to what William Gibson, cyberpunk author, said: "The future has arrived, it's just not evenly distributed yet."

In working to provide technology products to cities that each have their own unique character, and only so many dollars to invest, the importance of brand credibility is pronounced. Without a doubt, in a world where there is little differentiation between many sensors, devices, and software applications on a purely functional level, it is the solid, mature brand that will command the highest price premium from our cities. Why? Because every strong brand has defined itself in the market; it's distinctive and has evolved over time—and not just out of the mind of some great web designer. It enables all the other aspects needed to work with disparate stakeholders, politicians, partners, and financiers. Small companies simply have less to give, and a lot less room to make big mistakes. The smaller purveyor with a technology advancement that can benefit the smart city needs to be building relationships and ensuring interoperability with the predominant technologies and integration firms. By the way, there's an app for that (and if there isn't right now, there will be).

3.5 A Usable World

Earlier in the chapter, we compared the concept of usability for location-based services in the context of the GPS example. It's easy to argue that the tipping point for location services was not only the ability of a smart-phone to use GPS- and cellular-based technologies to pinpoint your place on Earth, but also the ability to leverage that information transparently and make it usable.

Usability simply means that the human-made object in question should be easy to learn and interact with. The vapid days of the early Internet were the domain of industrial engineers who were specially trained in cognitive psychology or even anthropology to provide the best possible construction of an application, website, e-reader, television, or set-top box to drive greater adoption and use (and often the sale of band-width). The earliest financial model for the Internet was the capitaliza-tion of access devices and web properties with e-commerce capabilities to allow customers with credit cards to buy things in exactly the same way as one would in a bricks-and-mortar store, but without the middleman.

The next real change arrived with the codification of personalization, the early analytical treatment of data, attempts at deeper customer seg-mentation, and advertising. When the idea of single-purpose applications began to emerge—and when Apple's App Store opened—the economy of very tiny things began to take root. To this day, apps tend to do one thing very well for a very low cost. As handheld-device operating systems and the cloud evolve to allow multitasking and ways of integrating applica-tion data, we see sharing across many channels. So when I take a digital picture with my phone, I can instantly share it on Facebook, Twitter, Flickr, and at least 10 other sites. The pic is also automatically backed up to multiple storage destinations.

In fact, we've gotten so good at incorporating standards into web design that usability itself has become a commodity skill. It's an accepted and required input into any new product design process, whether that product is a web page or a travel mug. Some will argue with this, saying that a pair of Levi's is distinctly different from a pair of Hollisters, but what really makes them different is how they're marketed and for what purpose (in this case, "I want to look like a cowboy" or "I want to look like a Venice Beach surfer," respectively). Less important is the fact that they're both denim pants.

In addition to being easy to learn and credible, a new product should be intuitive. There are many dramatic cases of user interface error, from Air Inter Flight 148, where a difficult computer system was blame, to a single misinterpreted light in the control room at Three Mile Island, resulting in a partial nuclear meltdown. A less well-known user interface error resulted in singer-songwriter John Denver's death in October 1997; the sad tale is instructive.

Denver's airplane—the no-longer-sold Rutan Long-EZ—was designed with the fuel selector valve (some aircraft require the pilot to switch the fuel source from the left tank to the right, depending on the distance of the flight) behind the pilot's left shoulder. Thus, to switch tanks, the pilot was forced to twist his head to the left, reach behind with his right hand, and turn the valve to the desired position. Unfortunately, pilots of a certain stature were required to brace themselves with their right foot in order to get the leverage to perform the action. Part of the directional control of an aircraft is managed through the rudders, which are controlled by the feet. Much like when you inadvertently stomp your car's accelerator instead of its brake, Denver pressed the right rudder pedal all the way to the floor while he was changing tanks, forcing the plane to jerk to the right and spin into the ocean. It's worth noting that the Long-EZ builder not only placed the valve behind the pilot, but also configured it such that turning the valve to the right actually turned on the left tank.[5]

3.5.1 Livability

It's not hard to understand that an intuitive, easy-to-learn, clear interface is always more pleasant to use, but sometimes it's the thing that stands between life and death. And in the smart city, the idea behind the importance of usability—and the aforementioned notion of transparency—is livability. This may be the most obvious component to a city (no people, no city), but strangely it is by far the most overlooked when the topic turns to technology advancement.

Although it's complex and multifaceted, this discussion really isn't as philosophical as it may seem. The significance of the city and the role of the public urban environment in shaping the world are known to most. Still, many cities have been run over by cars, pollution, and crime, nearly eliminating storied squares, soaring churches, public buildings, museums, and shops as key to the contentment of city inhabitants. It is easy to create an argument that a healthy urban environment can fight the

[5] Tognazzini, Bruce (1999), "John Denver: When Interfaces Kill," Ask Tog, blog. Retrieved October 19, 2014, from http://www.asktog.com/columns/027InterfacesThatKill.html.

insular, introverted world that's created by the soft exoskeleton of the city known as the metropolitan area, the megalopolis, and the megaregions that dilute our public spaces in conurbated municipalities. Examples of these regions include the Arizona Sun Corridor, the Colorado Front Range, Germany's Berlin-Brandenburg area, the Mediterranean Golden Banana, China's Pearl River Delta, and of course, Florida. Conurbation is an important issue, because it blurs the real definition of any city, smart or otherwise. The loss of a tax base is also part of the fallout; for all the issues that urban Detroit wrestled with after the Great Recession, the suburbanites didn't suffer nearly as much as the city dwellers.

The innovative initiative Cities for People describes the city as "a crucible for health, happiness and prosperity"; it further says, "We take livability to mean a city's ability to be responsive to the needs of its inhabitants."[6] Certainly there are fundamental aspects to that ability to be responsive, including the relationship of the natural environment to the built environment, social support across the range of human needs, recreation, and education. But for some reason, contentment and livability are often seen as trade-offs for sustainable development. These two paths have diverged, and there's not a clear way toward understanding the importance of design and structure to the functioning and well-being of the community that lives in the city's environment.

Community Research Connections (CRC) produced a variety of case studies in 2006 that demonstrate this issue. In its research of the city of Vancouver, CRC studied the city's position on the relationship between the "livability agenda" and sustainable urban development. The study largely casts the issue in extremes, not only from an ideological perspective but also from an intergenerational one. CRC stated, "The question, therefore, is how does the city shift from the current generation focused on liveability [sic], which is limited in its impact and not necessarily sustainable, to a position focused on sustainable development and making real advances in infrastructure and sustainable communities?"[7] Thus, Vancouver now fights for the good life, all the things that

---

[6] Cities for People (n.d.), "Livability." Retrieved October 20, 2014, from http://www.citiesforpeople.ca/en/themes/livability.

[7] Ling, Chris, Hamilton, Jim, and Thomas, Kathy (2006), "What Makes a City Liveable?" Community Research Connections. Retrieved August 31, 2014, from http://crcresearch.org/case-studies/case-studies-sustainable-infrastructure/land-use-planning/what-makes-a-city-liveable.

drew communities to the suburbs in the first place: parks, safety, low traffic scale, festivals, local food, and a community social life. Though it's unclear why these luxuries must come at the cost of livability in an urban environment.

Livability is essentially a way to measure whether or not a city is a good place to make one's home in. But what people want from their cities varies greatly, not just among cultures but among cities themselves. It's difficult, then, for a city designer to envision as solution that will be acceptable to all. Indeed, as many philosophers have noted over the eons, meeting everyone's needs all the time is nearly impossible.

Chapter Four

Why Design Thinking?

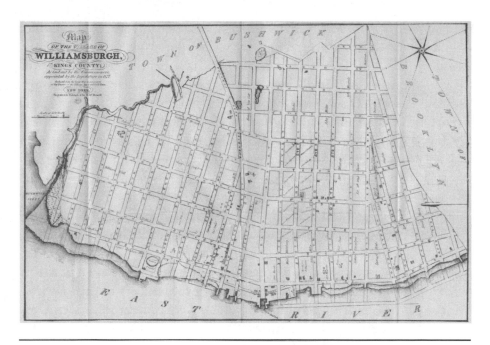

Historical map of Williamsburgh, Brooklyn, as laid out by the commissioners in 1827.[1]

[1] Image retrieved from the public domain as scanned by H. McDowell at https:// commons.wikimedia.org/wiki/Old_maps_of_cities#/media/File:1827_ Williamsburg_Map.jpg.

4.1 Chapter Goal

This chapter explores the fundamentals of the design-thinking process, from the initial perspective of empathy and inspiration, to the early stages of creativity and ideation, to the later stages of implementation that rationally meets the needs of people in their environments. In this chapter, we will discuss the repeatable elements of design thinking and begin to explore how it adds value in myriad settings, from classrooms to highways to urban living environments.

4.2 Thinking About Thinking

The term *design thinking* has a definition, but it's really just shorthand for human-centered cognitive processes that designers use to solve complex problems. This begs the question of just what exactly a human-centered cognitive process is. Tim Brown, the CEO and president of design and consulting firm IDEO, literally wrote the book on design thinking, and even he shirks off an exact definition of the approach. Instead, he tells us how it works. He describes a repeatable method that teams can use to create new products and approaches through an iterative process that flexibly drives new forms from the earliest stages of problem-shaping through ideation and, finally, execution. However, the history of what we now call design thinking is much older than the IDEO design firm. It actually finds its origins with the emergence of the post–World War II fascination with the creative process itself, documenting how it works, and understanding how it can be captured, studied, and implemented as a practice.

By the 1960s, society began marching toward the era of the machine, with digital systems in play that were designed to help solve seemingly unsolvable problems, such as unraveling human DNA, playing a decent game of chess, and working on a cure for cancer. Today, we find that the application of design methods and theories is the foundation of what has come to define our modern economy and technology-enabled way of life.

To demonstrate, let's do a quick search on Amazon. More than 6,000 English-language books have the exact phrase "design methods" in their title. A search of patents applied for in the US shows somewhat amusing evidence that plenty of people and companies have sought to protect their own novel "invention" for thinking processes that can be applied to making new things. Dismissed by some scientific thinkers as "art," yet rejected by artists who complain that the design process is unique and cannot be codified, design thinking rests somewhat awkwardly between science and the humanities, but may in fact be the key to future innovation and strategic thinking.

There are as many variations on design thinking as there are designers who use the process. This is not really surprising, since design thinking often represents the mere desire to transform our perspective from technology-centric to human-centric. This means creating meaningful products that strive to balance a world of constraints and competing requirements of both people and systems, in a way that is positive, useful, and viable within that world. Any other evangelistic touting of design thinking is likely to be gimmicky and an artificial manipulation of the creative process in the ultimate service of mediocrity. Design thinking is most useful when it maintains its focus on solution-based problem-solving for the built environment in a way that is appropriate and desirable for the people within that environment.

Using a templated and repeatable process for product development is common sense ("measure twice, cut once"), but by the turn of the most recent century, business processes aficionados (and CEOs) began turning their focus to services. Now, design thinking is being applied to more than just making things; it's being applied to how we carry out the business of life. Instead of designing a better pot for water, we want to figure out how to deliver clean water. Even university curriculum offerings have begun to integrate design thinking into their business programs, and within the past few years, design thinking has appeared within many a core curriculum for both the hopeful MBA and the aspiring MFA student at our leading schools of knowledge. We have learned to expect efficiency and optimization in everything. We want efficient energy, homes, web pages, organizations, and even our Olympians' swim strokes. We quest to produce, train, learn, eat, exercise, build, and move optimally. To be clear, design thinking is not always about optimization and efficiency; it's about balancing the forces and finding developing innovation in the space between what's desirable to our users, what's viable, and what's feasible.

This means that if we approach our problem of smart cities with design thinking, we will edge forward toward creating innovative environments that people enjoy living in that are realizable, practical, and economically and environmentally sustainable.

4.2.1 How Does This Working Definition Work?

For the purposes of designing smart cities, it's useful to be specific about how design thinking is not going to help us at all, especially in the context of a book that is geared toward the successful application of technology. First, for the engineers, it's not about the scientific method. We don't begin with all the parameters of the dumb-city problem because we don't always know them—and in every city, they will be different. Instead, the goal of design thinking as a process is to work to investigate all that is known and unknown about a situation in order to evoke all that is non-obvious about the needs of our cities. This is where we can begin to find the many potential (and often unexpected) pathways forward for solving our goals. With the more analytical scientific method, we are apt to let reality speak for itself by developing a theory, testing it, and adjusting when that theory is challenged. Ultimately, we want to discover a theory that can be confirmed.

While there are many creative theorists (the extent of their creativity usually depends on their feelings about risk), in general we will always find that analytical-prone people performing some variation of the question-hypothesis-experiment-theory process. Let's consider the problem of a lost set of car keys, with an example that is close enough to the truth:

Question. Where are my car keys?

Hypothesis. Well, my car is in the driveway. My house keys are on the same keychain as my car keys, and I obviously unlocked the front door because I'm standing in my kitchen. I put away all the groceries, took out the trash, and hung up my jacket at some point after I returned home. My first hypothesis is that they are in my jacket; my second hypothesis is that I put them in the freezer with the ice cream; my third is that I accidentally threw them away when I took out the garbage.

Prediction. If I search in my jacket, in the refrigerator, and in the trash, I'll find my car keys.

Experiment. I searched in my jacket pockets and the keys weren't there; I looked in the freezer and there were no car keys; finally, I dug through the garbage and they weren't there either. But there they were on the floor next to the trashcan.

Analysis. I lost my keys somewhere in my house, yet the experiment showed that my keys were not in any of the places hypothesized. Rather, they had dropped out of my jacket while I was throwing away the trash and were neither in my jacket nor in the trash. None of my hypotheses were correct, but I was able to move forward toward even with the theories I had until the real facts of the situation emerged, by being flexible enough to look next to the trash and not directly in it.

When a problem involves observable phenomena, when something can be tested by observable, empirical or measurable means, the scientific method is reliable and indisputably useful in solving the conundrum. That's because the truth can ultimately be verified.

But what happens when we instead want to solve for a goal, or even just solve a more ambiguous problem? Or what about the cases where the problem space is fairly unclear and we may be forced to define and redefine our initial understanding of the issues?

This is where a process of design can be helpful. As we have made clear by now, there is no canonical design-thinking process. And, just like every methodological approach, it too can be overthought and overwrought. However, at its most boiled down, there are three general stages of design thinking; they include an empathetic viewpoint, a creative ideation process, and a rational approach toward executing our ideas. What happens when we think about the lost keys with design thinking, focusing not on finding lost car keys, but on reducing the impact and frequency of losing them in the first place?

Empathize. In this early phase of the design process, a challenge is identified for some user or particular group of users. In our very simple example, I repeatedly lose my car keys, it makes me anxious, I run late, and I get upset when they're lost.

Define (or Interpretation). In this phase, we start to develop a meaningful understanding of the problem, one that gives shape to the challenge. When I'm running short on time or focused on something else, I'm not thinking about putting things back where they can be easily found; I'm rushing and things get misplaced or lost. Already in a high state of distraction, I'm not always even sure where to begin looking when I invariably misplace my keys.

Idea. Here, we begin to transition from problem definitions to solutions. Tools like brainstorming, sketching, and mind-mapping can bring shape to ideas. What if I could feel confident that I could always find my keys, even if I dropped them in the driveway? Maybe I could put some sort of clicker on my key ring, or a light, or a sensor. Maybe a wireless device that interfaces with my iPhone that is usually in my pocket and that I rarely lose!

Prototype. This is the experimental gadget stage, where a mock-up is produced that enables you to gain feedback from your target user. My design team cut out a small square and taped it to my key ring. Then, they mocked up a smartphone application that mimicked the behavior of a wireless sensor attached to my keys. The location of my keys is always being updated on the phone, and the sensor plays the game of cold, warm, hot as I get close to my keys. Additionally, I can find the keys by asking the app to play an audible tone on the sensor. I was able to imagine how useful this would be and I was enthusiastic about the idea.

Test. Like most projects, our key-finder initiative is a highly iterative and evolving process. The team made a sensor based on my initial feedback and hung it from my keychain. When I lost my keys, I used the app to play a tone, but at first it wasn't loud enough, so they fixed that. Then, I asked them to add a map to the app in case I dropped my keys while on a hike. That way, I'd be able to go back and find them. Turns out, I liked the solution so much, I put a sensor in my backpack, my wallet, and even hung one from my dog's collar.

Though the scientific method was very useful in solving the problem of finding my lost keys, it did nothing for me in terms of solving the conditions that created the problem to begin with, which is absent-mindedly misplacing my keys when I'm busy. Design thinking is not focused on excessive analysis or even on working it all out; instead, design thinking is about human-centered problem-solving. The problem began with my being unfocused, rushed, distracted, and stressed out—the perfect recipe for misplacing important items. With the scientific method, we were given a methodology to find the answer to a discrete problem—find my car keys by developing a hypothesis about where they might be—and then test it. With the design-thinking approach, the focus was instead on solution-solving, where we attempted to develop a way to either prevent the problem from ever occurring or make it easier to solve the issue when it happened. In fact, my stress-level dropped because I always knew I could find my keys.

So, what happened? The designers identified the human experience of distraction and stress and found a way to lower the anxiety related to the *prospect* of misplacing an important item. In ideating, the propensity for technology was accounted for as a guide to potential solutions. Then the designers created a paper prototype to form a basis for discussion about their ideas and how those ideas might work. The team took feedback and went back to ideation and prototyping. Then they delivered a sensor that could serve as a key fob that helped reduce my overall anxiety about losing things and provided a mechanism to easily locate important (and thus tagged) items with a map and a signal.

Figure 4.1 shows how the iterative process of design thinking occurs across the phases of empathy, creativity, and rationality—or what Tim Brown identifies as the spaces of inspiration, ideation, and implementation. Empathy-driven inspiration helps the design team understand the known parameters of the challenge and how best to approach it and interpret the information they receive. The structure of the process then leads the team toward a creative phase of ideation, which is where the opportunities to solve the problem begin to develop and thoughts emerge about what could be created to meet the challenge that was identified in the earlier phases of discovery. Once an idea is discovered, a rational phase of experimentation and implementation begins with simple prototypes and

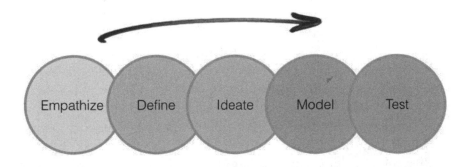

Figure 4.1 Design thinking is a human-centered iterative process that comprehends the phases of empathy, creativity, and rationality.

models that can be used to test the usefulness of the idea for actually solving the problem. Once the solution is proved to work, it can be built and incrementally adjusted as more is learned.

4.2.2 How the Best Technology Fails and Where the Better Solution Wins

These activities don't always happen in a linear or sequential manner, but without inspiration and a desire to solve a problem where real human need is at stake, empathy is the place where the process of design thinking must begin. Without empathy, there's no motivation to embark on this deeply human process—and this is where many smart cities have floundered. By emphasizing technology capabilities to achieve efficiency and optimization, smart cities neglect to consider how technology will succeed in a flourishing city full of people, and that is socially dumb. If I spend millions improving my transportation system into a revitalization project for the city center, but don't invest in cleaning up the trash, then people can get there, but no one will want to.

This may be a worn-out example, but the home video wars and the Betamax flame-out is a perfect example of design failure, but the story is much more interesting than many realize. Developed by Sony, Betamax hit the market in 1975 and was in many ways technically superior to the JVC Video Home System (VHS) product that rolled out soon after in 1976. Consumers had to choose: invest in the innovative Betamax format or the close-following VHS? Sony has been blamed for making key errors, including a slow move to license the technology (which seems hard to believe, given Apple's similar trajectory) and, perhaps more convincingly, an unwillingness to let the pornography industry use Betamax technology. But Sony's product failed for a simpler and more obvious reason. In the beginning, Betamax tapes could hold one hour of content, whereas VHS tapes could hold two. Consequently, dozens of production companies chose VHS over Betamax because they could store an entire movie on it. It wasn't until the mid-1980s that Sony started producing comparable-length tapes.

What Sony really needed to consider was how its product would be used by its target market—home consumers. It's annoying to change a videotape midway through a movie. With design-thinking techniques,

Sony would have begun at the definitive starting point with a document called a brief. For some reason, the construction of a brief is discombobulating to the bastion of people in the world who prefer to discuss and formulate specifications, but not necessarily create. The brief is just a definition of the problem, but the definition needs to be constructed in such a way that it doesn't overly constrain the design team but provides room for flights of fancy and inspiration. As the philosopher William Cowper is thought to have said, "If in this I have been tedious, it may be some excuse, I had not time to make it shorter." The author of the design brief cannot make this same excuse, because it is a key part of the process to avoid impeding on the imaginative process of how the goal of the exercise might be accomplished.

In the mid-1960s, the television serial *Mission Impossible* hit the airwaves in the United States. Each show began with the unveiling of the mission, the details of which were transferred to the Impossible Mission (IM) Force through a tape recorder and a bland envelope containing photos and information. The voice says to the agent—most famously Jim Phelps—"Your mission, Jim, should you decide to accept it . . . ," followed by a description of Jim's assignment and the desired outcome, but the voice doesn't tell Jim how to get any of this done. He's reminded, "As always, should you or any of your IM Force be caught or killed, the Secretary will disavow any knowledge of your actions." At which time, the tape recorder begins smoking and the theme music belts out. That tape recorder and the manila envelope? Collectively, those are a design brief.

Here it is more academically explained in the *Stanford Social Innovation Review*:

> The brief is a set of mental constraints that gives the project team a framework from which to begin, benchmarks by which they can measure progress, and a set of objectives to be realized—such as price point, available technology, and market segment.[2]

But perhaps most importantly, as the journal article goes on to point out, the key characteristic of a well-crafted design brief is that it never

[2] Brown, Tim and Wyatt, Jocelyn (2010), "Design Thinking for Social Innovation," *Stanford Social Innovation Review*. Retrieved November 22, 2014, from http://www.ssireview.org/articles/entry/design_thinking_for_social_innovation.

attempts to answer the question it has posed, only to establish the operating constraints of the potential solution.

4.2.3 Briefly on the Brief

Given the fundamental importance of the design brief, it's worth taking a quick look at a few examples of both successful and unsuccessful attempts at briefing the designer. It describes a problem scenario and sets up an opportunity for inspiration by including three discrete elements: what we want to make, why we think it needs to be made, and who it's being made for.

Let's consider a simple but interesting design situation and brief.

> *Traffic jams on the highway are often triggered when drivers are notified that two lanes will merge into one, yet the lanes of cars cannot merge because drivers don't offer sufficient gaps between their cars. Surface traffic in congested scenarios contributes to greenhouse gases, which are greatly increased in stop-and-go driving patterns. Motorists who merge early after seeing the merge sign tend to create the jams to begin with, and late mergers are often punished by the early mergers, who refuse to open enough space to allow the late-moving cars into traffic. This creates an even worse situation of tense drivers and higher carbon dioxide emission. Traffic congestion and greenhouse gas models have convincingly shown that the most effective solution to this problem is to keep drivers in separate lanes until the merge point, when drivers are forced to take turns moving into traffic. This solution keeps speeds consistent, improves vehicle performance, and gets cars off the road sooner as they reach their destinations.*

Now let's consider a very poor, but easy to fathom, design situation and brief. The project stakeholder calls in his team and says,

> *Getting drivers to merge into one lane at the appropriate time will make traffic flow more efficiently and reduce greenhouse gas emissions, so we need signage that will tell drivers how not to cause traffic jams. We would like to know the best language, color, and placement for these signs.*

The first case describes a situation that many frustrated drivers have experienced, whether they're early mergers or a late mergers. It leaves room for all kinds of inspired creativity, including social psychology, modeling, and simulation, and it does not prescribe in any way what the solution will look like, whether it's ultimately signage, a lighting application, or road paint or texture. We have defined what we want (better traffic flow), why we think it needs to be made (greenhouse gas reduction), and who the solution is for (happier drivers and society). The second brief tells us none of these things very neatly, only that merge-traffic problems are bad for the environment and that the design team should focus its efforts on improved signage—by the way, some inspiring words, thoughtful sign placement, and good colors would be nice too. We've got the exact same problem, but example one asks the designers to solve for a goal of better merge patterns, while example two just wants designers to solve a problem using the hypothesis that better signs will improve problematic merge scenarios.

What we achieve with an effective design brief is the establishment of a point of view. The design team feels emotion for the driver, society, and the natural systems of the planet that are challenged by anthropogenic climate change, and they want to help fix it. It's almost guaranteed, however, that any concepts for new signage will likely be incremental improvements from the signs that have already failed to help manage traffic. Hopefully, any seasoned design team will send the author of the second brief home to consider the question, "Are you sure it needs to be a sign?"

Of course, these are very simplistic examples. But a more complex goal (or example) doesn't necessarily require a complex design brief. The nature of the constraints is important, but so is trust in the design team. A higher degree of trust in the process will allow the design team to think about wild ideas that may be just the path to meeting the goal in a better way. What if a designer conceived of a magic car that would dump the driver's own coffee on him if he didn't leave enough room for a merge, causing the driver to brake and as a side-effect create room for a merging car? Not something likely to be implemented, but certainly something that might inspire solutions that move beyond simple incremental improvement. It's true that more-comprehensive and articulate briefs can indeed be important and helpful, but they run the risk of overburdening the intent of the brief. Some briefs may include elements such as budgets, styles, target audience, and goals. Anything that's a helpful constraint in terms of aims and desired objectives can be useful; anything that presupposes a solution will dilute the process and negatively impact the ultimate outcome.

4.2.4 Developing Empathy

Once an inspiring brief is in hand, the designers will want to better understand what the people in the situation are feeling and needing. More-conventional modes of research would call for a survey or a focus group, but even a well-designed focus group is susceptible to all sorts of effects, such as the Hawthorne effect, where the behavior of the subject in a study changes simply because of his or her cognizance of being observed. No, it's better if the team can go out and play in traffic, float deep into what Tim Brown calls the "first space" of empathy. Get into traffic jams, take videos of poorly executed merge patterns, create models with traffic simulations where variables can be turned on and off and visually observed. The design team needs to ride to work with everyday commuters, rush to the school play at 3:30 in the afternoon, or stand on the side of the road with the construction crew that put up the cone zone. In fact, based on the new clues they pick up in their observations, the designers may expand on their original brief, asking to include other goals such as road construction and maintenance workflows. It's at this point that we begin to see the power of a holistic, human-centered approach and to get a bead on some very simple tweaks that can encourage a breakthrough, reminding us of the importance of two hours of videotape over one.

4.2.5 Ideation

With a deep level of understanding for the humans who drive their cars and contend with merge zones, designers are well positioned to begin work in the "second space": ideation. This is the great stage of opportunity, but also the difficult stage of choices.

The American poet Mark Van Doren said, "Bring ideas in and entertain them royally, for one of them may be the king." This 1940 Pulitzer Prize winner for poetry clearly embraced the keystone value of the design-thinking process—that every potential solution that's brought to the table deserves equal consideration. The point is obvious: Maintaining the ability to consider a problem from more than one perspective instantly improves our ability to find a richer, more surprising result. Even if we think the problem is so straightforward that we just need new signs to solve it, innovation demands disruption, the willingness to step out of the shadows of the status quo, and the open-mindedness to distill and synthesize even amazingly far-out ideas, like what if we didn't need a horse to travel? What if perhaps we could fly a rocket to the moon? Or maybe we could carry our phones with us in our pocket. The design-thinking process enforces an environment where these ideas can come to light in a multidisciplinary environment.

With this process, we don't have to strain to hear the voices of our artists, engineers, city planners, street builders, and school teachers to help us design a solution to more effectively merge our cars. We seek out these voices. It sounds inefficient and downright painful for those who believe in highly structured and predictable ways of solving problems, but the path to breakthrough thinking is exactly the one that divergent thinking provides. While a structure is required for sorting through and choosing ideas, that framework should be the design team's (not the project sponsor's) choice, so it's not surprising that tools like Post-it notes are very popular. It allows a level of active shifting, prioritization, scratching out, and rewriting as some ideas naturally find the beach while others sink to the bottom of the ocean. This is very different than the customer relationship management crowd who will say, "If it's not in the system, it never happened."

This isn't as nebulous, immature, or counterculture a process as it first sounds. Open innovation has been around at least since the 1960s when Henry Chesbrough, author and faculty director at the Haas School of Business of the University of California said, "Open innovation is a paradigm that assumes that firms can and should use external ideas as well as internal ideas, and internal and external paths to market, as the firms look to advance their technology."[3] Meaning that breakthrough thinking is more likely to occur when the boundaries between entities are permeable, enabling those who can bring value to have the opportunity to do so. Despite the confounding issues of intellectual property, trade secrets, and commercialization, many firms have found ways to bring even the public

---

[3] Chesbrough, Henry William (2003), *Open Innovation: The New Imperative for Creating and Profiting from Technology*, Harvard Business School Press, Boston, Massachusetts, page xxiv.

into solving seemingly intractable problems. As a result, they've discovered innovative approaches at reduced research and development investments. One of the most common manifestations of this phenomenon is the "hackathon," where idea competitions bring in new talent to solve toward a particular goal, incentivizing the hackers with pizza, beer, and camaraderie (as well as ego and notoriety if a really great idea emerges). Facebook, ESPN, and various other wildly successful firms host hackathons.

In an authentically nurturing environment, great ideas will form, and the devil's advocate will be happily kicked to the curb. Often, this process of ideation requires many go-rounds, where ideas are presented, reworked, tweaked, promoted, and demoted until there's a handful of likely solutions that seem important to test.

4.2.6 Rational Implementation

Our "third space" is the moment when ideas begin to express themselves in action. During implementation, some prototypical form is developed that allows expression, testing, and refinement of what was in the mind's eye of the design team. Some will cut the process short here with a curt, "We've gone round and round enough. Let's get this thing done and out there." Or in the digital world, companies will produce a software prototype that looks good on the face, but has no legs to stand on. ("Pay no atention to that man behind the curtain.")

Now it's time to build something and see how it works, how our target market feels about it, and whether it helps us achieve our goals. However, functional prototypes can be quite dangerous from this perspective. The car design industry hasn't forgotten this important reality. Clay modeling for car prototypes began early in the life of the car industry, when in the 1930s the head of the General Motors' styling studio, Harley Earl (the father of the tail fin), began using industrial plasticine to allow designers to visualize their products in clay. In a 2003 interview, Alan D. Biggs, the North American design modeling manager for the Ford Motor Company, encapsulated the usefulness of prototypes quite succinctly, stating, "No one is willing to sign off on a production car looking at a picture."[4] (And

---

[4] McCosh, Dan (2003), "Driving: Most Cars Are Born as Models of Clay," *New York Times*. Retrieved November 23, 2014, from http://www.nytimes.com/2003/03/07/travel/driving-most-cars-are-born-as-models-of-clay.html.

that includes even your prettiest digital image on a large screen.) Models and prototypes can prove or disprove new concepts and reveal where the edges might still be rough. When an executive can walk around a clay model and see its potential to meet the needs of the target market, only then will she risk investment.

Yet prototyping can be tricky. They can be expensive and time-consuming to construct, and they can snuff out a great idea by not representing it in an understandable way. This is especially true when a prototype is unfamiliar, like the one Henry Ford probably presented to his buddies when he first sketched up his horseless carriage. Prototypes also may inspire new and better ideas, and the cycle of ideation and implementation may enter a phase of rinse and repeat. This can be a frustrating and lengthy process, but it deserves patience and trust in the right team.

Ultimately, what goes into production will more likely meet the initial goals of the project and even provide valuable insight into the marketing and communications strategies that emerge from the design process itself. By beginning with empathy and inspiration, the team understands the people and their unmet needs that your new product, organization, park, building, policy, or even traffic sign will fulfill. It's obvious how the up-front investment in human-centered design creates better outcomes not only from a social perspective but from an economic investment perspective as well, as many ideas are produced in the service of a greater goal.

4.3 So, What About Merging?

As to how solve our merge problem? Unfortunately, that's well outside the scope of this book, but it's certainly a problem many of us would like to see solved. Henry Barnes, the traffic commissioner of New York City in the 1960s, observed, "Traffic was as much an emotional problem as it was a physical and mechanical one." People, he concluded, were tougher to crack than cars. "As time goes on the technical problems become more automatic, while the people problems become more surrealistic."[5]

---

[5] Vanderbilt, Tom (n.d.), "Why I Became a Late Merger (and Why You Should Too)," excerpted from *Traffic* (2008), Alfred A. Knopf, a division of Random House, New York, New York. Retrieved November 22, 2014, from http://tomvanderbilt.com/traffic/excerpt.

Chapter Five

Design Thinking Applied

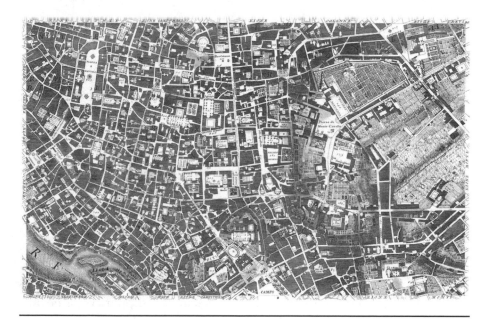

Before Giambattista Nolli, the cartographer of this map of Rome, most representations were bird's-eye views, instead of ichnographic, as in this drawing.[1]

[1] Nolli, Giambattista (1748), *Nuova Pianta di Roma*. Image retrieved from the public domain at http://commons.wikimedia.org/wiki/File:Giovanni_Battista_Nolli-Nuova_Pianta_di_Roma_(1748)_05-12.JPG.

5.1 Chapter Goal

This chapter discusses the real-world applications and possibilities of using design thinking to identify new opportunities for urban environments. The examples provided in this chapter show that information and communications technology (ICT) solutions are best designed and deployed in a manner that's appropriate for and sensitive to context. They should be implemented in a way that not only drives down risk but also ensures that there's a true demand for the proposed solutions in our shifting economic landscape. Finally, we'll propose the notion of utilizing neighborhood engagement as an innovation hub, and we'll discuss how engagement can be used as a tool to scale new products and services across the globe.

5.2 A Method, Not Magic

The architects who designed Grand Central Station, or Pierre Charles L'Enfant (the architect and civil engineer who conceived of the layout of Washington, DC), or perhaps the creators of the Herman Miller chair you may (if you're lucky) be sitting in all showed an incredible attention to detail, a vision, and perhaps even a level of obsession in their design. What's clear is that they were focused, they had an intention to their plans, and they were attentive to how their ideas were realized. L'Enfant envisioned a great public walk and placed key buildings in strategic areas—a concept so otherworldly that some believe he incorporated secret Luciferic design into his streets and cul-de-sacs. Artists across the millennia have decorated our public squares with national symbolism and anti-monuments both. Urban painters spray murals on our architecture. And building designers endeavor to make our structures more efficient and supportive of healthful and productive environments. All of these creators have a purpose and objective, whether it's to tell a story, remember an important historical moment, increase worker contentment, or use our resources more efficiently. Yet when it comes to designing smart cities, there's a lack of precise intention in exchange for platitudes, and we certainly find a lack of story that talks about how we might actually live in our more advanced spaces.

Without these stories, we will have profound difficulty realizing a better vision. In the previous chapter, we discussed the role of design briefs as a way of setting intention. Here we'll discuss two examples of briefs, one explicitly intended to serve as a guide to the design exercise for a project, and one that could best be construed as a design brief for smart cities.

The first is from OpenIDEO, which is an online collaborative design environment sponsored and curated by the design firm IDEO. This brief is entitled, "How might we make low-income urban areas safer and more empowering for women and girls?" Here is an excerpt:

> [F]or the millions of women and girls living in low-income urban communities across the world, personal safety can be difficult to achieve—giving way to gender-based violence, social isolation or a lack of basic social services. [We want to] design solutions that enable women to feel safe and empowered.[2]

There are many marketing vision statements produced for the myriad of smart city ventures. Below, we present a select example from the Brookings Institution, a self-described centrist think-tank formed in 1916. While not explicitly framed as a design brief, it is fairly representative of the oft-repeated vision for the economically viable and hyperproductive smart city, which comprises:

> a focused, forward-looking economic vision that targets long-term productivity, inclusivity, and resiliency [as] the first step in making cities smarter . . . [with] purposeful integration between technology and sustainability departments and their peers in other agencies.[3]

Both these statements promote a vision. The first envisions a safer, less violent world that empowers women, and the second conceives of an urban environment that is highly productive, resilient, and connected. There is a somewhat subtle different in these concepts. The first describes a new experience—more empowerment for girls and women—whereas the second describes an outcome that is driven by purposeful integration. Meaning, we have already presupposed that it is the binding of technology

[2] OpenIDEO (2014), "How Might We Make Low-Income Urban Areas Safer and More Empowering for Women and Girls?" Retrieved December 6, 2014, from https://openideo.com/challenge/womens-safety/brief.html.

[3] Puentes, Robert and Tomer, Adie (2014), "Getting Smarter About Smart Cities," Brookings Institution. Retrieved December 6, 2014, from http://www.brookings.edu/research/papers/2014/04/23-smart-cities-puentes-tomer.

with other agencies that will bring the good things we assume come with a smarter city, such as economic and social benefits.

Although this is a technical book that focuses on technology solutions to enable smart cities, there's room here to think about designing our smart cities in terms of the experiences we hope to drive. What if we refuse to settle for what often feels like just an incremental improvement on what we already know how to do quite well, which is create software platforms and analytic solutions to manage and respond based on new kinds of data about people, places, and things? Instead of focusing on technology prowess, what if we focused on how technology can enable people in urban environments to be productive, socially connected, and economically successful?

To accomplish this, we must put design rather than technology capability at the heart of our smart city ventures. And we should define an accessible vision that brings together many new urban experiences in a context where the sum becomes greater than the parts. This is not madness or magic; it's just a method that puts new options on the table that perhaps we never thought of before—instead of striving to find optimal solutions from our existing collection of well-understood approaches.

As discussed previously, design thinking isn't really new; it's just newly popular. This is likely because our expectations about new products and services have become quite high, so it's impossible to bring a poorly conceived idea to market and expect much success. As consumers living in a largely digital world, we're tolerant of prototypes, but we expect them to be well conceived and quickly and incrementally improved. In the software world, these expectations aren't demanding. Over the past two decades, patterns have emerged as a way to quickly build very complex systems that incorporate reusable solutions in new ways for new outcomes. Patterns are not recipes; they're general concepts for software design that are focused on solutions rather than problems—much like design thinking. Further, the role of agile software development practices has encouraged engineers and corporations to embrace the notion of incremental delivery.

5.3 Ways That Design Thinking Has Been Used in Cities

Within the past decade, we have seen progress in the willingness to solve difficult problems in new ways. Take, for example, the reimagining of gross domestic product (GDP) as the primary marker for the health of a nation. In an effort already under way, economists are expanding GDP with questions related to safety, human rights, and environmental sustainability. For the first time, there's a worldwide effort to index our basic human needs and enhance our personal freedoms and choice. The willingness to establish new guides to progress and wellness doesn't necessarily imply improvement, and not all populations agree on what the most important underpinnings of a society are, especially when it comes to issues of gender equality and education. This is yet another reason why a normalized approach to urban environments is so tightly bound to local needs, especially when it comes to sanitation, personal safety, education, and access to information.

But has design thinking been helpful? How has a focus on experiences and solutions proved to be valuable to enhancing urban living? The following examples describe new approaches to crime, economic value, and health and well-being.

5.3.1 Designing Out Crime

In 2007, the New South Wales Department of Police & Justice Initiative in Australia established the Designing Out Crime (DOC) research center to use a design-thinking approach to help solve the state's seemingly intractable problems of crime. New South Wales wanted to explore new solutions to problems that included an in-depth understanding of all kinds of potentially obscure factors that could contribute to crime in specific situations. The research center describes its goals:

> This research is . . . used to widen the problem context and create new frames. Reframing a problem context allows for totally new solution scenarios to be developed. DOC tests these solutions for validity, integrating them in to the problem context. Through this process DOC creates new solutions to old problems.[4]

These solutions may be physical in nature (as in a security product such as a door lock), but they may also be system- or policy-based. In many ways, this is the revitalization of an age-old scheme. As shown in

[4] University of Technology, Sydney (n.d.), "Designing Out Crime." Retrieved November 22, 2014, from http://www.designingoutcrime.com/about-us.

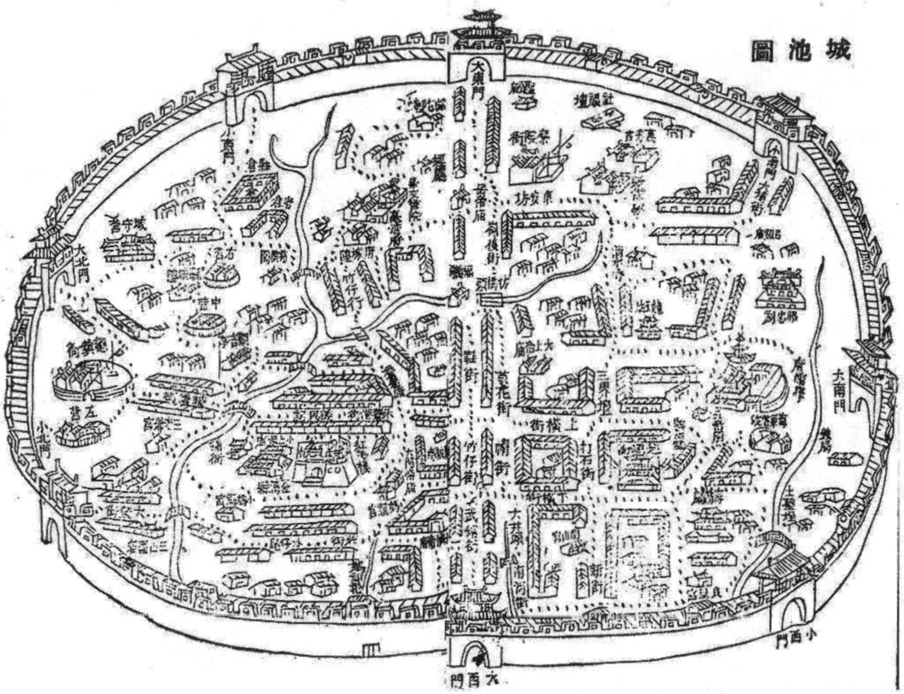

Figure 5.1 Tainan during the Qing dynasty, which lasted from around 1683 to 1887.[5]

Figure 5.1, the 15-foot-thick and 25-foot-high walls around Tainan, the oldest city in Taiwan, replaced a ring of bamboo constructed to keep out marauders. There were large spaces for the principal temples and some pleasant walks to enrich the living conditions.

Designing out crime—also known as crime prevention through environmental design (CPTED) —is based on research that indicates that, despite a societal propensity toward reactionary approaches to crime, crime prevention is the most effective and economic way to reduce crime. In New South Wales, stakeholders felt that the right design and use of the built environment could reduce the incidence of crime and, subsequently, the resulting fear that created emotional difficulties for their citizens. Thus, they believed that this approach could encourage an overall improvement in the quality of citizens' lives. Using the disciplines of criminology and psychology, the government explicitly promoted and invested in the

[5] Image retrieved from the public domain at http://en.wikipedia.org/wiki/Tainan#mediaviewer/File:1807_Taiwan_city_fortifications.jpg.

design and management of the built environment. It also improved product designs to help directly reduce the opportunities for crime.

Taking a systems approach, the initiative focuses on a variety of strategies, such as creating safer public spaces by designing structures that inhibit conflict and encourage a sense of ownership and community responsibility. The initiative also supports technology monitoring and so-called natural surveillance as a part of a proactive physical protection scheme. Further, ongoing management and maintenance patterns are used to enhance public health and discourage crime and incremental degradation of public space through acts of vandalism and petty theft. To achieve this, policy changes were enacted to promote community-minded experiences, such as initiatives supporting children and young people, projects to revitalize neighborhoods, strategies to target high-priority offenses, approaches to reduce recidivism, and technology innovations to support all of these efforts.

The actions taken to implement these initiatives were extensive, and some are especially noteworthy:

- The program encourages property owners to restore rundown properties and provides incentives and options to help owners manage and maintain their properties in an effort to reduce the number of vacant and neglected buildings.
- The program aims to improve the accessibility and usefulness of crime data at the local level through spatial and geographical analysis.
- A collection of standard crime prevention principles has been created to help reduce opportunities for crime through the improved design of products and processes.

Further, the state went to great lengths to enhance measurement criteria, including a carefully tuned set of key performance indicators (KPIs) to track how communities were adopting the designing-out-crime principles.[6]

Many jurisdictions across the globe have adopted and adapted CPTED principles, and while Western Australia has reported variable success

[6] Cozens, Paul, Thorn, Michael, and Hillier, David (2008), "Designing Out Crime in Western Australia: A Case Study," Emerald Group Publishing. Retrieved November 22, 2014, from http://www.academia.edu/7193966/ Designing_out_crime_in_Western_Australia_a_case_study.

rates with the program, other adopters have reported crime reductions by nearly half. It's quite possible that this disparity is due to the number and variety of measurement points used in Western Australia versus, say, Savannah, Georgia. In Savannah, "CPTED principles can be applied easily and inexpensively to building or remodeling. . . . The results have been impressive; in some CPTED communities, criminal activity has decreased by as much as 40%."[7] Also, the government of Australia was looking at more than just criminal activity, including an extensive list of goals and measures ranging from financial assistance, building rehabilitation, and restructuring public spaces. Many other CPTED implementations are focused more on creating spaces that discourage crime through the sheer preponderance of people in the area through better management of space and community activities, underscoring the need for contextually relevant solutions.

In 2005, the parliament of the Commonwealth of Australia suggested that the concepts of designing out crime should be considered a key part of establishing sustainable cities and central to promoting healthy communities.

5.3.2 Collaborative Consumption

Design-thinking methods may not always be practiced explicitly; they may emerge from our own personal stories. Truly, design thinking has stirred much excitement at TED talks and within the pages of coffee table books featuring slick photos of white men in expensive jackets and great hair who have used the approach to invent new espresso makers and lemon squeezers. We've heard many dramatic stories that serve only to increase the mystery around design thinking. But design thinking is for anyone who wants to create something of value, and it's often very simple. One of the simplest applications is an emerging economic force called collaborative consumption—also known as sharing—with a technological twist. There are several remarkable examples demonstrating how this model is actively strengthening neighborhood and community connections, driving down consumption, and creating new opportunities for reducing carbon loading and increasing efficiency.

[7] "CPTED" (n.d.), City of Savannah, Georgia. Retrieved December 8, 2014, from http://www.savannahga.gov/index.aspx?NID=685.

In some ways, the emergence of the new sharing economy is part of our forgotten history, but it's one that ironically will be critically important to the growing urban population. This reemerging construct involves the sharing, bartering, lending, and trading of goods instead of outright buying them with an exchange of currency. The idea of collaboration takes the concept a step further with services such as Uber, Lyft, Airbnb, Meal Sharing, and Rewear that use analytics, open data sources, global positioning system (GPS) coordinates, maps, and visualizations, all delivered to smartphones and often including Short Message Service (SMS) capabilities to facilitate economic exchange. This peer-based economy and approach to doing business employs age-old skills that humans tend to cherish—cooperating, collaborating, and sharing—to meet our individual goals.

The emergence of enabling technologies, the ubiquity of smartphones, the availability of data, the rising inequality of income, the growing population, and the spread of urbanization are the driving forces behind the expansion of the sharing economy. Letty Reimerink, a journalist who writes about global urban environments, shares the example of the mobile app Peerby. The application is the brainchild of Daan Weddepohl, who found himself without a home when his apartment burned in a fire. Without possessions, he learned to ask his neighbors for help to meet even his most basic needs and realized that the human contact and expression of vulnerability led directly to an improved quality of life for him. The vision for the app is simply to facilitate sharing among strangers, but, unlike many other collaborative apps, Peerby is focused on micro-communities. It requires at least some neighborhood involvement, yet it can have a deep impact on the way a city block or apartment building consumes. Reimerink says that the transactions on the system can be much more than a spurious exchange of goods,

> [Weddepohl] sees them as a form of community building, in which each borrower and lender can experience a bit of the neighborly good will that he discovered back in 2009. He figures sharing more and buying less will also save people money and help cities lower their carbon footprints.[8]

8 Reimerink, Letty (2014), "Can an App for Borrowing Housewares Make Neighborhoods Stronger?" Citiscope. Retrieved December 8, 2014, at http://citiscope.org/story/2014/can-app-borrowing-housewares-make-neighborhoods-stronger.

Weddepohl's design brief might have easily been, "I want people to help people meet their simple needs while enjoying the same connections I had with my neighbors." And apparently he's not alone in his goals. In 2014, more than 100 applicants submitted applications to be considered for a seat at the New Cities Summit, the leading global event of the New Cities Foundation, whose sole mission is to help find solutions and ideas to "shape a better urban future" by bringing together many participants in the urban environment, including the media, arts, business, and government. A consortium of public, nonprofit, and private-sector participants—including Cisco, Ericsson, Google, and Schneider Electric— expect to play a significant role in the world of the smart city.

Whether they're motived by entrepreneurism or something more personal, urbanites in all economies are using technology to improve their communities. And smart city developers are learning from this example, and beginning to make efforts to engage their citizens more positively in order to maximize developer investments.

5.4 When Urban Design Rises Above Imposition

One of the most implausible things in approaching the smart city with a suite of technology products, applications, and services is the notion that a broad solution can bring all things to all people. In fact, that notion is disturbingly implausible. Economies of scale is the classic reason for looking for cost advantages where increased output will decrease as fixed costs are spread out across more units. This theory is especially useful when all other factors are equal in that increased scale will naturally create cost advantages.

There are very clear limits, though, and many convincingly argue that indeed the philosophy falls short in the services sector when a services-oriented company tries to manage unit costs that can paradoxically raise overall costs through a phenomenon called failure demand. This is when demand for a service increases because of a failure to do the right thing for the customer in the beginning. A classic example of failure demand was first identified by John Seddon, British occupational psychologist and author, who found that when telephone work was moved to call centers from local bank branches, the total number of calls soared. Why? Because people weren't getting their problems solved the first time, as they were when they engaged directly with the local bank branch. Thus, in the end, the quest for efficiency drove up overall costs.

To confound the problem, in the smart city market, we have classic solutions providers that are accustomed to selling widgets, implementers and strategists that partner with those providers to build solutions, and city governments that must write convincing business cases in an emerging market. Additionally, these government entities have to answer to accounting departments that are steeped in traditional notions about measuring return on investment in order to ensure that taxpayer dollars are well spent. For example, we know how to measure whether the number of crimes committed has gone up or down, but what we're not good at measuring is how certain efforts may have prevented the opportunity for crime.

Seddon encouraged organizations that are focused on services—and what entity should be more service-focused than a city government?—to break away from seeking efficiencies through economies of scale and instead begin looking at what he called economies of flow. Economies of Flow is a way of looking at optimization that diverts the focus from the volume of transactions and instead looks at ways to streamline the flow of a process to the point of interaction between the customer and the provider. Thus, although an economies of scale perspective demands standardizations that may actually increase the amount of fragmentation in the process of delivering a service, economies of flow eliminates waste by successfully absorbing unique customer requirements, limiting overall complexity, and reducing rework and duplication of efforts (which is inherent in failure demand). Seddon further advocates a local level of engagement in optimizing flow, noting that when citizens are able to enjoy good service in their immediate environment, their behavior becomes more positive, and they eschew indifference for awareness and engagement.

To achieve this, cities that want to deploy ICT to become smarter and more efficient in delivering their services are best to reject solutions that advocate driving up transactional volume. For example, if a wireless sensor network (WSN) is being deployed to measure the soil moisture dynamics of rooftop gardens in an effort to improve automated watering schedules, then the placement of the sensors must be suitable to enable soil moisture analysis and other dynamics within the growing operation. An informatics specialist might walk into the garden and place sensors equidistant from one another throughout the plots and at a few key areas of operation. An agricultural master would enter the same garden and place the sensors in clusters at various depths in the soil. The informatics specialist is motivated by having data for the topsoil model. The agricultural expert is interested in learning how to create the optimal conditions to grow tomatoes on the top of a skyscraper, where the prevailing conditions are much different than those on the surface of the Earth.

In an analytics-driven smart city, this would also likely involve combining the historical and real-time data with meteorological data and other operational information. Though there are various schools of thought on this issue, all can agree that analytics are not necessarily more effective when you have all possible data versus some relevant data. In fact, you may end up reducing the utility of the models you are hoping to improve by including irrelevant data or redundant measurements of the identical values.

5.4.1 Creative Capetonians

Cape Town, South Africa, serves as a remarkable example of the power of design thinking, technology, and powerful partnerships between public and private enterprise. By drawing on human-centric solutions thinking, the city is working on housing, arts, livability, and urban migration issues. It's creating community by cleaning up neighborhoods without violating unique cultural identities; it's looking for ways to help strangers engage in meaningful conversation; and it's moving toward a low-carbon city profile. Cape Town uses design storming, design dialogues, and ethnography as tools to improve the urban environment, and it uses technology to create better support systems.

Creating a wireless infrastructure for the public good is the key to improving many of the services in Cape Town. Not only does broadband connectivity promote digital inclusion, it also enables all forms of economic growth and improves business development opportunities to enhance the overall health and cohesion of the city environment. At a cost of R1.3 billion, the Digital Inclusion Project is scheduled to be completed by 2022 and will facilitate the city's universal broadband network strategy to deliver Wi-Fi connectivity to more citizens. Free public Internet improves educational outcomes for children, and increased digital literacy boosts economic growth and opens more opportunities for all residents. Once Cape Town begins connecting public spaces, the city will be able to improve transportation alternatives and applications, increase tourism, and enhance collaborative apps that provide visitors and citizens with essential information. Once the ICT infrastructure is in place, the plethora of unimagined smartphone apps will develop.

5.5 Assessing the Usefulness of Design Thinking

An important partner in the efforts to improve the city for Capetonians, Creative Cape Town nails the issue in its statement, "Design for change cannot happen simply on computers in chic shiny studios in hipsterville. Solutions need to be prototyped, tested by the end users and improved on, over and over . . . because things will change and the product will need to grow again."[9] But when it comes to spending serious money on research and development on serious problems like urban decay, energy poverty, crime, and sustainability, it's very difficult to embrace what feels like just another buzzword to describe yet another failed business case.

The methodology known as design thinking and its application are really just a matter of appropriateness. Yes, smart cities offer a new promise for urban citizens with technologies. We can expect to use our resources more efficiently, and connectivity between people, places, and things brings opportunity to many who have been greatly disenfranchised. Cities that adapt to this reality will experience better economic growth. But achieving these goals will require capitally intensive investment and appropriate policy, with very little help from national governments. One way to manage the risk associated with such expensive and complex ventures is to start small. In many ways, smart cities will benefit greatly with an initial focus on the needs of neighborhoods, which make terrific technology incubators. Design thinking calls for iterative development to get things right, and engaged neighborhoods can help unlock the potential of new thinking with smaller projects, easier-to-implement policies, and palatable price tags.

Additionally, a community engagement approach can reduce political risk by helping to identify small-scale, neighborhood-embraced best practices and moving them upward to greater scales through city-level

[9] Creative Cape Town (n.d.), "Design Thinking for Better Living." Retrieved December 10, 2014, from http://www.creativecapetown.com/design-thinking-for-better-living.

collaboration. Solutions can be identified and adopted in one city and tuned to fit the unique needs of other urban centers. Thus, neighborhoods can become hubs for innovation, and also prove out the demand for new solutions.

5.5.1 Measuring Success

Design thinking isn't a trick, a magic bullet, or even very new. Unfortunately, any organization that incorporates design thinking into its work stream with the goal of increasing efficiency will be sorely disappointed. Adopting design thinking also means adopting messy failures and the emotions that come with what can sometimes be a fickle creative process. It's the same messiness, in fact, that has driven many very bright technologists and companies to make the startling decision to invest billions in building efficient cities from scratch, solve the big problems, and just move people in later.

On the other hand, for any enterprise that's willing to venture into exploring the urban place where people live, work, and play and is intent on finding solutions that effectively address urbanization, global warming, overpopulation, and the erosion of many of our familiar social and economic systems, design thinking would be immensely helpful and perhaps even unavoidable. This is a business philosophy that recognizes that designing, implementing, and driving long-term value from technology solutions for the urban environment means necessarily acknowledging both the people and the cultures for which these designs are being generated. And believing that there are many sources of wisdom and knowledge that will produce real sustainable solutions to seemingly intractable problems.

Section One

Key Points

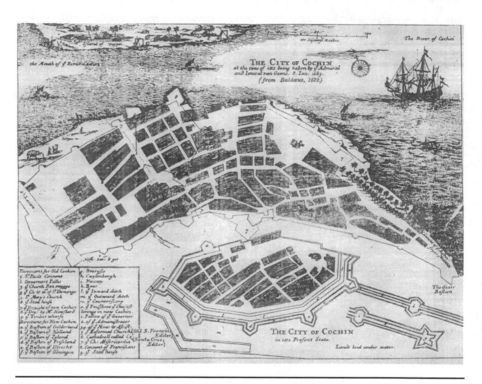

A map of the Dutch-occupied Fort Kochi municipality in 1672.[*]

Section One

Key Points

A Large and Accurate Map of the City of London, created in 1908 by Ogilvy and Morgan Maps.[1]

---

[1] Image retrieved from the public domain at http://commons.wikimedia.org/wiki/File:City_of_London_Ogilby_and_Morgan's_Map_of_1677.jpg.

Chapter One
Growing Urbanization Concentrates Sustainability Challenges in Cities

Poorly managed urban growth creates human and environmental challenges, especially when the infrastructure is insufficient or when policy is inadequate. Cities are already seeing growing sprawl, pollution, and unsustainable production and consumption patterns.

- According to the United Nations, for the first time in measured history, global urban populations now hold over 50 percent of the world's population.
- Between 2007 and 2050, it is estimated that the world's urban population will double from 3.3 billion to 6.4 billion, meaning that the world's urban areas are absorbing the majority of the population growth over the next several decades as rural populations continue to decrease.
- Urbanization is not just about large cities. Even as megacities continue to increase in population, over half of the urban dwellers live and will continue to live in smaller urban environments that have less than half a million inhabitants.[2]

Smart Cities Tend to Be Technology-Centric and Early Efforts Are Falling Short

Many real-estate speculators, urban planners, master architects, and global purveyors of advanced technologies have spent billions of dollars on smart city efforts that have fallen short of their goals.

- Smart city concepts focus on reduced operational costs, resource conservation, and decreased consumption. These plans also tend to be highly technology-centric.

[2] United Nations (2014), "World Urbanization Prospects: The 2014 Revision, Highlights." Retrieved on February 6, 2015, from http://esa.un.org/unpd/wup/Highlights/WUP2014-Highlights.pdf.

- A schism of sorts has developed between civil engineers, planners, policymakers, and information management experts, and important stakeholders have been isolated from the process, including schools, hospitals, and other providers of public services.
- Planning and building a smart city in the same way one might develop a computer operating system overlooks the complex forces in the urban environment, which starts with the people.

The Vision for Smart Cities Must Include Its People

The principles of design thinking help us reframe the problems of smart cities to capture the needs of people and how a highly efficient urban environment can serve them.

- While the ubiquity of sensors in our cities promises a high degree of coordination and the ability to make smart decisions automatically, many early projects have suffered because their ideals fell short when it came to creating vital and livable cities.
- Technology has extraordinary potential to make cities safer, healthier, more affordable, and more beautiful for many urban communities, but the diversity of cities makes even fundamental challenges like waste, water, sewage, and crime very difficult to address.
- Smart city designs that consider technology as well as the lives of the human beings living in the environments hold the greatest chance of creating sustainable and vital communities by helping reframe problems and deliver solutions that bring all stakeholders to the table.

Chapter Two

Technology Advancement Encompasses Both Form and Function

> *Systems that have been deployed to manage things like surveillance can also be used to monitor other activities such as vehicle traffic flows or the movement of people through a park.*

- It's often assumed that smart technology advancement requires robust processing power, communication speed, and ubiquity. However, it is the preponderance of a variety of systems with different forms of data that, once brought together and analyzed, can provide the most powerful capabilities.
- New use cases for existing data don't rely on infrastructure changes, just in imagining new ways that we might leverage existing capabilities.
- Measuring complex phenomena with greater precision may not always bring us the value we desire, since many issues in our cities depend on helping people modify destructive behavior.

Smart City as Mediator: Moving from Sensors to Services

> *People are unpredictable. Society would be easier to manage if we were machines, but our essence as individuals, as partners in relationship, and as members of our communities breathes life into our urban environments.*

- We have a tendency in a technocentrist world to use point solutions to solve problems such as transportation, waste, and poorly maintained infrastructure. This is a short-sighted and reactive approach to urban design that doesn't always account for deeper human needs.
- Sensors don't mean anything to people. How we interact with our world is what gives meaning.
- The truly smart city is much more than a billion chattering sensors; what really makes a city smart is the way those devices mediate their

data and actuations into positive intelligence for people in a way that smooths the challenges and complexities of the real world.

The Smart City Stack

The technology stack for the urban environment synchronizes the environment with people by gathering data about the natural and built environment and delivering valuable information for both computer consumption and human enablement.

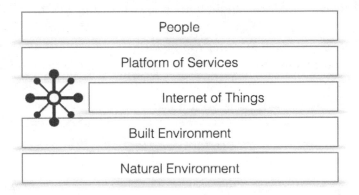

A smart city technology stack that synchronizes the natural environment with people.

Chapter Three

Smart City Technologies Should Focus on Improving Human Society

The application of sensors and analytics alone will not solve any of our pressing urbanization challenges. However, advanced technology applications may be the foundations of our desired transformation.

- Sensors, technologies, and analytics alone cannot solve our challenging urban problems, though they are fundamental to meeting our societal goals.
- Technologies such as water monitoring, chemical leakage detection, air quality monitoring, traffic management, resource integration, financial engineering, and automated balancing of energy supply and demand are key enabling technologies.
- Many technologies that create smarter cities are neither obvious nor apparent to urban dwellers, but they're deeply important to creating the foundations for a sustainable urban environment.

The Approach to Bringing New Technologies to the Smart City Is Time-Tested

When designing for smart cities, we can forget about the enabling technology, especially in the long run. It's more important to deliver data-driven applications without necessarily focusing on adapting to a source.

Some things to consider:

- How can technology from one domain be transferred to another domain in order to drive new forms of innovation?
- How can we best access as many sources of data in a responsible and openly shared way, without restriction, to create the best chances for widespread economic benefit?

- Who else in the city government or community might be interested in data that has traditionally only been used in one functional area? How can we use data to build bridges across our city government?
- What are ways that data and information can be reused to benefit as many stakeholders as possible?

Smart Cities Are Really About Smart Management

Striving for efficient, optimal, and effective cities does not mean that we will have to be living inconvenient and unpleasant lives. To achieve our goals of driving down resource costs (in dollars and impact), it's best to focus first on what we want to achieve and then on how to achieve it.

- Too often, the mandate for smarter cities places pressure on efficiency of infrastructure and services that can be delivered more cheaply, causing downward pressure on providers and the development of reactionary solutions.
- Novel financial engineering approaches can play an important role in funding the development of the smart city by focusing on incentives for real sustainable change instead of greenwashing.
- The companies that run these projects and that expect to succeed in a variety of cultural and economic environments should be organizations with solid product and service offerings, but also with access to financial depth and seasoned teams.

Chapter Four

Design Thinking Is a Repeatable Method for Creating New Designs

Design thinking describes a variety of human-centered processes that are used to solve complex problems.

- Design thinking isn't new. It's a time-tested approach to documenting the creative process, and it can be implemented as a practice in developing products and services.
- The application of design thinking in the context of advancement toward the smart city represents an opportunity to transform our perspective from technology-centric to human-centric.
- If we use design thinking to solve our smart city problem, we can edge forward toward creating innovative, livable environments that are realizable, practical, and economically and environmentally sustainable.

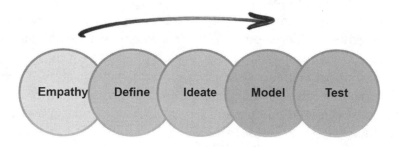

Design thinking is a human-centered iterative process that comprehends the phases of empathy, creativity, and rationality.

Design Thinking Is Different Than the Scientific Method

Design thinking is appropriate when we want to solve for a goal or an ambiguous problem. When the problem space is fairly unclear and we may be forced to define and redefine our understanding of the issues, the scientific method is not the right fit.

- Problems with potential solutions that can be tested by observable or measurable means are well suited to the scientific method.
- Because there is no design-thinking canon, we can adopt general principles of design thinking that include an empathetic viewpoint, a creative ideation process, and rational execution.
- Design thinking is a human-centered iterative process that comprehends the phases of empathy, creativity, and rationality.

The Best Technology Fails When It Solves the Wrong Problem

By emphasizing technology capabilities to achieve efficiency and optimization, smart cities neglect to consider how technology will succeed in a flourishing city full of people.

- Design thinking begins with a design brief that helps define the problem in a way that doesn't overly constrain the design team, leaving room for inspiration.
- The brief gives the project team a framework to begin its process. It helps team members gauge whether they're making progress and provides clear objectives that they aim to realize.
- A well-crafted design brief will never attempt to answer the question it has posed, only provide constraints for the solution.

Chapter Five

Smart City Design Tells a Story About the People Who Live and Work Within the Environment

><<<<<<<<<<<<<<<<<<<<<<<<<<<<<<<<<<<<<<<<<<<
>
> *All great designs show intention in their plans, and they are attentive to how their ideas are realized. Efficient and productive designs in the realm of ICT should not be an exception.*
>
> <<<<<<<<<<<<<<<<<<<<<<<<<<<<<<<<<<<<<<<<<<<

- Many smart city designs lack precise intention, instead focusing on platitudes. They lack a story that is engaging and inspiring.
- Personalized stories help us understand how we fit into the city narrative, and they promote a vision of how we might actually live in advanced cities designed for our mutual benefit.
- Designs for deploying ICT in a city can and should show the same attention to detail, vision, and commitment to good design as any other useful product or solution. This requires putting design rather than technology capability first.

Design Thinking Techniques Have Already Brought Measurable Impact

><<<<<<<<<<<<<<<<<<<<<<<<<<<<<<<<<<<<<<<<<<<
>
> *Design thinking principles have already shown themselves to be useful. Focusing on human experiences in creating solutions to enhance urban living shows success in fighting crime, economic value, and new levels of health and well-being.*
>
> <<<<<<<<<<<<<<<<<<<<<<<<<<<<<<<<<<<<<<<<<<<

- The Designing Out Crime initiative focused on reframing the problem of crime so that they could find new solutions to age-old problems of crime in urban environments.
- Early approaches in using designing thinking to treat crime showed that using design to build a physical environment that helped prevent crime could also reduce the fear that crime inspires, improving the overall quality of life in these areas.
- Physical changes support technology monitoring but also use space to create a protection scheme that discourages crime and the incremental degradation of public space that increases crime.

Design Thinking Isn't About Being Slick; It's About Creating Value

Often, the solutions generated by a process of design thinking aren't really all that complicated, but they can have far-reaching results. In fact, many of the best tools for bringing improvements in resource efficiency involve simple acts of sharing with a technological twist.

- The sharing economy is a reemerging construct that involves the sharing, bartering, lending, and trading of goods, and it's fully enabled by technology.
- Despite decidedly technology-driven underpinnings, collaborative applications are facilitating new engagement among strangers and even creating new communities of interest.
- Urban designers interested in using ICT to further their goals can learn from entrepreneurism, and make efforts to engage their citizens more positively to maximize their investments and their efforts.

Section Two

A Review of Smart City Technologies

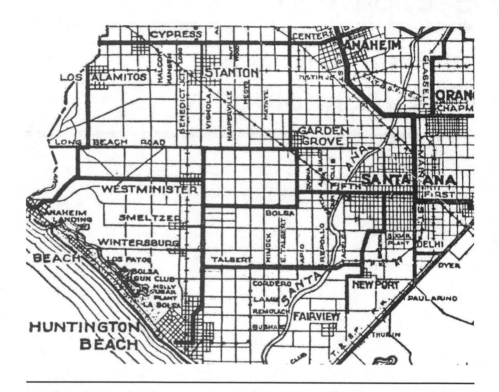

Map from the 1921 brochure "Orange County California, Nature's Prolific Wonderland - Spring Eternal."*

* Image retrieved from the public domain at http://en.wikipedia.org/wiki/File:Midway_City_CA_map_1921.jpg.

Chapter Six

Smart City Planning and Management

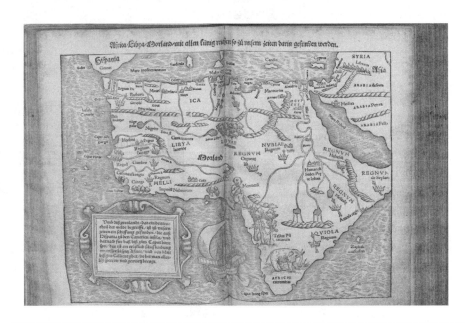

A map of Africa, as shown in Sebastian Münster's *Cosmographia*, 1545.[1]

---

[1] Image retrieved from the public domain at http://en.wikipedia.org/wiki/Cartography_of_Africa#mediaviewer/File:Cosmographia_(Sebastian_Münster)_p_120.jpg.

6.1 Chapter Goal

This chapter discusses the challenges for urban planning activities when using information and communications technology (ICT) to resolve safety, regulatory, and social issues. The application of technology has often been considered a largely neutral activity, but it is, in fact, much more complex, and often has political implications. In this chapter, we'll discuss the weaknesses of a technology-centric planning approach when compared to a human-centered solutions-oriented approach. When a technology is selected for pragmatic reasons, it's prudent to question the political implications of the deployment and governance of technology.

6.2 Smart Cities and Their Role in the Creation of a National Identity

The solutions-oriented approach of design thinking shifts the focus from scaling outcomes to scaling the process. The way we frame a problem that's common across many urban environments can be documented and referenced innumerable times. But the implementation of a solution to that problem can be refined to suit the context. The result is that instead of solely looking at a problem from the perspective of technology, design thinking ensures that the primary focus is on the people who are being served by the solution, and that the best solution is desirable to people in a way that increases positive impact.

There's lots of evidence that the nation-building approach to enforcing change through policy is not only difficult, but when it fails, it can be in dramatic ways. The term *nation-building* comes from academia and means many things to many people, but at its kernel, it's a revolutionary (versus evolutionary) model for constructing new independent nations that better reflect an integration of people by identity. In the 1930s, the approach was used to deal with unraveled states and resulted in the aftermath of European colonialism. Nation-building efforts center on constructing and supporting a homogenous population with updated flags, anthems, new stadiums, a common language, and even resurrected cultural myths.

More recently, nation-building has become popularly aligned with armed occupation and interventionism, or *state-building*. This newer interpretation provides an interesting point of instruction for building cities, namely, that much of nation-building involves the creation of a system of democracy. One can legitimately question the usefulness of employing force to impose democracy on a province of people. Similarly, we must question the efforts of city planners to use a system of regulation and law to encourage citizen engagement, especially if the goal is to enhance more-effective systems of transportation, energy, healthcare, and water and waste management.

Carolyn Stephenson, PhD and professor of political science at the University of Hawaii at Manoa, has written about the importance of identity in developing long-term stability. Typically, communities focus solely on infrastructure, where success is measured by economic health, primarily by gross domestic product (GDP). The impulse to overlook the critical role of societal engagement and civil well-being is quite similar to the tension experienced in the realm of urban development under the auspices of technological advancement. Stephenson says, "The importance of democratic values, of the civic culture and civil society that develop and sustain them, the importance of increasing social, political, and economic equality, and of human development, rather than just economic development or state-building, are key in any successful strategy for long-term democratic nation-building."[2] She underscores the lessons learned from authentic nation-building efforts (as opposed to those that are whitewashed excuses for external intervention), namely, that when the basic needs of a nation's people are met, those people will act not from conditions of poverty or inequality but from a desire to participate in a full democratic process. These basic needs include a functioning infrastructure, access to resources, and safety and security, but they also include the development of influential institutions that consistently advocate and design services for the welfare of the nation's citizens. It seems as close to a truism as one can assert in the study of human progress that a nation can best contribute to a stable international peace by creating the conditions for a sound and thriving civil society at the community level.

[2] Stephenson, Carolyn (2005), "Nation Building," Beyond Intractability. Retrieved December 21, 2014, from http://www.beyondintractability.org/essay/nation-building.

6.2.1 World Cities

There's another compelling reason to examine the role of smart cities amid a rising incongruity between federal and global policies and their ability to guarantee human survival. Enter the rather awkward portmanteau glocalization. This term was first introduced by economists in a 1980s *Harvard Business Review* article. It was later defined more precisely by sociologist Roland Robertson, who said that glocalization "means the simultaneity—the co-presence—of both universalizing and particularizing tendencies."[3] A more familiar term—internationalization—is most often used by economists to describe a variety of economic theories related to taking a product to international customers. Colloquially, this practice is known as thinking global. However, the most important thing about glocalization is that it describes the need to adapt a product to meet the needs and desires of local consumers. Meaning, in Korea, you'll enjoy a kimchi burger and in France your Happy Meal will be served up by Asterix the Gaul, but you're still eating at McDonald's.

In our increasingly connected world, other forms of glocalization have emerged related to our extended social networks and a sense of local responsibility for the greater rights of people in far-off places. In both cases, the challenge is similar: people are attempting to balance the desire to bring what is relevant in their daily lives to a level of global consistency—or, they're taking the "think globally, act locally" approach. In fact, many cities around the world—including Tokyo, Japan; New York, New York; Los Angeles, California; and Toronto, Canada—have coined themselves global cities and are part of a virtual social movement to express the solidarity of local populations with those across the globe. This is somewhat of a federative structure (also sometimes called mundialization) and though it lacks a governing body per se, it expresses a sense of shared responsibility. At an even more individual level, many of us maintain deeply personal relationships through our online social groups from around the world; these bonds are effectively erasing the boundaries inherent in nationalism.

[3] Rouse, Margaret (2013), "What Is Glocalization?" WhatIs.com. Retrieved December 22, 2014, from http://searchcio.techtarget.com/definition/glocalization.

In many ways, our federal governing bodies have been left behind. Never able to agree on meaningful climate-change accords, world cities have organized into collaborative networks that are defining a collective agenda for a sustainable urban future. One forum, called the World Cities Culture Forum (worldcitiescultureforum.com), convenes senior policy-makers and others who are able to speak in depth about the conditions of their cities. They're also able to work in a collegial environment to compare techniques and approaches that focus solely on increasing opportunities to impact their collective urban environments through enhanced cultural influence. The group produces research; writes policy briefings; and sponsors events, workshops, and ongoing summits, demonstrating clearly the power of how the destiny of our cities rests not in national or supranational influence, but in local governance that is profoundly influenced by a growing urban internetwork.

6.3 A New Role for City Government

Governments have been planning cities since King Gilgamesh ordered a massive wall to be built around the city of Uruk in Mesopotamia. Although city governments have long been creating regulations and frameworks for providing city services, they must now comprehend the profound technological advances that have emerged in ICT, including the Internet of Things (IoT), machine to machine (M2M), and big-data analytics. In general, city governments will need to focus on three general tracks of emphasis to discover and plan for the best applications for ICT with a coordinated approach to smart city design. These tracks are social, regulatory, and safety. The social aspect refers to those innovations that use data collected from citizens for the improvement of their everyday life. Regulatory design, often an exercise in trade-offs, addresses the consent and privacy issues that result from ambient monitoring, as well as the overall societal benefit of such things as improved infrastructure operation. Public safety, which is often synonymous with smart cities, protects citizens from public crimes and terrorism. As described in Figure 6.1, these forces are blended under the auspices of the city-planning process.

In light of new technologies, the city's tools of innovation have changed dramatically—as have the expectations that cities build environments

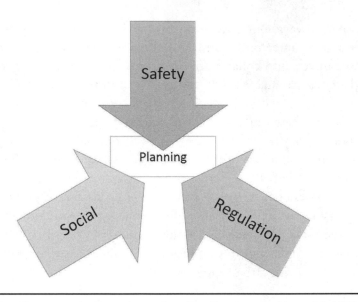

Figure 6.1   Three tracks for urban planning for smart cities with ICT.

that are responsive, useful, and seamless in their operation. Further, these tracks must be analyzed for both short-term and long-term advantage. For example, ICT can provide instantaneous information and alerting functions. It can also inform the city of its progress toward improving problematic conditions using technical solutions. Moreover, ICT can help drive an understanding of what the next-best high-value plans may be. ICT has the potential to change not just the design of the city, but the way the design is implemented, and, ultimately, the new urban narrative that will emerge.

6.4 Balancing the Forces

When one takes the view that technology innovation is best facilitated by a low level of regulatory impulse, then—when a social or other concern emerges during implementation or deployment—one is forced to deal with the problems as they arise. However, deploying technology with the user in mind implies that a technology deployment will necessarily support social values, including privacy and democratic issues, wherein the concerns of the people are dealt with directly by their elected representatives.

This shift in perspective can be quite problematic for the highly fragmented and specialized world we live in, affecting everything from design, architecture, and engineering to academics. At the same time, these disparate approaches are converging in the smart city, where they're impacting myriad stakeholders. And, in the end, those stakeholders can include every one of us, as devices and people grow evermore connected.

Because the citizens of the city are now also users, the important role of addressing the societal aspects of planning cannot be underemphasized in planning exercises. In the smart city, the role of people individually, and in some cases collectively, concerns not what the smart city can do for them or to them, but how they will participate in the environment. Smart cities that have been built from scratch are avoiding this reality, assuming that once they get the infrastructure correct, people will move in and interact properly. This is the big-green-brother approach to energy management that Masdar City took, but it's likely to become the preferred strategy by many in both Europe and the United States. It's a technophiliac's dream to know who is using which devices and to determine ways to directly control or cleverly influence consumption patterns.

So how can ICT-enabled smart cities improve everyday life for the urban citizen? There seem to be endless things we can connect to the Internet (hence the term, IoT); some offer incremental improvements, while others are entirely disruptive. And like many technology-enabled shifts, many of these solutions exist within the realm of city intelligence and will be startling at first. If successful, they'll slip into the background of our lives just like any other commodity. Similar to electricity, which is available nearly everywhere in the developed world, Internet-enabled things will become expected, part of the fabric of our everyday lives. And if they fail to perform, we'll respond with angst.

Smarter city operations related to energy, water, transportation, and public safety are all parts of the smart city vision. But the operational efficiencies, environmental advantages, and service improvements that are designed to provide low-intervention or completely automated solutions will only be of benefit if they improve some aspect of our lives. To achieve this result, solutions providers will need to deliver more than just their technology solutions; they'll need to offer follow-through and create insightful new plans. Typically, this isn't the case. Consider the following excerpt from telecommunications company Alcatel-Lucent's statement about smart cities and their ability to improve our lives:

[M]achines will enable better services to citizens by managing operations automatically, without human intervention. Intelligent lighting can automatically manage an organization's electricity with technology such as activity sensors which turn off all the lights when no one is physically nearby and humidity sensors which adjust to find the perfect temperature.[4]

While there's nothing particularly egregious about this statement, as there are hundreds of similar examples repeated in marketing materials, they represent little more than broad excited statements by smart city advocates working to build business cases and offer a future vision of their urban communities. The devil is in the details.

Recently, more than 1 million streetlights were dimmed in the UK to conserve money and to meet energy goals, including limiting light pollution. The decision to reduce streetlighting is difficult, but more than 100 UK councils participated in the initiative, with some claiming that economic stress required the action. Money saved, they said, could be used to provide social care, including child protection. But as a result of the light reductions, visually impaired citizens complained of comprised nighttime vision, coroner inquests suggested that low-lighting conditions were contributing to accidental deaths, and cautious citizens expressed concern about their well-being while outside at night. UK's *Daily Mail* summarized the situation:

[T]he accident rate on roads where street lights are switched off or are unlighted in towns and cities continues to go up, and it's particularly bad on roads which are 40mph or faster. . . . [I]nsufficient or broken street lighting or lighting turned off was an issue for over a quarter of people; it makes them feel unsafe and deters them from walking.[5]

In light of the backlash, some councils are now looking at more-energy-efficient lighting technologies such as light-emitting diode (LED)

4   Trinh, Anthony (2014), "Smart Cities Will Make Our Lives Better," TMCNet.com. Retrieved December 31, 2014, from http://blog.tmcnet.com/next-generation-communications/2014/09/smart-cities-will-make-our-lives-better.html.
5   *Daily Mail* Online (2014), "Safety Fears as Councils Cut Lights." Retrieved December 31, 2014, from http://www.dailymail.co.uk/wires/pa/article-2883042/Switch-leaving-shires-dark.html.

streetlights. This is a viable alternative for many communities concerned about energy consumption and related costs because these bulbs can use between 65 percent and 85 percent less energy. But even LEDs aren't without challenges. When the city of Berkeley, California, began its roll-out of LEDs, replacing upwards of 8,000 old streetlights, it discovered new issues related to bulb brightness.

Not surprisingly, safety-oriented planners were excitedly recommending the lights for many reasons, especially because they're brighter and cover more area. Yet these advantages became handicaps, as residents in all jurisdictions where the lights were installed complained that the LEDs were irrepressibly bright when they shone in places other than the street. Some homeowners hung blackout curtains to reduce glare from the high-output lights. One Berkeley citizen stated, "I'm all for efficiency, but accompanied by sensitive design, or careful fixture selection."[6] In the UK, older residents muse that it's just like World War II blackouts, except this time, citizens are fighting to keep the light from coming in instead of seeping out.

6.4.1 The Temptations of Reductionism

It seems unfathomably difficult to meet universal needs in an urban environment. But perhaps that's because it's an impossible goal. It's worth reflecting for a moment on why we still cling to the ideal that a technology, if sufficient and necessary, will alone bring the profound social change we claim we so desire. In fact, if this were this true, it would render the application of policy, rules, regulations, and urban planning useless. All that would be necessary is some equipment, some applied knowledge, and some money. How often have you heard engineers boldly claim that with enough money and time, they could do almost anything? This is a common theme in our era of rapid technology capability, but often these same technologists are deeply frustrated when they work to cross the chasm from the early adopter to the mainstream user. Worse, if technology alone were the solution, it would pit the forces of visionaries and idealists against the people they are purportedly trying to benefit.

[6] Jaffe, Drew (2014), "Berkeley Residents Weigh In on New LED Streetlights," *Berkeleyside*. Retrieved December 31, 2014, from http://www.berkeleyside. com/2014/08/06/berkeley-residents-weigh-in-on-new-led-streetlights.

Perhaps most cynically, this form of technological determinism is nothing more than a rhetorical device used to justify expensive decisions, with the full expectation that the public will show early resistance.

Technological determinism is a philosophy that asserts that a society's technology drives its social structure. This reasoning is considered to have its roots in Marxist theory, but the term was invented by Thorstein Veblen, an American social scientist who was active in the early 1920s. It generally embraces two concepts: 1) that technology is inevitable and exists beyond culture and politics, and 2) that technology affects society, which will organize itself around the application once it has been introduced into the community. Some go much further and credit technology as the determinant of history, saying that we, as a society, are powerless to its vicissitudes.

The oft-repeated example that serves as proof of technological determinism is the horse stirrup. According to author Lynn Townsend White, the invention of the stirrup created feudalism. The proof is extensive, but it results in the conclusion that the riding stirrup made combat a much more effective and vastly superior form of attack. Thus, this substantive shift in military techniques sparked the emergence of feudal townships. This is a vast oversimplification of White's proof, but it has set the foundation for an ongoing debate on whether an entirely new societal system rode in on a technological innovation called a stirrup. The equipment could not alone have *caused* the emergence of feudalism any more than dead flesh *causes* the emergence of maggots. The stirrup may have been useful for the implementation of feudalism—it may have even been crucial—but to reduce the evolution of an entire social system to a single technological advancement can be deeply disconcerting.

As rigid a position as this is, a softened perspective has been suggested by others. They believe that it simply takes time to adjust to technology changes, but that in the end, technology will be the divining force that propels us forward. Softer, yes, but the idea still falls into the reductionist assertion that technology is the principal determining factor in how a social system will evolve. And yet, it is equally possible to cast a deterministic outlook as either cynical or supremely hopeful, depending on one's point of view about technology and where one falls on the age-old debate about free will and determinism. Technology itself is morally neutral—it doesn't take a position on how we use it. However, our viewpoint on technology rarely stays in the neutral zone. For example, a gun may not shoot someone, so we argue that it is ridiculous to legislate a gun. But, if we're honest, we know that the function of a gun is to kill. We're left, then, with the nearly definitive comment of Melvin Kranzberg's first law of technology, "Technology is neither good nor bad; nor is it neutral."

The application of technology can never be as simple a method as cause and effect. Systems, especially human systems, have demonstrated repeatedly that they are complicated. Humans respond to many applications of technology, even if the technology is designed to be transparent. Did the invention of the printing press cause democracy to take hold? Or, rather, did the printed word bring new ideas to large swathes of people who gave meaning to texts by exerting their collective will to foment social change? Will the mere existence of Internet-enabled devices cause our cities to be more-efficient operations, to achieve greater sustainability, and to improve the delivery of important services to citizens? Probably not. A flashlight sitting in a drawer shines no light, just like the existence of a mobile phone in my hand doesn't shape my conversations or how I express myself, even though it has changed the way I relate to my intimate connections. Technology innovation affords change. It tells us what can be done, but people decide what will be done.

6.5 The Politics of Artifacts

If we can dispense with the overly simplistic concept of rigid technology determinism, then we must also discard the notion that technology advancements provide us anything more than the possibility for change in how we carry out our lives in the urban environment. At the same time, one is well served to be particularly wary of the role of politics in technology innovation, regulatory design, and planning. Langdon Winner, author and humanities and social sciences chair in the Department of Science and Technology Studies at Rensselaer Polytechnic Institute, published an article in 1980 titled "Do Artifacts Have Politics?" He resolved that there are certain technologies that have such profound societal implications that they take on political dimensionality.

Winner's article provides an excellent example of this phenomenon. In the 1930s, Robert Moses designed a series of expressways in Long Island, New York. Moses designed the overpasses to be low to the ground so that public buses could not pass under them. The political result of the bridges was that low-income people who did not have cars could not access the beachfront, which became the playground of the middle and upper classes.[7] Winner's examination also explored the fact that some technologies, such as nuclear generation, require a hierarchical system—including highly trained technicians, specialized regulators, and security functionaries—in order to operate. Solar technologies, on the other hand, are distributed, require no special skill set to generate or provision power, and need no security. Solar is inherently democratic, accessible, and populist. Despite making this observation in 1980, Winner's conclusions are more important than ever. Even if one rejects the quite naïve viewpoint of technological determinism, one cannot refute the reality that technology can be consciously political in design. Technological design can surely enforce a political agenda. Winner says:

> The things we call technologies are ways of building order in our world. Many technical devices and systems important in everyday life contain possibilities for many different ways of ordering human activity. Consciously or not, deliberately or inadvertently, societies choose structures for technologies that influence how people are going to work, communicate, travel, [and] consume.[8]

Without careful and equitable planning, technology that's introduced into the urban environment will reinforce political realities. And even with such planning, the outcome could be the same. When we experience backlash for smart meters and healthcare system efficiencies, it's important to realize that people rarely accept technology at face value. In fact, it's unusual to find a technological advancement that's globally embraced without regard for its political implications. Even though we seem to accept radical technological change at a high level, we also reject technology simply because it violates our political sensibilities.

Our common, everyday experience shows us that technology innovation is almost always mediated by societal factors that—at least in the short term—tend to suppress the true potential of the raw technology.

[7] Winner, Langdon (1980), "Do Artifacts Have Politics?" *Daedalus*, vol. 109, no. 1, "Modern Technology: Problem or Opportunity," MIT Press. Retrieved January 1, 2015, from http://innovate.ucsb.edu/463-langdon-winner-do-artifacts-have-politics.

[8] Winner [7].

This is because in nearly every conceivable case, we are responding to technology, and in many cases, we're taking it by the scruff of the neck and forcing it our own way.

6.5.1 The Politics of Safety

Safety in the ICT-enabled smart city is both the raison d'être and the tragic weakness of intelligent urban design, and it tends to be profoundly political in nature. The technologies of smart cities, including video surveillance, remote security monitoring, smart streetlights, mass alerts and notifications, and emergency response, are not just tools; they're also systems that can be used for enforcement and maintenance of certain social conditions. The Amber Alert GPS (https://www.amberalertgps.com) can help save the lives of abducted, wandering, or lost children. The device can be placed in a backpack or on the body, and it provides continuous surveillance. If the monitor leaves a safe zone, it sounds an alert. The device can be tracked with any smartphone, it can listen in on conversations using a two-way voice system, and it posts an alert whenever a child gets within 500 feet of the residence of a registered sex offender. Marketing this product is a no-brainer in the context of ensuring the well-being of innocent children, but what about other contexts? What if your boss were monitoring your whereabouts, receiving alerts every time you wandered out of a safe zone?

It's certain that cities can theoretically be managed more efficiently and intelligently on the back of a well-orchestrated digital infrastructure. Indeed, we know that motion-sensitive streetlights, especially LED lamps, save significant amounts of energy, and a personally identifying chip in my car streamlines my use of roadways and highways. But access to data and mapping systems; collaboration with cutting-edge corporations that know how to design, deploy, and run smart infrastructure operations; and partnerships that aim to achieve city sustainability goals are not likely to characterize the smartest cities. Instead, we will find that the most successful urban environments are those that accept the inherent political forces found within ICT systems, and that the deployment of a technology can be akin to a political act.

When city planners pragmatically choose to deploy a certain technology because it's the most cost-effective, or drive efficiency goals, or help create a safer city, then it's incumbent upon them to explore all the possibilities and characteristics of that technology. They need to ask themselves, "How is it best governed?" "What is its correct role in society?" and—of preeminent importance—"What is the technology's relationship to our political preference?" The answers to these questions can drive an important discourse that casts the role of technology in the context of its value to societal configuration and evolution. They can also help planners understand the justifications for the technology, and encourage them to contemplate objections that people may feel when asked to embrace at every level a proposed technological advancement.

Chapter Seven

The Fundamentals of Smart Infrastructure

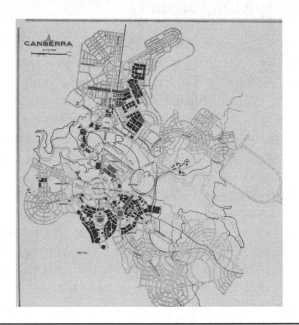

Streets of Canberra, Australia, in the 1940s. The city was originally designed by Walter Burley Griffin in 1912 after he won the Federal Capital design competition.[1]

[1] Image retrieved from the public domain at http://commons.wikimedia.org/wiki/File:Canberra_NCDC_1940_MAP.jpg.

7.1 Chapter Goal

This chapter provides a foundation for understanding how we can best measure from a holistic perspective the success of designs that we bring to our plans for the smart city, including our treatment of the important issues of energy efficiency, energy intensity, and emissions intensity. Further, we probe the information communications technology (ICT) aspects of building design, exploring how ICT informs a full and positive integration with the lives of urban citizens. We also discuss the relationship between our fundamental resources of energy and water and how they can be optimally managed.

7.2 The Energy Opportunity

In the context of the smart city, the generation, distribution, and consumption of energy are all elements of a fully converged digital technology strategy within the power industry value chain. In the urban environment, the impact of demand-side management (DSM) and prosumer activity will be more impactful, at least in the next decade.

Much ink has been spilled in discussion of the energy savings that could be achieved in smart cities, due mostly to energy-efficiency and conservation opportunities in buildings. The overwhelming impulse has been to convince energy consumers of every ilk that they need to conserve energy and that to do so, they must fully orchestrate their buildings. Indeed, many trials and pilots have consistently shown that automation is a reliable technique for obtaining energy-related savings than feedback systems that show consumers or facility operators how well the building is working in the hopes that someone will take action or corrective measures. Recent studies indicate that automation increases energy savings by around 20 percent over feedback systems, which may include in-home displays (IHDs), paper reports, web-based consoles, and most significantly, automation.

Consequently, prodigious sums of money are being invested in smart home orchestration devices and services. But frankly, even the engaging and exciting Nest thermostat isn't going to significantly impact homes that consume at intense levels, at least not in the short term. Still, interest in using smart devices to encourage energy efficiency and conservation is growing. This trend is leading many to conclude that the Internet of Things (IoT) exists to serve our most personal needs and that a world of network integration is about connecting us to the world through devices like cellular phones, tablets, and computers. Instead, we should invest in improving our economic output while simultaneously lowering our consumption. Our persistent focus on the residential sector has given short shrift to other sectors, especially to commercial buildings, and neglects the opportunity for comprehensive energy solutions in the urban environment. Instead, it's the networked sensors, centralized monitoring, and unified control of our buildings that will provide us with profound energy-efficiency gains.

7.2.1 Why So Intense?

In the energy sector, we talk a great deal about energy efficiency and much less about energy intensity. The difference between the two concepts is subtle, but they're inverse concepts. However, energy efficiency does not always explain a decrease in energy intensity. Structural and behavioral factors, can also reduce energy, which is discussed further. First a little clarity:

- *Energy intensity* is a measurement of the quantity of energy that's needed for every measured unit of activity. When we use less energy to produce a product, for example, we reduce energy intensity.
- *Energy efficiency* is an improvement in process that maintains the level of service (the amenity) when the amount of energy required for the service is reduced. The effect is the same if a service is enhanced with the same amount of energy input. Thus, we are either doing the same amount of work with less energy or doing even more work with the same amount of energy.[2]

An example can help explain why it's important for us to be precise in our use of language. I can achieve 44 miles per gallon (mpg) of gas in my plug-in hybrid electric vehicle (PHEV) and 17 mpg in my four-wheeler.

[2] US Department of Energy (n.d.), "Energy Intensity Indicators: Efficiency vs. Intensity." Retrieved January 20, 2015, from http://www1.eere.energy.gov/analysis/eii_efficiency_intensity.html.

It's easy to say, then, that my PHEV is more fuel efficient, and as an individual unit, it also has a lower energy intensity. However, when we talk about an entire city, we can't meaningfully say it's more energy efficient. A city is a combination of people, and buildings, and cars, and even various microclimates; it is not in and of itself a level of service. It makes no sense to compare the energy efficiency of a jet engine with that of an electric bicycle. We can, though, use energy intensity to start measuring the energy intensity of transportation.

Further, energy intensity can be improved by factors other than an increase in energy efficiency. As mentioned, structural and behavioral changes can affect energy intensity and are equally important when we're considering alternative design for our cities. For example, demographic changes can have a surprising impact on energy use both structurally and behaviorally. In our family homes, as children grow up and move out of the house, the household size changes and overall energy use decreases. But as people age, they tend to turn the heat higher. So the heating bill in a 65-year-old woman's house will likely increase as she nears 80, but nothing has fundamentally changed with the underlying efficiency of her house.

Energy intensity is most often expressed as energy divided by gross domestic product (GDP), where the fewer units of energy for each dollar spent, the better. It's a way for us to compare the performance of a sector without the underlying detail—that is, without zooming in too far to be able to examine broad-scale improvements in areas such as transportation, manufacturing, and service delivery. In fact, many would argue that this is the most useful way for us to measure the impacts of our intended efficiency, behavioral, and even structural improvements. It requires us to consider myriad factors and not just how well a motor works.

It is an interesting fact that the more resources a nation has, the worse its intensity score. For example, Saudi Arabia, Canada, and Russia have relatively cheap energy, but because they have extreme climates, remote cities, and mostly non-energy-efficient vehicles, their energy intensity is high. European nations pay much more for their energy, but because they have denser city distribution and a modern electric infrastructure—which was installed after the devastation of World War II—their energy intensity is less than half of their more-abundant counterparts. For obvious reasons, the use of energy intensity as a metric can become political very quickly, depending on how the score is correlated with per-capita income. Thus, it should be evaluated only with a deep understanding of context. Just on the basis of energy intensity, a preindustrial economy may prove to have extremely low intensities, but it may not provide anything close to a healthy, safe lifestyle for its inhabitants.

This is where a related measure can be useful to factor into the mix: emission intensity (sometimes called carbon intensity). Emission intensity is used to express the weight of the carbon dioxide (CO_2) released for any given unit of measure. It's possible to measure the intensity metrics of all sorts of things, from every can of soda produced on an assembly line to every kilometer or mile driven in an automobile. One of the reasons to calculate an emission intensity metric rather than an absolute measure of emissions is to avoid misinterpreting results among products that may have longer lifetimes. For example: Two washing machines are manufactured by two different companies. One of them is less durable than the other, so in absolute numbers, the longer-lasting product would have a higher lifetime emission value. Clearly, data can quickly become misleading. It can be more useful, then, to look at a number of units over the lifetime of the sold product, and then divide the total lifetime emissions by the number of units per lifetime of sold products.[3]

Let's calculate an intensity metric for an automobile. First, we determine the gas mileage of the vehicle, then we factor in how far the car is driven per year, and finally, we apply a multiplier that is derived from how many grams of CO_2 per liter of fuel are liberated into the environment when the car is running. We can then start to chase up the value stream and evaluate other factors related to emissions intensity for the extraction of the fuel, its transportation to the filling station, and the manufacturing process of the car itself, depending on what we want to demonstrate with our derived intensity metric.

The key point in this discussion is that we can't measure a green city based on superior efficiency alone. Rather, we need to use various metrics—including energy-efficiency improvement values, energy intensity, and emissions intensity—to better understand our goals and our progress. It's easy to see how the subject can get confounding and cause designers, planners, and technologists to get quickly mired in difficult complexities.

A city that is economically healthy and productive, with a temperate year-round weather cycle and a density that can drive down transportation costs while encouraging walking, will have a far lower energy-intensity

---

[3] The Greenhouse Gas Protocol (n.d.), "Appendix C: Calculating Emissions Intensity Metrics." Retrieved January 21, 2015, from http://www.ghgprotocol.org/files/ghgp/AppendixC.pdf.

measure than a city that is similarly productive but experiences more-extreme weather conditions and longer commutes. As already mentioned, Canada tends to have a high energy-intensity score, as do Sweden, Norway, and France, but all of these countries have transitioned rather dramatically toward low-carbon energy generation, such as utility-scale wind and hydro power. Thus, these countries produce a fraction (in some studies as little as a fifth) of the carbon that's produced by other countries that have not made such rapid shifts to renewables. It's worth noting that energy-intensity measurements are changing rapidly, especially in the major world economies such as China, Japan, and Germany, where a shift away from nuclear has occurred since 2012.

Consequently, more-holistic measurement protocols must consider more than efficiency. In addition to energy intensity, metrics should include emission intensity, which takes stock of a variety of pollutants and seeks to produce some insight into the environmental impacts related to fuels and other activities. Let's say I own six high-rise condos. My cousin invented an unbelievably efficient engine that can provide air conditioning to the entire fleet of buildings at a fraction of the electrical requirement. Unfortunately, the engine spews large quantities of methane gas during its process, and I choose not to deploy it over a concern for its overall negative impact on the environment. This kind of trade-off will always occur, unless some magical change in how we power our world happens. We must be willing to undertake the complex evaluation required to understand how our designs serve our goals of a more sustainable urban environment.

It is still a fair statement that one of the primary goals of the smart city is to find quick, clean, and economical resources to power our urban environments. There is no doubt that energy efficiency—sometimes called the first fuel—is that virtual resource. It's obvious that building new power plants is more expensive than increasing efficient technologies consistently enough to have an overall impact on decreasing energy intensity. There is plenty of evidence that energy efficiency can produce significant savings, especially in decreased carbon emissions and reduced peak electricity demand. The trends are clear, showing a 58 percent reduction in US energy intensity from 1950 to 2011, mostly attributable to more-

[4] Alaska Renewable Energy Project (n.d.), "What Is Energy Efficiency?" Retrieved January 21, 2015, from http://alaskarenewableenergy.org/energy-efficiency/what-is-energy-efficiency.

efficient loads.[4] But there are still dramatic improvements to be made in how we design our cities to take advantage of opportunities like tree shade, insulation, window technology, and green space.

7.3 The Building Opportunity

The United States, second only in energy demand to China, consumes 20 percent of worldwide energy resources. The buildings sector, including residential and consumer buildings, accounts for over 40 percent of that consumption—more than either the transportation or the industrial sector. Heating, cooling, and lighting comprise about half of that usage, especially in our office spaces, retail operations, and educational institutions.[5] Of course, given that information, it's tempting to use automation to directly attack the problem of efficiency in buildings. If we can install the appropriate technology in buildings that "just works" to control our end uses, we will surely make exceptional and meaningful gains. In short, an appropriately orchestrated building, house, or commercial structure will prevent the excessive use of energy beyond what is required for the amenity of the occupants.

This makes sense, but like so many instances where we fire a magic bullet, we miss the target. Building management systems (BMSs) have been around for decades in the commercial enterprise, but they have not had the kind of impact that one would assume, given their level of penetration. And despite a new generation of highly connected and remotely controllable buildings—whose systems can be tinkered with via iPhone or facility command center—even well-designed BMSs aren't showing major energy reductions. In a number of case studies, reductions are reported to be as high as 40 to 50 percent, especially if lighting is considered in the management strategy. But these systems are failing to consistently and broadly perform. There are two reasons for this. One, a poorly configured BMS, usually the result of control errors, can actually raise energy consumption. Second, the human occupants of our well-engineered or upgraded buildings have thrown our dreams of the simple, refined, and easy-to-manage technology-driven solution asunder.

[5] US Department of Energy (n.d.), "Buildings Energy Data Book, Chapter 1: Buildings Sector." Retrieved January 18, 2015, from http://buildingsdatabook. eren.doe.gov/ChapterIntro1.aspx.

In earlier chapters of this book, we talked about how building smart cities from the ground up poorly serves their human constituents yet fails to create rich, satisfying, livable environments for human beings. Urban communities evolve over many years, they can change dramatically under cultural influences, and people are constantly adjusting within them. Similarly, buildings that have been carefully designed to incorporate both passive and active measures for efficiency and greater sustainability can still fail to reduce energy use. That's because it's difficult to account for human behavior, which can drive the energy use of a building five times higher than what was expected.[6] Anyone who has ever worked in an office building has likely made adjustments to their environment, as journalist Simon Brammer describes of his own experience. He says we waste energy in myriad ways, including,

> —not switching off lights or computers, propping doors open, or . . . running a fan heater under your desk when the air conditioning gets too cold. This creates a huge energy-use loop of one system trying to cool and the other, heat. We are simply never going to be "passive players" in our environments.[7]

Every energy conservation specialist, product designer, policymaker, and facilities manager has been frustrated by building occupants' blatant disregard of BMS controls to conserve energy. Brammer breaks it down to trust: engineers' trust in building users, the lack of which is shown by how little manual override the engineers provide. Thus, if you don't have a thermostat in your office, you might end up using a space heater to warm your feet under the desk, running a cord across the office and tripping anyone who walks by. And surely, many will cringe to recall the motion-sensor lights that are so cleverly installed in company restrooms,

---

[6] The Carbon Trust (2012), "Closing the Gap: Lessons Learned on Realising the Potential of Low Carbon Building Design." Retrieved January 19, 2015, from http://www.carbontrust.com/media/81361/ctg047-closing-the-gap-low-carbon-building-design.pdf.

[7] Brammer, Simon (2014), "How Riding Elephants Can Help Energy Efficiency in the Office," *The Guardian*. Retrieved January 18, 2015, from http://www.theguardian.com/sustainable-business/riding-elephants-energy-efficiency-office.

creating compromising situations that involve groping around in the dark at the worst moment imaginable. Too many of us have been there, waving our hands futilely in the dark, hoping the sensor will switch the lights back on. After a while, someone will wrap a piece of duct tape over that sensor, ensuring that the lights remain on forever.

Brammer quotes Jonathan Hines, director of the award-winning, UK-based architecture team Architype (www.architype.co.uk), who closely monitors the firm's structures to track their performance. He provides further insight:

> We found that the more automated and complex the systems and controls, the more likely they are to go wrong and not work effectively. Occupants need to both feel, and actually have, sufficient control of their own environment. They need to be helped and supported to understand how to best control their environment.[8]

The obvious conclusion is disturbing for the many who prefer the predictability of an automated world and who yearn for a simpler worldview that doesn't involve the capricious actions of the human being. It's a daunting task to design a building that incorporates multiple and varied types of occupants with different habits, behaviors, schedules, and preferences. It's even harder to incorporate these variables into a system that is both comfortable and energy efficient. Workarounds and accommodations are inevitable in human life, but anticipating them and designing toward them requires a certain degree of trust and confidence that people will make the "right" choice. And as the world becomes even more networked and connected, the problems are becoming more complex.

7.3.1 New Models, New Ways Forward

The way we generate, distribute, and consume electricity is changing at a rapid pace, even in our most sophisticated cities. And it's being informed in surprising ways by some of the most underdeveloped regions of the world. For example, in sub-Saharan Africa, the upsurge in mobile phones has brought advancements in distributed solar to overcome the issue of a

[8] Ibid.

lack of reliable energy sources. In fact, only about 25 percent of the population in this region of the world even has access to electricity. Meanwhile, power outages can add up to more than 50 days of blackouts per year in some places, coupled with very high power tariffs. Users who want to acquire mobile technology must consider how they will power their phone before they ever purchase a device.

This combination of forces has compelled more consumers to adopt mobile devices that use very little energy and remain charged for longer periods of time. As a result, solar- and hybrid-powered telecom installations are booming, and more-advanced deployments include remote monitoring, system analysis, techniques to extend battery life and reduce downtime, and high-tech sensors that can respond to environmental events to decrease site maintenance and operating expenses. Further, the desire of mobile network operators to increase their market sphere have caused renewable options for electricity generation to scale very quickly. In fact, some African nations may get their first electricity from a remote solar grid.

7.4 Orchestrating Our Lives, Not Just Our Buildings

Early BMSs handled fairly rudimentary tasks, such as heating, ventilation, and air conditioning (HVAC); security; and sometimes lighting. Now, a BMS may be charged with many responsibilities, including biometrics, access control, metering, video systems, elevators, and even some communications systems. We count on them to secure us, keep us warm, cool us down, adjust our mattresses, and even turn out the lights in the bathroom. As described in Figure 7.1, these activities are carried out over an Internet Protocol (IP)-based network, and although they're distributed, they're often managed centrally through a complex cloud-based system that channels our wishes through our smartphones or advanced consoles. While a fleet of buildings may be under the auspices of a service provider, the residence may be under the control of an app that we interact with right after a quick Facebook post updates our current location. The principles of operation are precisely the same, even if the extent, context, and level of complexity are not.

Integrated BMSs for complex buildings like high-rises or fleets are most often under a centralized command-and-control system. While

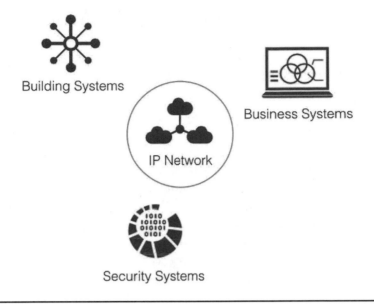

Figure 7.1   Integrated building management systems are about more than energy.

HVAC control used to be the primary consideration, lights are now regularly managed for optimal energy usage over time. Additionally, BMSs now monitor a broad range of building system functions such as temperature control; door control; fire systems; elevators; security systems like access control and closed-circuit TV (CCTV) surveillance; business systems such as asset management, communication, and help-desk function; as well as sewage, parking control, electric vehicle charging, plumbing and water management, backup generation, or any imaginable device that can communicate with a standard protocol over the IP network.

7.4.1 Resource Infrastructure

The performance gap between the level of overall efficiency gain expected by orchestrating a building will continue to grow as more and more systems come under the auspices of centralized command. Let's revisit the important delineation between intensity and efficiency: Sooner or later, as the underlying systems under control become more disparate, the issues and determining the appropriate measures can become more confounding. Further, many buildings do not behave as designed, either because the facilities management team is not operating the building in the way the planners and architects intended, or because the occupants are not occupying in the expected manner. More likely, it's both.

As this problem becomes more easily recognizable, many non-government organizations (NGOs) interested in low-carbon buildings have been working to develop strategies to improve how these buildings are designed. Yet even when modeling, training, building-bedding measures, and processes, there still seems to be a blind spot to improving our level of achievement over time. Unfortunately, so far none of these recommendations, processes, or approaches fully comprehends the human-device interactions, or other behavioral principles that may improve building outcomes.

The Rocky Mountain Institute (RMI) was established in 1982 with the primary focus of researching, consulting, and lecturing on energy and resource efficiency. However, the institute's work is extremely varied, addressing everything from building technologies to designs for a super-efficient automobile called the Hypercar, the science of which was commercialized in the 2014 BMW i3 family of automobiles.[9] Despite its sometimes controversial positions, RMI has never failed to push the envelope of what we can achieve in making the direct connection between our quality of life and the way we consume our resources, especially energy. Amory Lovins, the progenitor of RMI and the brains behind the Hypercar, and his team have introduced many important ideas that can help us evolve our thinking about our natural resource; If we consider human behavior, happiness, and even productivity up front, we will think of our resources as part of our infrastructure rather than commodities. Essentially, we need a strategy that decouples the financial health of a utility from the amount of resources it sells, be it electricity, gas, or water.

The Renewable Energy Alaska Project (REAP) is as un-urban as one can imagine, but the organization is encouraging local builders to design structures that reduce the region's energy intensity, which is elevated due to the area's extreme temperatures and high fuel costs. REAP has investigated the benefits of the well-insulated home and as a result proselytizes many

[9] Vidal, John (2014), "Amory Lovins: Energy Visionary Sees Renewables Revolution in Full Swing." Retrieved January 21, 2015, from http://www.theguardian.com/environment/2014/feb/17/amory-lovins-renewable-energy.

of the design practices discussed by RMI, such as capturing waste heat and chemical energy to turn it into tiny, other usable forms of energy during industrial processes, improving fuel economy without compromising function for varied transportation needs, and enhancing air and lighting systems. REAP is also encouraging builders to employ behavioral and structural mechanisms, which—as noted earlier—can also greatly affect energy intensity:

> These include the psychological benefits of using natural lighting sources, including making a home or office more comfortable, increasing worker productivity, or making a retail store more appealing to customers. Other benefits include healthier, better-ventilated buildings, food that stays fresher in more efficient refrigerators, and motors that run quieter.[10]

7.5 The Bonds of Energy and Water

It's impossible to truly divorce water from energy. We make efforts to increase the efficiency of our lighting and air conditioning, and we diligently fix our leaky faucets and turn off the tap when we're brushing our teeth. But we're never quite sure what the relationship is between water and energy.

First off, it takes water to produce energy and it takes energy to produce drinking water. And anyone who is living in drought conditions—such as California, where residents are experiencing one of the most severe droughts on record, precipitating a state of emergency—knows that we're facing pressing problems related to the limitations of our current technology to access the water we need to support life, our ecosystems, and the processes and systems that underpin our society and our economy. The situation in California, which itself carries a GDP of nearly US$2 trillion, has shown how deep the links between energy and water go.

In the course of generating electricity, water is used to cool the steam that is produced by the generators; it's also required in the production of fuel, specifically, in the mining of coal, the hydraulic extraction of natural

[10] Alaska Renewable Energy Project [4].

gas and oil, and even the growing of crops for biofuels. As the Union of Concerned Scientists reminds us, "Using water in our homes and business requires getting there, treating, [and] heating it."[11] So it's not surprising that if there's stress on the energy system, there's stress on the water system. If water becomes scarce, competition rises for the share of what is available, whether it's used to water crops, mix concrete at construction sites, facilitate manufacturing processes, or generate electricity itself.

In the smart urban environment, the nexus of energy and water requires a process of co-planning and management. There are a variety of new initiatives emerging that aim to address this linkage and propose approaches to coordinating plans for energy and water infrastructure. Internet-based control and monitoring strategies are at the foundation of what will be required for smart cities to manage our resources. Part of what will enable this will be regulatory constructs and standards that will not only quicken the adoption of renewable energy generation, but will also allow innovation to thrive. Standards are not only relevant and important in the smart city; they're also critical in enabling new collaborative designs to emerge. Standards begin with ICT and engaging the built environment, the energy and water infrastructure, and transportation by collecting, analyzing, and responding to issues in their own functional and operational domain. Then, that information must be shared across domains.

7.6 Full Convergence

Researchers have been raising the issue of information technology–operations technology convergence (IT-OT) for several years, and it's unhappily yet another term that defies industry standard definition. IT-OT is relative. As the smart city emerges, it will be tempting to draw stringent lines of demarcation between functions. If that occurs, programs that manage the transactional side of the city's technology—billing, accounting, asset management, human resources, and records

[11] Union of Concerned Scientists (n.d.). "The Connections Between Our Energy and Water." Retrieved January 21, 2015, from http://www.ucsusa.org/clean_energy/our-energy-choices/energy-and-water-use/energy-and-water.html#.VMAgM8YeWlI.

and licensing—will not benefit from the operational forms of data that include distribution operations, infrastructure and control center monitoring, and essentially any machine-to-machine (M2M) interaction.

Creating a human environment with ICT as the keystone drives not only operational changes but also changes throughout the knowledge-based infrastructure. Departments and systems must be integrated and work well together. There are many crosscutting business processes, and a lack of integration results in poor or uninformed decision-making, difficulty in meeting compliance requirements, poor communications, inefficient field operations, and the inability to effectively report to external stakeholders.

At the simplest, making operational data available to systems that directly support public processes will contribute to improved situational awareness. A key example is asset management analytics to support electricity distribution. Asset health models can be constructed by analyzing and seeking patterns in operational data based on information such as temperature, pressure, loading, short-circuiting, and fault events—all data that drives improved decision-making about how to manage a particular asset and conduct replacement scheduling. In fact, asset analytics characterizes one of the most important early smart grid wins for the business, reducing catastrophic outages while managing capital and maintenance outlays.

Designing infrastructure services to make a city more livable includes not just finding ways to make a city more comfortable and environmentally friendly, but also ensuring that even the design of utility services such as water and energy are viewed holistically. This means designers must aggregate, integrate, and analyze data from end to end, considering how people operate, consume resources, and integrate with the environment around them. In a sense, citizens are part of the fabric of the infrastructure itself, from generating renewable electricity to building efficiencies, and the behavioral role of humans as active participants in how resources are consumed, is a key consideration in smart city design.

Chapter Eight

The Urban Life Force

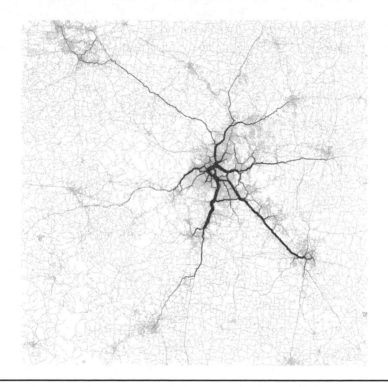

Data visualization of transportation flows through the Nashville, Tennessee, metro area; created using the Twitter streaming API in 2011.[1]

[1] Image retrieved from the public domain at https://www.flickr.com/photos/walkingsf/6882607681/in/set-72157628993413851.

8.1 Chapter Goal

This chapter takes a novel approach to investigating the role of advanced transportation flows within the smart city by considering them holistically. Designing for smart cities is not only about picking the most efficient, least polluting fuels, nor is it just about commercial telematics and toll collection—it's mostly about goal setting. Designing smart cities focuses most on helping to solve high-impact human problems, such as decreasing pollution and traffic congestion, improving access to social services, preventing urban food desertification, and increasing public safety with a comprehensive understanding of events and incident management. How that gets done is largely tactical. Additionally, from an information communications technology (ICT) perspective, the use of data analytics greatly enhances transportation networks. We also examine how to reach goals with the best application of technology and analytics by integrating the most powerful forms of data, giving special latitude to perhaps the most innovative sensor system technology ever available to the city—the city dweller and her smartphone.

8.2 Transportation as Animating Principle

Life force represents our sense of vitality; it's the thing that separates the living from the nonliving. In our cities, our collective life force is demonstrated by the quality of our lives, as measured by the health of our society, economy, and our relationship to the environment; it's the vital force that spurs continued growth and well-being for communities. Typically, in a discussion of smart city technology, transportation and human services aren't explored as one unit, and that means that some legwork is in order. But if we're committed to designing a smart environment that's founded on empathy for our citizens, we must first consider how our design influences the movement of people through the city. We also need to account for the subsequent impacts on fundamental transport issues as well as public health and wellness. How we organize a smart city's transportation system determines how the city develops and becomes sustainable over time. Our design affects land-use policies and myriad elements of the built environment. It also forces us to face the truth about how transportation can segregate disadvantaged neighborhoods and how that isolation can limit ready access to hospitals, community clinics, public parks, and even food.

In this light, the concept of urban transportation must go one step further than our traditional thoughts about conveyance, because wherever the transportation infrastructure accommodates and encourages non-motorized transportation, positive impacts on public health result. Physical activity improves citizens' health, but equally important is the decrease in transportation-related pollution that results in asthma, respiratory illness, heart disease, lower healthy birth rates, and cancer. Further, multiple studies have shown that a limited access to affordable transportation creates health inequity, decreased access to education, and fewer recreational opportunities for all populations, especially disabled and senior citizens. Transportation has always been job one for urban designers, but if we believe that smart technologies should improve livability and increase resource sustainability, there may be no more impactful a goal for transportation design than improving health outcomes by how we move people around.

The traditional vision for treating transportation-planning problems in urban environments is to focus on traffic mitigation, outfitting highways and roads with intelligence such as roadside sensors, and installing radio frequency identification (RFID) tags and global positioning system (GPS) devices in vehicles. Mostly, planners are thinking about how to connect shipping, rail, and air transportation to most efficiently get people, products, and services from here to there. Data about location-based, real-time conditions can improve the use of existing infrastructure, but it can also serve to build out new, almost fantastical systems of transport. For example, consider the Hyperloop, Elon Musk's conceptual high-speed transportation system. It was conceived to run from Los Angeles to San Francisco in just 35 minutes, covering nearly 360 miles (570 kilometers [km]) at an average speed of around 598 miles per hour (962 km per hour).

Under the auspices of a research company called Hyperloop Transportation Technologies (HTT), approximately 100 engineers are designing the Hyperloop. These professionals were selected from several hundred who applied to participate through the JumpStart Fund. While Musk's West Coast vision may have been the fodder for the collaborative group of members, the company is also researching intercity transport and urban Hyperloops that would carry travelers between suburban areas. Essentially, the concept proposes to push capsules through a steel tube at a partial vacuum, where the capsules float on a thin bed of air and glide down the tube at an extremely high rate of speed (with solar-powered linear motors). Although the science sounds like fiction and there are significant technological challenges and costs related to constructing an elevated tube, the goals of the project seem worthy: a transportation solution that's weatherproof, faster than a jet airplane, and has low power requirements.

Unfortunately, it's the humans who aren't up to it: If you're the sort of person who finds a magnetic resonance imaging (MRI) test a bit challenging, you will likely find it unpleasant to step into a narrow, sealed, windowless capsule to shoot down a closed steel tunnel at near-sonic speeds with high noise levels. Of course, at 900 feet per second, you're not going to be standing in the aisles, going to the restroom, or even moving. While the Hyperloop doesn't pull enough lateral G's to cause a passenger to black out, the vessel would be estimated to pull a little less than half the g-force of a roller coaster—for the entire duration of the ride. To sum that up, the Hyperloop may be perceived as nothing short of a terrifying shot through hell, complete with dramatic acceleration, braking, and very likely quite a bit of nausea. You will, however, reach your destination in an unbelievably short amount of time.

Truly, a "cross between a Concorde and a railgun and an air hockey table" is the vision of one of the most innovative thinkers in the world, who doesn't seem to mind all sorts of political or naysayer pushback.[2] Musk finds ways to fund his projects, out of his own wealthy coffers and the fortunes of private funders. But the project raises the kinds of issues we see when we confuse the important role of "future thinking" with the immediate need to use technology to solve real human problems. Regardless of whether we're tantalized or horrified by these futuristic visions, we need to be open to their possibilities. However, future-think doesn't solve immediate problems, and is a deeply insufficient tool for addressing the major problems we have today.

For some, fast trains and spacecraft are science fiction in a time of uncertainty. For others, their creation is an absolute necessity to the evolution of the human race. We want breakthrough technologies, but we

[2] Gannes, Liz (2013), "Tesla CEO and SpaceX Founder Elon Musk: The Full D11 (Video)." Retrieved January 31, 2015, from http://allthingsd.com/20130530/tesla-ceo-and-spacex-founder-elon-musk-the-full-d11-interview-video.

need immediate impact of our technology-based designs on society, the economy, the environment, geopolitical situations, and even technology itself. So it may be that the Hyperloop is ultimately the best solution to meet a transportation goal, but the principles of design thinking implore us to consider alternative starting points. When it comes to the use of ICT to improve transportation infrastructure, it is best to think of break-through technologies as a side-effect of the quest to create and deploy innovative services while building a coordinated and efficient system of transport networks, whether they are Hyperloop trains, hovercraft, trains, shared rides, bicycles, or roller skates.

8.3 Innovative Transportation Services

The world over, organizations have been working to improve transporta-tion infrastructure, but it's the European Union (EU) that has been the most intentional about actually creating a unified framework of thought. With the EU Directive of July 2015—named 2010/40/EU—the organi-zation specifically recognized the importance of intelligent transport sys-tems (ITSs), describing the framework, in part, with the following:

> Intelligent Transport Systems (ITS) are advanced applications which without embodying intelligence as such aim to provide innovative services relating to different modes of transport and traffic management and enable various users to be better informed and make safer, more coordinated and "smarter" use of transport networks.[3]

This is a brilliant (though awkwardly written) piece of legislation because it begins to define transportation differently. The EU points out how transportation scenarios must begin to embrace smart technology for advanced coordination through a service model—this is quite a shift

[3] European Parliament and the Council of the European Union (2010), "Directive 2010/40/EU of the European Parliament and of the Council of 7 July 2010 on the Framework for the Deployment of Intelligent Transport Systems in the Field of Road Transport and for Interfaces with Other Modes of Transport," Official Journal of the European Union, pp. 1–13. Retrieved March 30, 2015, from http://eur-lex.europa.eu/LexUriServ/LexUriServ.do?ur i=OJ:L:2010:207:0001:0013:EN:PDF.

from the past approach to the mechanics of moving people and things around, because it includes consideration for the habits and behaviors of drivers and riders themselves. The problems for which we seek solutions through smarter transportation in our cities include:

- Creating healthier, more-walkable, and more-livable cities
- Improving transportation infrastructure to reduce congestion and enhance public safety
- Reducing urban food deserts and improving access to social services

The specific characteristics related to transportation innovation include increased access to transit and improved street design. Traditional transportation management and design techniques, include such measures as counting for the general number of automobile trips (called vehicle miles traveled or VMT) to calculate impact on congestion and air pollution. That is just part of the story when we include human behavior in our models. Possibly an even more direct correlation with public health are the transportation-related benefits relevant to the higher density of the city are decreasing VMT by eliminating the need for automobile ownership outright through an extended system of public transit networks, walkways, and bicycle routes.

One of the most important roles for urban transportation-related technology is to help control the movement and speed of vehicle traffic throughout the roadway network. A broad review of the literature shows that vehicle speed and volume are the primary levers for influencing congestion and crashes, including pedestrian-involved accidents. While much of this influence can be asserted through streetscape design that affects both driver and pedestrian behavior, the movement of vehicles can be optimized through traffic-calming initiatives, improved controls, and an overall network redesign to facilitate connectivity and offer more route choices.

The computational technologies in play include the usual suspects: sensors, closed-circuit TV (CCTV); cellular data; wireless, Bluetooth, and GPS technologies; and other forms of detection such as inductive loops. Eventually, these loops will be able to estimate vehicle characteristics such as speed, car length, and vehicle class (passenger car, truck, or motorcycle). By extension, creating new services with this data becomes an intriguing possibility. Intelligent transport applications are already being and built and include emergency vehicle notifications, traffic enforcement, and variable speed limits that change with road congestion and driving conditions. Collision-avoidance systems and technologies that enable dynamic traffic-light-sequencing for driverless cars and freeway management are also being developed.

8.3.1 Transportation Analytics

The transportation industry has long been a provider of big data. Sources of this information include infrastructure sensors as well as databases that track the tickets we buy, the fares we pay, and the apps we run on our smartphones, which are enabled with powerful sensors and location services. From a planning perspective, transportation planners have leveraged data since the first slabs of concrete were poured. However, the fusing of unexpected and surprising data sources is beginning to provide a richer picture of how people move through the cities and the services that can be deployed to help the urban environment better respond to human needs.

Twitter, for example, is a surprisingly powerful source of information. Tweets contain geolocation information that can be used not only for planning but also for real-time operations. Eric Fisher, a data-mapping expert and self-proclaimed aficionado of failed transportation plans, used the Twitter application programming interface (API) to find and map the most frequently travelled routes in the United States. Basically, Fisher uses geotagged tweets collected over a period of time to indicate traffic levels, showing the load of existing transport networks, and providing an alternative view of movement. Mashing millions of these tweets with data already known about the transportation system, Fisher plots the data into striking cartograms.

Although some might find Fisher's efforts gratuitous or redundant, he demonstrates the possibilities for analytics to help us spot emerging trends, draw new conclusions, and cross-reference the data we already know with other sources of information for powerful new insights. In Figure 8.1, Fischer's map of Chicago includes 10,000 Twitter points plotted on an OpenStreetMap grid using the Dijkstra shortest-path routing

---

[4] Fisher, Eric (2012), "Is This the Structure of Chicago?" Made available through the Creative Commons License. Retrieved February 1, 2015, from https://www.flickr.com/photos/walkingsf/6747156223/in/set-72157628993413851.

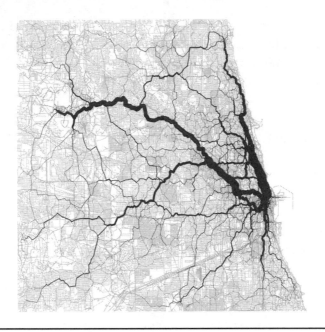

Figure 8.1 Eric Fisher's 2011 plot of Chicago from the Twitter-streaming API.

aggregation method (the data is from the Twitter streaming API and comprehended 10,000 points with 30,000 vectors).[4] The map tells a story about transportation route demand, but it also provides underpinnings for deeper studies that could be achieved by overlaying ethnicity, drivers versus train riders, and precise demographics of Twitter users in Chicago. For example, are these tweeters youngsters with stigmatized dialects or business professionals off to a meeting?

8.3.2 The Most Powerful Sensor in the City Is in Your Pocket

Just into 2015, Facebook announced that it would be testing a digital presence service that would allow it to deliver information about surrounding shopping opportunities and landmarks through localized transmitters called "beacons." The company is calling its service Place Tips. When one of the largest Internet properties in the world attaches the physical environment to the mobile environment through the company's social media platform, it is further indication of how the smartphone has emerged as one of the most powerful sensors available. This is true now for two reasons: smartphones are ubiquitous and they reliably broadcast our personal location data on a continuous basis.

The location-based activity stream that smartphones produce is easily captured. As a person walks around the city, her cellphone, Wi-Fi, and Bluetooth signals can be mashed with GPS data to provide great real-time precision. Facebook's service isn't novel, except in one way. The company is focusing on the service, not the enabling technology. This isn't the first time that such technology has been used—it's appeared in sports stadium applications as well as retail in-store marketing plays—but it's the first time the technology has been used to find 1.3 billion people through their Facebook app. This advancement enables a whole new level of data collection, tracking not just our physical bodies in space but also our relationships, preferences, likes, and conversations.

From a deployment perspective, the physical cost of the beacons is absurdly low (around US$5), which allows Facebook to provide them to their target purveyors for no cost. Providing cheap devices is a clever move, since the use of the beacons and the immediacy of being able to measure the result to a beacon ad will allow Facebook to charge a premium for its services. It's not hard to imagine that the company will sell not only for the placement of an ad in its social network, but for the measurement data it can further sell since the company now owns a description of the entire loop of a sale. Facebook can now analyze customers from the street, encourage them to walk into a store at just the right moment, and provide real-time incentive for a purchase: "Like that watch you're looking at? Here's a 10% off coupon."

Given this initiative by Facebook, even the staid *Wall Street Journal* is captured by the whimsy of the moment:

> Beyond such commercial uses, a street artist could place a beacon near a new work, broadcasting information extracted from the artist's Facebook page. An architect could place a beacon on a new building and tell passersby about the construction process. Cities could place beacons on little-known historical sites that go otherwise unnoticed."[5]

[5] Albergotti, Reed (2015), "Facebook Tests Bluetooth 'Beacons' to Feed Users Local Content," *The Wall Street Journal*. Retrieved February 1, 2015, from http://blogs.wsj.com/digits/2015/01/29/facebook-tests-bluetooth-beacons-to-feed-users-local-content.

It feels that we have traveled far afield from transportation, but it's a small leap to pull these strands together. People already use their phones to manage their own movement through the city, report potholes, call for rides, and purchase tickets. With the addition of powerful locational data available through social media services, city planners can now understand how and why people are moving around and begin to manage transportation at a personal level with mass impact. It is not difficult to stipulate that the smartphone-wielding city resident is potentially the biggest disrupter to the delivery of transportation services since the mass production of the motorized vehicle itself. Aggregating transportation data and other information provides the ability to predict, manage, and plan our transportation systems in real time.

8.3.3 Serious Planning with Our Playthings

Despite the inextricable link between the smartphone, the movement of vehicles and pedestrians through the city, and transportation policy, most major cities are not excited about the prospect of playing either app designer or developer. Eric Goldwyn, an urban planning expert at *CityLab* who writes about the role of the smartphone in urban development, has noted that even in New York City, with its tremendous public transit ridership, the private sector—including Google and Uber—is leading the shift toward new mobility applications. Goldwyn observes that despite some investigation and false starts, city spokespeople are now calling it inappropriate for the city to take an active role in app development and are expressing a preference for private-sector leadership.

Why aren't city infrastructure departments seeing the obvious benefits of aggregating and fusing data from external sources with their own data for planning and operational benefit? Not only is this a potentially huge missed opportunity from an economic perspective, it also fails to recognize that in order for public agencies to do their jobs effectively, they must learn to become data driven. Even public infrastructure companies such as utilities are moving toward a full embrace of big data. For example, the very conservative energy industry has made dramatic moves toward big-data analytics with smart meter consumption data as well as grid sensor data to help integrate intermittent renewable forms of energy and improve efficiency and conservation outcomes. While in the early stages of learning how to benefit from data-driven strategies, the energy industry is finding that without data analytics to drive both the business and operations to unprecedented levels of efficiency, it simply cannot find a meaningful return on investment from its infrastructure and modernization upgrades. It's a matter of fiduciary responsibility at the very least.

Goldwyn presciently points out the dangers of this essential blindness of handing over public data to private entities and hoping for the best. He says, "[a]s more and more of the transport system falls into private hands and becomes fragmented . . . cities will lose out on valuable data on where people want to go, how they travel, what's slowing them down, and how the network is operating."[6] He could have gone farther. These same private entities are driven by profit, not by the social contract. They want to increase users and usage, and drive up their value as a company by selling advertising, licensing deals, and microtransactions. Uber isn't interested in adding new bus routes or installing bike-sharing docks, and it likely doesn't care about improving route efficiency as long as the drivers of this unregulated car service make money based on the length of the trip.

Silicon Valley—not the public transport agency—now seems to be responsible for accessible and affordable travel. Services such as Uber and Lyft are not likely planning to subsidize access for any citizen who can't afford to pay surge-pricing rates, nor are they required to provide nondiscriminatory service. Further, nonparticipation in the apps business is pushing even licensed taxicab drivers into service through networks like Hailo, which has promised drivers more jobs and passengers by electronically mediating the relationship between the passenger and the cab driver. Like similar services, Hailo demonstrates clearly that people want a quick and interactive response from their driver, even if it requires the cabbie to drive distractedly as they interact with their device as they hunt for their next fare instead of focusing on the road.

It is tempting to view smartphone apps for transportation as playthings for the few who can afford them. But in developing economies, the mobile phone infrastructure has already proved itself to be a key lever for development. For example, the adoption of mobile phones in Africa

---

6 Goldwyn, Eric (2014), "The Most Important Transportation Innovation of the Decade Is the Smartphone," *CityLab*. Retrieved January 31, 2015, from http://www.citylab.com/commute/2014/09/the-most-important-transportation-innovation-of-this-decade-is-the-smartphone/379525.

has been transformative not only for individuals but also for entire countries and regions. With very poor overall infrastructure—from roads to electricity—in Africa, mobile telephony has brought a wide range of new possibilities to the continent. Across urban/rural and rich/poor divides, mobile phones are connecting individuals to other individuals, markets, services, and local and global information. For many people, the mobile phone is raising standards of living that have long been among the lowest in the world. The telecommunications industry is driving economic growth and enabling the development of a burgeoning middle class.

A publicly operated unified mobility app has enormous potential to eliminate barriers between modes, use existing infrastructure more efficiently, and bring the entire transport network to the smartphone in both developed and developing economies. The fact that there has been no serious, major effort in any city to integrate the smartphone with urban mobility is not just a failure to grasp the dramatic impact of the mobile phone on how transportation systems are used; it's also a missed opportunity to integrate all our resources toward benefiting as many people as possible across the city population.

8.4 Transportation Connects

It was argued early on in this chapter that transportation may be one of the most important influences of community well-being by almost any measure. Unfortunately, increased systemic pressure on budgets and resource stress has created a chasm in our view of how instrumentation and improved interconnectedness can be significant contributors to improved health and human welfare outcomes. For many social services organizations, this means introducing efficiency and improved client care by providing access to better information, but also by improving a client's ability to access services. Finding ways to incorporate urban activity from people and the broad activities and events within the city also touch on issues of public safety. Understanding human movement helps manage food-poisoning outbreaks; mass outbreaks of illnesses like measles, pertussis, and Ebola; and create successful strategies for managing police and public safety response.

Even under stress, public health agencies have shown greater propensity to embrace social data and analytics to help improve their operations.

Stephen Goldsmith, director of the Innovations in Government program at the Harvard Kennedy School and author of *The Responsive City*, encourages a form of "listening to the urban airwaves" through social media. Using data analytics to understand salient details from tweets and Facebook posts, agencies can help uncover and correct public health and safety challenges. As a contributor to Data-Smart City Solutions—an initiative by the Ash Center at the Harvard Kennedy School—Goldsmith describes how the New York City Department of Health and Mental Hygiene used local business reviews on Yelp (www.yelp.com) to root out restaurants that weren't up to code. The agency deployed a system of sentiment to find establishments whose reviews included terms such as "sick," vomit," and "food poisoning." After scanning the text of over a quarter million restaurant reviews, the department flagged three restaurants whose reviews contained a high number of references to foodborne illness and discovered rather shocking health-code violations.[7]

In addition to public health problems, data analytics can be used to address complex environmental health interactions and—in more-dramatic instances—school safety. Proactive arrests have been made in jurisdictions for threats made against communities or schools over Facebook and Twitter. It's not just listening, though; public safety can be greatly enhanced by talking. Countless tragedies have been averted by pushing out Amber Alerts (integrated directly in Android and iPhone units) and emergency management systems messages, as well as other information such as police activity updates, traffic alerts, weather notices, and general safety communications.

Goldsmith makes an important point about what happens when cities become aware and learn to productively hear their citizens through social channels. He notes that, "[a] new image of the city emerges from this collection of citizen-generated data and presents an opportunity to better understand urban activity."[8] The most crucial thing about creating a new view of the city through the eyes of the citizens is that it enhances the relationship between public agencies and citizens. This allows city functionaries to become more responsive, especially where city dwellers

---

[7] Goldsmith, Stephen (2014), "How Social Media Listening Can Improve Public Health." Retrieved February 2, 2015, from http://datasmart.ash.harvard.edu/news/article/how-social-media-listening-can-improve-public-health-540.

[8] Goldsmith [7].

frequent social channels to log their life stream and are likely to geo-tag this information. Given the increasing ability to provide analytics on unstructured data sources like Yelp and Twitter, this is data that cannot be ignored.

8.4.1 Getting to Well-Being

Urban food desertification is another unique problem, predominantly in cities with blighted areas. These areas have many fast-food restaurants, liquor stores, and gas stations, but are largely devoid of access to even moderately healthy, whole food. This is a transportation issue. If a mother wants more than beer and junk food for her children, she's going to need to travel out of her neighborhood to get it. That means she must either own a car (the likelihood of which is low, given the demographics of these areas) or be able and willing to navigate a system of buses to get to a store and then transport everything home. Even still, providing access to transportation out may not be the sole solution to food deserts. Local initiatives can help solve these challenges by creating community opportunities to bring healthy food into the environment and by providing opportunities for families to purchase food from mobile vendors and co-ops. Communities can also sponsor initiatives to open up grocery stores and sit-down restaurants in these underserved communities.

Transportation policies have historically had an impact on shaping dietary conditions for inner-city residents, yet little has been done to address the problem. Policymakers can help improve the food desert problem, including making way for mobile food markets and optimizing transportation alternatives to improve food access. Also, social media channels can be leveraged to alert community groups and other agencies to mobilize in real time to accommodate surplus food and supplies that would otherwise go to waste. Food excess can be collected from restaurants and farms and moved directly to those who can benefit. These are all small efforts, but they can provide improved immediate access with an eye toward improving the mass-transport infrastructure through goal setting.

Denver, Colorado, provides an excellent example of how incremental improvement to advanced transportation systems revitalized a distressed downtown area, creating a vibrant city center. The Lower

Downtown (LoDo) area developed a partnership that established many small goals to improve the area, ultimately leading to the redevelopment of Union Station, a public transportation hub with Amtrak service, a bus pavilion, and a light-rail stop that carries passengers regionally. All these services contribute to a vital landscape of mixed uses and mixed incomes. Previously isolated local residents can now use light rail to get to work, school, or shopping destinations, and trendier folk have moved into the neighborhood, creating an economy that supports evening visitors and tourists.[9]

8.5 Where Do We Go Now?

Transportation analytics provide the tools and models that bring nontraditional data sources to our well-known operational systems. These analytics encourage smarter traffic data systems and adaptive technologies, with social media feeds that can tell us where people are going and where they last ate tainted seafood.

The impacts are data driven and holistic. Data allows us to get to our bus on time, but it also enables improved predictions about which roads will be impacted by the construction of a Hyperloop and how to adjust other transit schedules and communicate with the pubic about how they can best cope with the major construction impacts. When unplanned incidents and events occur, such as accidents or strikes, traffic can be rerouted and other utilization decisions can be made in many planning horizons, from budgetary cycles to real time. Data-informed transportation planning is able to account for comprehensive land-use development strategies, such as understanding how to account for the transit requirements that will result if we build a new hockey rink in an outer downtown ring, or look to modify our streets to create public spaces for mobile food trucks in blighted areas.

The design opportunities only become greater as more data is brought under consideration. And designers can become more capable as analytics techniques improve and people understand how to better access data, use

---

[9] Peterson, Eric (2014), "What Smart Cities Can Learn from Denver," Pop City. Retrieved February 2, 2015, from http://www.popcitymedia.com/features/SmartCitiesDenver080714.aspx.

it properly, and improve their interpretation of it. How cities access and activate the data that's available to smarten our cities determines the rate and depth at which favorable change can occur. Advanced transportation systems are a key element of an enriched and vibrant city and an opportunity for high-impact solutions that can reach almost every urban dweller.

Section Two

Key Points

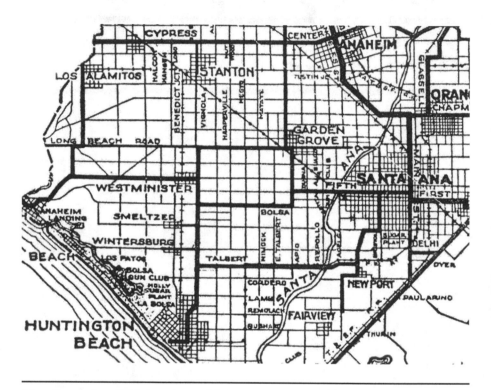

Map from the 1921 brochure "Orange County California, Nature's Prolific Wonderland - Spring Eternal."*

* Image retrieved from the public domain at http://en.wikipedia.org/wiki/ File:Midway_City_CA_map_1921.jpg.

Section Two

Key Points

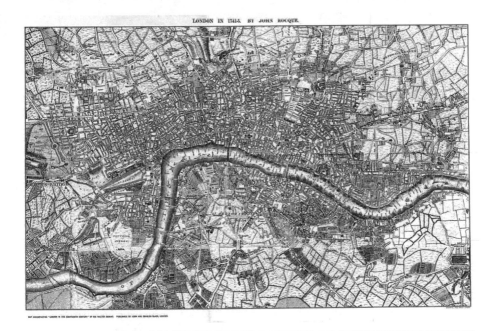

John Rocque's map of 1741–1745 London, found in the British Museum. Rocque only blocks in buildings on his map where they are attached to open ground, gardens, and fields.[1]

---

[1] Image retrieved from the public domain at http://commons.wikimedia.org/ wiki/File:Rocque's_Map_of_London_1741-5.jpg.

Chapter Six

Technology-Centric Planning Is Not a Neutral Exercise

Smart cities are challenged when technology-centric planning is pursued without regard for broader implications in the safety, regulatory, and social spheres. By nature, technology choices may be pragmatic, but they should be considered as part of an overall solution that includes human attributes.

- Design thinking encourages city planners to shift their thinking from outcomes to process by framing smart city issues in the context of goals rather than discrete problems.
- It is a common approach to try to solve human problems by instituting change through policy. Whether the adoption of certain technologies violates fundamental values of civic culture and society is a legitimate concern to city planners.
- By definition, smart cities aim to improve the functioning infrastructure, access to resources, and safety and security for the population. To succeed in creating a sound and vibrant civil society, urban planning for technology application must account equally for the goals of all citizens and their disparate needs.

Thinking Glocal Increases Our Sense of Responsibility

Glocalization describes the adaptation of broad solutions to local needs and desires. With advanced technologies and especially social media, what is local is quickly shifting as we learn about the lives and struggles of others across the world and move to influence them.

- Glocalization, similar to internationalization, describes several economic theories related to adapting a product or service to meet the needs and desires of people in their particular cultural context.
- With the Internet and social media, we are connected to people on a daily basis across the world. This connectivity is broadening our sense of what is local as people become more interested in the lives and conditions of populations in far-flung places.

- As a result of this new level of global consistency, cities across the world are starting to adopt a federated structure. Local citizens are behaving quite collegially and collectively, comparing and sharing techniques, research, and workshops. Which technologies are adopted where and for what use will be profoundly influenced by this growing urban internetwork.

Safety, Social Factors, and Regulation All Influence Technology Planning

Safety, social factors, and policy considerations are all key in technology planning. Although today's technology is highly specialized, fragmented uses will diminish as our cities grow evermore connected and new uses for data emerge.

- The benefits of information and communications technology (ICT) in the smart city are both short term and long term. While certain city functions benefit from instantaneous information, others use ICT to influence the next-best high-value plans for the city.
- The shift in demand for data and the corresponding ability to analyze and serve data to both cities and citizens means that every sensor may contribute to meeting unanticipated goals. These sensors will also be expected to perform to unconsidered levels.
- Fundamental infrastructure operations like energy, water, transportation, and public safety are becoming integrated into consumer-focused services that will improve lives, not just provide a commodity. City plans must reflect this important shift.

Chapter Seven

Resource Issues Can Best Be Treated with Integrated Solutions

Designs for smart cities must include treatment for energy efficiency, energy intensity, and energy emissions intensity. Resource issues must be well defined and understood if they are to be optimally managed.

- Energy is changing in every way, from how it is generated and distributed, to how it's consumed in the context of converging digital capabilities. This is especially true in the urban environment as renewable generation is deployed—especially small solar—and energy-efficiency and conservation opportunities in buildings expand with ICT.
- Energy consumers show little interest in hands-on management of their resources, but they have shown a greater propensity toward orchestration technologies, which are more reliable in producing meaningful energy savings.
- Smart devices for the home will continue to become more interesting to consumers, but other sectors—especially commercial buildings with networked sensors, centralized monitoring, and unified control—will find significant savings of both cost and resources, primarily energy.

Increased Energy Efficiency and Decreased Intensity Are Both Key Levers

Solutions providers and utilities talk about energy efficiency rather than energy intensity, but a sole focus on efficiency will not always help us reach our goals. Structural and behavioral factors related to intensity will also help.

- Energy intensity measures the quantity of energy we need for every unit of activity, while energy efficiency measures the amount of energy required to deliver a particular service. It's a subtle difference, but it's important in resource-sensitive design.

- Understanding energy intensity helps us compare the performance of a sector without the underlying detail because it is an expression of energy divided by gross domestic product (GDP). As such, intensity metrics help designers understand the high-level impacts of efficiency improvements that are not measurable by microlevel metrics.
- Although energy intensity is a useful measurement, it should only be considered with a deep sense of context and in concert with other metrics, including emissions intensity and other values that help understand progress to goals.

The Building Sector Provides Significant Opportunity

The buildings sector accounts for nearly half of the consumption across the world. Building management technology can provide meaningful gains, but it requires a strong understanding of behavior.

- Heating, cooling, and lighting comprise a significant opportunity to automate office spaces, retail operations, and educational institutions, but solely relying on automation for positive change may not work well if the behavior of the occupants is not understood.
- Building management systems can put the Internet of Things (IoT) to good use to mitigate poor configurations, and help account for behavior issues that can trouble even well-engineered buildings.
- Design thinking can be very useful in addressing building management challenges by accounting for human habits, behaviors, schedules, and preferences. Human-centric design helps anticipate these activities, and may even help build trust and confidence among occupants to positively influence their behaviors within the building.

Chapter Eight

Smart Transportation Solves High-Impact Human Problems

Urban transportation is about more than efficient fuels, telematics, and toll collection. It's about helping urban citizens get to work and gain access to social services and more-healthful food. It's about improving public safety outcomes and general well-being.

- Transportation and human services are usually not considered holistically, but it is transportation that impacts our urban quality of life as measured by the health of our society, economy, and relationship to the environment.
- The urban transportations system affects how a city develops and becomes sustainable over time, from land-use policies to the long-term health of our natural and built environments.
- Poorly conceived transportation systems can segregate disadvantaged neighborhoods and limit access to hospitals, community clinics, public parks, and even nutritious food.

ICT Brings Transportation Technologies to the Masses

Traditionally, transportation-related technologies focus on problems such as traffic mitigation, and the gathering of road intelligence. However, they can also be used as a source of information to improve real-time operations and planning.

- Emerging transportation technologies embody intelligence that is goal driven to provide innovative services across the spectrum of urban movement issues, from transportation mode to transportation management.
- Transportation innovation includes designs to create healthier, more-walkable cities that reduce congestion and enhance public safety.
- Transportation planning with ICT even treats questions of social policy by reducing urban food deserts and improving access to social services.

Transportation Analytics Can Benefit from Wide Sources of Data

The transportation industry has long been a generator of big data, but from a planning perspective, the influx of new forms of human-centric data and powerful analytic capabilities are helping urban transportation planners respond even better to human needs.

- Access to urban transportation data has brought new forms of data to the mix, including geolocation data from social media sources like Twitter.
- Such agglomerations and analytics allow planners and designers to spot emerging trends, draw novel conclusions, and cross-reference data for new insights and integrated city solutions.
- Cell phones are important new sources of information for transportation planners because they're ubiquitous and reliable broadcasters of personal location data. Additionally, we can now integrate relationships, preferences, likes, and conversations directly into serious city infrastructure planning, especially transportation.

Section Three

Data Analytics and the Smart Urban Dweller

A city planning map for Hamar, Norway, first drafted by planning engineer Røyen in 1848.[*]

---

[*] Image retrieved from the public domain at http://en.wikipedia.org/wiki/File:Original_city_map_for_Hamar_Norway_1848.png.

Chapter Nine

Smart City Analytics

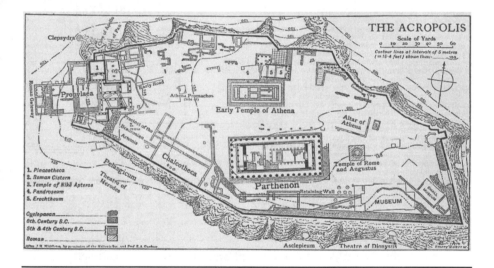

The Acropolis in Athens. Built on a hill with precipitous sides, an acropolis is a settlement that can be easily defended.[1]

---

[1] Image retrieved from the public domain at http://commons.wikimedia.org/wiki/File:1911_Britannica_-_Athens_-_The_Acropolis.png.

9.1 Chapter Goal

This chapter discusses the common analytical approaches used in large enterprises, including utilities, governments, and smart cities. Typically, advanced analytics is used for major events, such as storm recovery, riots, and major threats to public safety. These same principles can be used to establish a baseline and operate the smart city on a daily basis, and can be implemented cost-effectively and securely using a platform approach to access disparate data and delivery analytical value through a framework of services.

9.2 The Vocabulary of Analytics[2]

Uncertainties complicate our lives. As much as we might prefer a deterministic view of the world, we rarely have complete command of the consequences of everyday life. It's no different with analytic models, which must be flexible enough to provide strategic value under varying conditions. To make things simpler, we organize analytic approaches into categories. For the purposes of smart city data analytics, we maintain four model categories: descriptive, diagnostic, predictive, and prescriptive. We define a model as a symbolic representation of the relationships, systems, and structures that we find in the urban environment. These models help us simplify the real world so that we may better explain what is happening and more accurately predict what might happen in the future to better inform our decisions.

There are two important things about categorization: First, analytic systems rarely use only one category of analytics to produce useful results in a specific problem domain. Second, there is no real progression in terms of value from one category to the next. That means that despite the fact that predictive and prescriptive analytics may be more complex in design, they fill specific needs related to solving particular problems. Descriptive and diagnostic analytics may be better understood as a discipline, but they are not less valuable. Table 9.1 describes the analytic systems we

---

[2] Modified from *Big Data Analytics Strategies for the Smart Grid* by Carol L. Stimmel, with permission. ISBN: ISBN 9781482218282. © 2014 Taylor & Francis.

Table 9.1 Basic Analytical Approaches

Analytic Approach	Function
Descriptive	What happened or what is happening now?
Diagnostic	Why did it happen or why is it happening now?
Predictive	What will happen next? What will happen under various conditions?
Prescriptive	What are the options to create the most optimal or high-value outcome?

will discuss in this chapter and how they function to help solve problems found in urban environments.

There are many examples of how these models can fit together to solve a business problem. Consider a problem that might be found in a city's office of energy and sustainable development. To help offset the need to build fossil fuel–based generation, the city is requiring that new and renovated property be equipped with smart thermostats that enable participation in demand-side management programs. The local utility has agreed to subsidize the rollout with the ultimate goal of using automation to create a reliable source of demand-side relief for days of high stress and high consumption. This is an expensive endeavor for the utility, which knows that just because some customers have thermostats installed that can respond to the utility's signals, there's still a low likelihood that customers will actually enroll in a program. The utility wants to determine which consumers will be interested in the program and which are likely to participate. Also, what are the best messages and incentives to encourage customers who may show a propensity for implementing conservation and efficiency measures in their homes?

Using analytic models, here are some steps that a utility analyst could take to answer these questions:

1. *Descriptive modeling.* Of the customers who have previously participated in demand-response programs (such as a one-way pager switch installed on an air-conditioning unit), what happened? Did they answer surveys, cooperate with the setup of the equipment and its signals? Did they override the response? How often did they override it? Tracking this information provides a basic understanding of customers who participate in demand-response programs.

2. *Diagnostic modeling.* Prudently, the analyst would then want to determine why certain customers behave in certain ways. Are they hardly ever home? What's the impact of the incentive on their overall bill? Did they sign up for the incentive but then resist providing the utility access to their equipment? Are they sensitive to temperature fluctuations? What was the weather like during the opt-out behavior? Did they express dislike for utility control mechanisms? At this point, the utility knows some characteristics about the customers who participate in the program, but they also have a sense of why they make some of the decisions they make in terms of their participation.

3. *Predictive modeling.* Having a sense of the what and why of consumer behavior, the analyst now has the appropriate inputs to devise a model that will attempt to predict how consumers will behave under certain conditions with smart thermostats placed in their homes. Specifically, under similar conditions, how can we expect consumers to respond to smart thermostats? Manipulating the variables in the model allows the analyst to create a precise segmentation of customers who are likely to embrace the utility's control of their home's smart thermostat. In fact, a comprehensive model can help identify segments of consumers that the analyst might never have considered before.

4. *Prescriptive modeling.* Finally, the analyst endeavors to understand what the next best steps are to take to drive program success. Based on what is now a deep understanding of customers who are likely to want to participate, a prescriptive model can provide insight into the best marketing or engagement strategies and their relative trade-offs for reaching the appropriate people.

Figure 9.1 describes how an analytics program can be structured to drive fully optimized business insights and outcomes. As insights are turned into action, these actions will change how the business operates (sometimes unexpectedly), and filter back through the analytical process in a cycle of continuous change and improvement. This is called generativity. The feedback loop of generativity may be one of the most important motivations for developing a comprehensive analytics program in the utility: As new structures and behaviors emerge under the forces of a shifting operations and forecasting, new problems and states emerge,

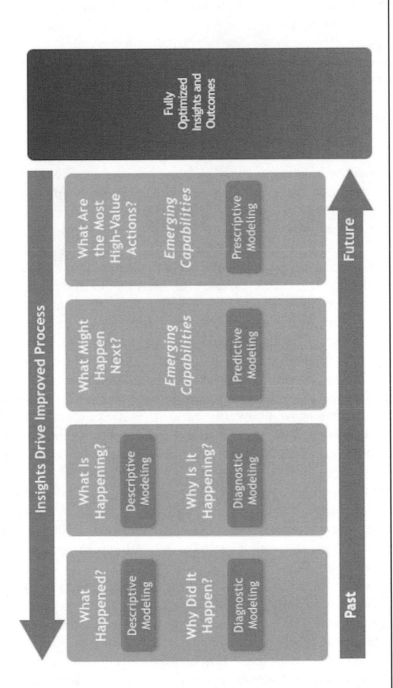

Figure 9.1 Analytic models use the past to prescribe the best business actions.

driving the city to new insights into ways to improve the value and operation of the urban network.

9.3 Analytical Models

Models are the heart and lungs of advanced analytics. They use various algorithms and statistics to uncover the patterns and relationships we hope will bring increased value. But the best models aren't just the application of pure math. Yes, modeling is science, but it's an art, too. Like the master craftsman, the data scientist must have the ability to envision how the data pieces fit together; she must measure and construct a vision, and then produce something of long-lasting value that will be functional for the user.

To build a worthy model, the data scientist must be able to select the right data sources, algorithms, variables, and techniques that fit the business problem in question. These are the mechanical components, but they still require that the scientist have well-developed domain knowledge of the utility enterprise. Both the development of the model and the communication of the model's results tell a story. The storyline is constructed by pulling through the right data to estimate and classify values.

Trust of the output that a model produces is perhaps the most difficult part of any analytics modeling process. For maximum perceived reliability, the model must reflect business realities—for example, showing how an asset maintenance model can drive down operating costs and demonstrating the value of the model's output. It is, in fact, a lack of business connection that can explain much of the fear and distrust of analytics. Sometimes this "value" is not always expected. A very good asset maintenance model may expose issues that the utility has not anticipated and has not grappled with, causing unforeseen workflow disruptions and expenditures.

It's worth pointing out that even a very good model is not some sort of mythical panacea; breakthrough discoveries are simply not a day-to-day expectation. Such expectations clearly defy the very definition of breakthrough. Models can be valuable for the organization even if they serve to reinforce and concretize implicit knowledge within the company. As discussed previously, this contributes greatly to improving and generating new insights for the system that makes up the utility business. To achieve this, the utility must hire or partner with data scientists who understand utility problems, data, and—perhaps even more importantly—utility processes and workflows that help them map analytical models to useful and trustworthy tools to improve the business.

9.3.1 When Cancer Causes Smoking

Part of the communication challenge for data modelers is helping analytic consumers understand the distinction between causation and correlation. These two terms are so often conflated that it can cause seemingly hopeless confusion. Causality and correlation confusion can disrupt the very goal of analytics, which is to transform correlation into causality. But sometimes there is a rush to provide an explanation for an observation. Usually, that's achieved by claiming false causality.

By way of definition, correlation simply describes how two sets of data are related. Causation, on the other hand, defines a relationship between two sets of data wherein one creates the conditions for the other to occur. Consider the following simple example: A study shows that as ice cream sales increase, so does the rate of drowning, indicating that the consumption of ice cream causes drowning. We understand intuitively that this is foolish. However, this sort of leap happens frequently with less understood data. In our example, we have not taken into account two important data points: time and temperature. Consider, then: Ice cream is sold at a higher rate during the warm months of summer than during the colder months. During these warmer months, more people engage in water-related activities, such as swimming and boating. The increased drowning rates are caused by an increase in human exposure to water during the same period of time that more ice cream is sold. This is the structure for a very common kind of causality fallacy called the "lurking variable"—a variable that, once known, disentangles the issue.

In fact, no matter how excellent a correlation may seem, there may be one of several logical fallacies that create false interpretations of data. When considering causation, it's helpful to think of the construct of cause and effect. Such as, when I throw a ball, it moves. Cause-and-effect relationships are rarely equally valid when inverted. Just because the ball moves doesn't mean it was thrown. Think about it: There's a well-established causal relationship between obesity and an increased risk of gallstones. However, I may have gallstones and not be in the slightest bit overweight. The causative relationship is not true in either case.

No matter how profound the conclusion, it is obviously important to be wary of the logical pitfalls in rendering a series of correlations as causation. So the real question, it seems, is how do we safely conclude a causal relationship? It's difficult, but there are reliable methods we can use to prove that a correlation is causation, including randomized controlled experiments or the application of causal models. Put simply, the more powerful and robust we make the correlations, the easier it is to confidently draw a causative conclusion. Serious mistakes have happened, especially in medical science, where epidemiological studies have attempted to draw conclusions from data without fully understanding other factors that were responsible for the issue at hand. Remember, if smoking is the cause of cancer, it is quite unlikely that cancer causes smoking.

9.4 The Analytics of Things

It is becoming increasingly important to understand that without analytics as the motivating force behind widespread data collection initiatives, very little stands to be achieved from Internet-of-Things (IoT) deployments. But, it's not always glamorous. In the context of the smart city, most people imagine operations rooms with huge video screens, alerts, and control modules—lots of maps and video footage showing criminals being caught in real time. But, not all of the smart city's apps and widgets need to run complex algorithms to be helpful; an app that allows city dwellers to report potholes or one that collects detailed location information for emergency services is a straightforward tool. But how can we best learn from the data collected so that we can predict and prescribe future actions—such as forecasting crime outbreaks, planning better transportation solutions, or using facial recognition software to help police find a face in a wave of people?

Some experts refer to the activity of deriving insights from the high volume of information that is increasingly collected in cities as "pulling signal from the noise." But more importantly, perhaps, is establishing a baseline for improvement. While many might be looking for breakthrough value, such as managing riots, storms, and terrorism, the real value in combining many datasets is to create a picture of our cities that can improve our everyday lives, as well as manage the edge cases that may occur in our urban environments.

9.4.1 It's Not Just Your Things

Many of the discussions so far logically lead us to the equation of "the most compelling sensor is a person and his smartphone." Consider the following description of federal activities after the Boston Marathon bombing in April 2013, and this may become clearer. According to an *FCW* article, the Department of Homeland Security (DHS) deployed tools through its on-the-ground teams to act as field sensors that could interact in real time with a centralized operations hub. The article says, "Through a smart phone, a user's position can be triangulated by the central network, and the user can push alerts to the network via text, image or video, for instance, or view where other mobile device users with the application are located via mapping technology."[3] Using the field investigators as smart sensors, the department generated a virtual map of all the "sensor" activity and the investigators' observations on the map.

A full-scale indexer of Twitter data from Topsy Labs was used during the investigation to sort through the related tweets. If we believe Topsy— that the organization has saved every tweet since July 2006—it stands to reason that every reference to the word "bomb" could be tagged, retweets could be tracked, and, most importantly, tweeters who were engaging with the suspects could be readily identified. Reportedly, Topsy even deployed a geo-inferencing analytics engine that produced accurate tweet maps even when Twitter users did not geotag their tweets. All sorts of terms were monitored, according to *FCW*, including words like "explosion" and "shelter in place," as shown in Figure 9.2. Corroborating the many, many hours of data-driven analytics, an injured citizen provided the fundamental lead for the case. Then, a coincidental investigation at a convenience store showed the suspects on closed-circuit TV (CCTV), and later, a man reported the cover on his boat flapping in the breeze, revealing the secreted last suspect.

[3] Konkel, Frank (2013), "Boston Marathon Probe's Big Data Use Hints at the Future." Retrieved February 8, 2015, from http://fcw.com/articles/2013/04/26/big-data-boston-bomb-probe.aspx.

Carol Alfonso @caa1000 · 18 Apr 2013
RT @cnnbrk: FBI: Call 1-800-CALL-FBI if you have infomation about the 2 suspects. on.cnn.com/175CKDq **#BostonMarathon #Explosion**

Lolly Daskal and 1 other follow
Kim Fox @kimfox · 18 Apr 2013
I'm fascinated by how the @imgur community are coming together to try & analyze photos of **#bostonmarathon #explosion** imgur.com/QvTOzKo

Islam Delenda Est @velvethammer · 18 Apr 2013
FBI To Release Video Images Of 2 **#BostonMarathon** Bombing Suspects ironicsurrealism.com/2013/04/18/fbi... #crowdsourcing #bostonsuspect #tcot **#explosion**

Figure 9.2 Twitter stream and hashtags from the Boston Marathon bombing in 2013.

The Boston Marathon bombing case demonstrates how data can be fused from many unstructured sources, such as CCTV footage, Twitter streams, smartphone triangulation, and digital images. Not only does this example underscore the value of humans as sensors, it also shows how descriptive and diagnostic analytics can be used to improve the urban environment. This example alone demonstrates how quickly the infrastructure for data analytics can scale up for predictive value. Clearly, the DHS agrees. In its Privacy Impact Assessment in 2013, the department revealed that the National Operations Center (NOC) Media Monitoring Capability (MMC) monitors social media platforms in a variety of ways, including "publicly available online forums, blogs, public websites, and message boards. Through the use of publicly available search engines and content aggregators, the [DHS] monitors activities on the social media sites for information that can be used to provide situational awareness and establish a common operating picture."[4]

[4] Triner, Donald (2013). "Privacy Impact Assessment for the Office of Operations Coordination and Planning: Publicly Available Social Media Monitoring and Situational Awareness Initiative Update." Retrieved February 8, 2015, from http://www.dhs.gov/sites/default/files/publications/privacy/PIAs/privacy_pia_ops_NOC MMC Update_April2013.pdf.

9.5 The Analytical Intersection of Human and Machine

We have discussed both the current and emerging role of the human sensor in the networked system of the smart city. Almost every idea for applying technology in the smart city must find its way into the nexus of IoT and analytics where human behavior is of immediate interest. But even though technology is designed to help humans, technology development is not always designed to maximize societal goals. Usually, this is due to a market failure where it is too expensive to build an application for its perceived benefit. However, this is changing quickly. Not only are the barriers to technology diminishing, the plethora of smart devices intended to be attached somehow to a human or a home (some will not surprisingly call this the Internet of People) is growing. These devices—although they're not purchased, owned, or maintained as city assets—spill their data freely into public forums, rendering the information easily available for investigation by anyone with access to computing power and an Internet connection, including our city government. What's more, the initial cost of these devices is the only deep financial cut, as the applications are exceedingly cheap to purchase—the real currency is data.

Clearly, analytics can be integrated deep into the hardware layer of the network, such as in the routers or the devices themselves. They can also be integrated closer to the outer edge of the network devices that are generating data, such as within a command and control center that manages a fleet of buildings or multiple units in a high-rise condominium. There is a broad array of practical and powerful uses for this form of end-to-end connectivity, but from the perspective of smart city design, these sensors become multipurpose data feeders to sectors across the city, including transportation, energy, water, public spaces, healthcare, controlled environment agriculture, and retail.

But, so often, our greatest technology minds seem to lead us away from simplicity by driving us toward data specialization and silos. This is not surprising, but still troubling, because if we really wish to design our cities from the perspective of goals, specialization lends itself more to confusion and missed opportunities as we lose awareness of what data, information, techniques, and solutions may help us move forward. Data may be organized by sector, source, user, or owner, but rarely by solution or benefit; thus, it's difficult for design-thinking principles. Unfortunately, right now, data is not well integrated and our systems are not adaptable enough to easily acquire information from physical, machine, or social data without a decent understanding of the nuances of the data sources themselves.

9.5.1 Organizing by Scale

Even when we try to expand our perspective and use metadata systems to organize by market (economic characteristics), hazard (such as traffic, crime, or poverty), or even technology ("What can we do with a CCTV camera?"), we don't always get the answers we need. What if instead we view our data through a lens of issues and goals? From there, we can begin to define and build our analytical models, which represent the scope of urban problems by characteristics such as impact, consequence, and benefit. An example of this is proposed in Table 9.2, where, by using this approach, we rise far above the constantly confounding issues and limitations of data silos and technology descriptors and focus on where our most pressing problems are, what their impact is, and how we can prioritize and plan to solve them.

When contemplating design within these levels of scale, it's more useful to think about how our data is relevant to a type of user or users operating in that scope who want to achieve a benefit. Once that is understood, we can more easily define a pathway to get there based on our data and analysis.

Table 9.2 Example of a Goal-Driven Approach to Urbanization Issues at the Level of Issues and Goals

Scale	Issue	Goal
Home	Energy efficiency	Reduce heating bills in cold winter months
Neighborhood	Food deserts	Provide development support for new grocery stores
Workplace	Biological pathogens	Improve ventilation to reduce viral transmission
City	Chemical pollutants	Identify and mitigate pathogens in open water bodies
Regional area	Waste management	Reduce pollution from dumping household wastes
Global issues	Fossil fuel use	Reduce carbon-emitting and stratospheric ozone depletion

Each one of these examples could be sorted and parsed to meet any number of needs, especially when it comes to harvesting new ideas for exploration. The advantage to the perspective of scale is that it reduces the distractions that occur when people view problems through the lens of technology ("What data can we collect with this gadget?") or economics ("Will it make money?"), essentially reducing the presupposition of a solution. Take the first example of scale: the home. In this case, we raise the issue of energy efficiency and state that the goal is to reduce heating bills in cold winter months. If I were a thermostat dealer, I might have restated that solution to focus on my smart thermostat product. If I'm an insulation provider, I might say that the goal is to use hot water heater wraps to reduce heating bills. If I'm a utility subsidizing solutions, I'm likely going to look at economic impact as measured against my cost to buy, deliver, install, and maintain my energy-efficiency program or solution.

By focusing on goals, we leave the door open to the power of the design-thinking process. As discussed earlier in the chapter, in the context of analytical models, we strive to know what is happening, why it happened, what might happen next, and what we might do about it. It's a seemingly straightforward practice where empathy and creativity can play an important role because as every model is being developed, it's informed by the compelling needs of the domain and question. Simply put, every model has a point of view. A good model is one that exceeds mechanics and represents the data scientist's knowledge of the specific users and systems in question and provides a much more meaningful construct of the person or thing being represented.

9.6 Analytics as a Service

While it is out of scope for this book to travel into the far regions of data collection, storage, and transformation processes, the value of information and communications technology (ICT) data for smart city will come from analytics and the delivery of analytical conclusions through services. This value will be delivered through a platform mechanism that comprises a foundational base upon which other applications and process are developed and provisioned. The platform approach is already a blossomed reality in the private sector—consider Facebook, Uber, and Netflix. All of these platforms strive to enable value for both developers and users by making it easier to create applications and tools that benefit from a network effect. For example, the more applications that interface with Facebook, the easier it is for me to post and read my friends' posts or find their locations, thereby increasing the depth at which Facebook is an indispensable application for me. Other users benefit similarly, driving up the interest in and viability for more applications. This effect keeps Facebook relevant and provides the kind of investment needed to make sure that the platform drives solid standards, security is enhanced, and user needs and interests are known and fulfilled.

There are many, many other similar examples that go far beyond social networking, including business-to-business platform services and consumers and data information exchanges. There is plenty of solid evidence by now that a platform approach—using a robust application programming interface (API)—is a flexible and secure approach that can accommodate the fluid requirements of data analytics applications. And it is also the ideal foundation for analytics: flexible for the data consumer, easily secured, and able to accommodate both custom and packaged application projects.

9.6.1 Platforms Are Cost-Effective

Today, it is not at all atypical for large, expensive projects to be very custom in nature. It is also often true that these projects include nonstandard implementations, are expensive, and cause lock-in to a particular hardware solution and development team. This approach is usually called bespoke software (in reference to tailor-made clothing constructed to a user's specifications), and until the past decade, it was not a bad strategy, as it allowed applications to be developed quickly, cheaply, and even more securely than commercial off-the-shelf (COTS) software or canned platform applications. COTS usually fell short of providing a full solution for most enterprises. Bespoke software provided flexibility, but it also was often risky, expensive, and took a long time to develop. Platforms are the antidote to COTS shortcomings.

Platforms allow the sharing of components across many different business lines and across functional silos; as mentioned earlier, they have both technical and business benefits. Preconceived analytical applications will always require customization to meet utility needs, and it is an absolute that customization will be expensive, resource intensive, and likely to create unintended security loopholes. Figure 9.3 describes in general how sharing components changes the focus from the heavy lifting and security concerns of monolithic application development toward flexible services that address the needs of uses across the spectrum, from city operators such as asset managers, to city service providers such as child protective services, to the citizens themselves, who must desire to avail themselves of these services.

For the reasons discussed above, cities have long used integrators for custom projects, and this often results in high initial costs for system design, coding, and deployment, as well as steep maintenance costs over the lifetime of the software. This is work that usually stays with the integrator because no one else really understands it. The expense and locked-in nature of custom development are at the root of the raging argument that has gone on for decades in business computing: build versus buy. Cities certainly can't afford this level of custom development and maintenance, and COTS is inflexible, expensive to customize, and hard to upgrade once customized. Neither choice provides the kind of rapid return on investment (ROI) required in today's financial ecosystem and crimps strategic innovation.

The demands of enterprise-class data management have the potential to lock out financially constrained cities from benefiting from an effective analytics strategy. This inability to make the required expenditures can also slow the pace of innovation in the sector. Early big-data players are

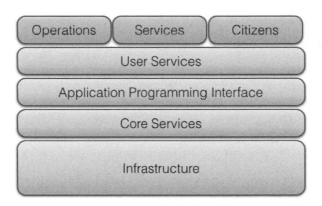

Figure 9.3 Example of sharing components through a service layer.

orienting their offerings toward more immediately lucrative opportunities such as the financial services industry, healthcare, government, and retail. The reason is obvious: most cities are slow moving and can be perceived as draconian. Furthermore, the diverse economic constructs and regulatory forces within the industry are difficult to cope with; application providers and integrators have a hard time identifying the key industry requirements that allow them to build cost-effective solutions.

Given boundless financial, IT, and infrastructure resources, utilities would likely always select the bespoke way. But, a more reasonable solution from ROI, speed-to-integration, and long-term viability perspectives is packaged software that can be quickly customized to meet unique requirements (including financial constraints) without impacting a forward migration path. This is possible with the use of reusable application services that can be adapted and extended to create many distinctive applications.

Traditional bespoke projects require cadres of programmers who understand the underlying data structures, relationships, and workflows, but an application platform automatically handles arcane issues, including data quality, data consistency, and security. And it is by far more quality-assured, consistent, and secure to solve these challenging issues in one place rather than within many applications. Programmers instead focus their skills on responding to business demands and building useful applications, including applications that can readily link to service layers from a variety of sources, converging and mashing data from disparate systems to create a richer, more valuable result.

9.6.2 Services Require a Platform

A platform provides more than just packaged applications. A platform can be thought of as the foundation upon which to build applications complete with the required computing operations. This amounts to an analytics engine combined with a services layer, as well as a toolkit to integrate the custom applications built on those services. While a hosted infrastructure that provides facilities, power, and bandwidth is one way to achieve this, because of cultural and governance challenges, cities are also experimenting with other methods to incorporate a platform approach, including licensing schemes and preloaded appliances that are managed for the utility but that physically reside within the enterprise.

No matter where it lives, this service approach is beginning to make a lot of sense. Some of the large solution providers and integrators are even offering analytical packages that can be easily customized to help utilities get started with their smart city efforts, especially for high-value problems like traffic management and electricity demand analytics.

9.6.3 The Foundations for Scale

Building the foundation for an enduring data analytics program within a smart city is not trivial, and it's one of the reasons why many have looked for investments in less complex places, such as Masdar City and Songdo, where there is no traffic, no crime, and no people. Some might think that the entire scope of the company must be considered, including operations, service functions, and tools for urban dwellers. This is true when wanting to avoid expensive missteps and provide as much future-proofing as possible. Indeed, these considerations and the decisions that city stakeholders make about how to design an enduring analytics architecture will undoubtedly affect the future ability of the city to make the best use of its ICT as it comes online in a cost-effective and efficient manner.

Cities now find themselves at the center of a complicated and critical network of smartphones, traffic lights, and every single operation in the urban environment from managing crime, to feeding the disenfranchised, to moving the school buses. Smart grid data analytics are changing the nature of how the city will ultimately make every decision. If analytics are done poorly, the city's agility will be inhibited and the realization of the smart city will stall.

Chapter Ten

Technology, Social Inclusion, and the Wisdom of the Urban Community

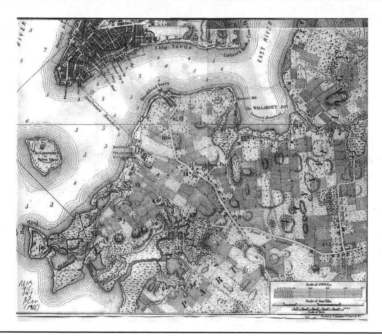

Map of Brooklyn, New York, created in 1766.[1]

[1] Image retrieved from the public domain at http://commons.wikimedia.org/wiki/File:BrooklynMap1766.jpg.

10.1 Chapter Goal

This chapter focuses on the role of technology in the urban community and how it impacts city dwellers' day-to-day lives. Technology—smartphones especially—provide the unprecedented opportunity to include people in defining and helping to solve urban issues. As mobile connectedness climbs to higher and higher rates, in both the developed and developing world, the ability to assess individual behaviors in a positive way also increases. We discuss the levels of community coordination and the new models for leveraging technology for community-driven planning, design, and change.

10.2 Technology in Social Inclusion

One of the most important concerns regarding social inclusion since the widespread rollout of the Internet and other technologies is the digital divide. This term describes the gap between those who have access to information and communications technology (ICT) in a particular community and the skill to use it versus those who do not have either the access or the skills to use technology if it's made available to them. The divide has demonstrably created both economic and social inequality. However, technology-enabled inclusion is more complex, especially for older age groups or those who may have a disability that makes access to technology difficult or impossible. Yet in many ways, the digital divide is quickly being bridged and a different dynamic is emerging.

A lack of access to computers to the poor and the less educated in cities has resulted in the so-called digital divide that is responsible for major negative shifts in social engagement and opportunity among these groups. Policymakers, nonprofits, and communities have focused on filling this divide, and according to the US Office of Science and Technology Policy and the National Economic Council, major government and private investment has enabled broadband networks to now reach 94 percent of US homes.[2] Similarly, in most Organisation for Economic Co-operation

---

[2] Sterling, Gene (2013), "Four Years of Broadband Growth," Office of Science and Technology Policy & The National Economic Council. Retrieved February 14, 2015, from https://www.whitehouse.gov/blog/2013/06/14/four-years-broadband-growth.

and Development (OECD) countries, broadband penetration is up significantly. This uptick is due in large part to the rapid growth of wireless broadband penetration, which is now over 72 percent in OECD countries. In Finland, Australia, Japan, Sweden, Denmark, Korea, and the United States, multiple smartphones and tablets per person have pushed penetration rates to over 100 percent.[3] This is remarkable growth, but not surprisingly, those lagging behind include people with lower education completion levels, low incomes, and a sense of disenfranchisement. It seems, then, that the digital divide is no longer about differential access to the Internet; it is instead about differential allocations and patterns of use.

In many ways, this mirrors our core premise that in designing the smart city, it is not the preponderance of sensors, their type, or even the massive volumes of data they collect. Instead, it's how we use the information we collect to provide opportunities for engagement. Without careful attention to how we engage various populations of people, the digital divide may become a fissure that cuts along race, class, and ethnic lines. For example, many train services offer discounts only to those who purchase their train tickets online, and many museums allow visitors to reserve their spot for an exhibit, get discounts on ticket prices, or gain access to fast-track lines if they buys tickets online. Further, many job applications must be either printed online or submitted via a website or e-mail address, underscoring the impact on those whose only Internet connection is via their smartphone.

Further, as many cities look to technology to help deliver better services to their citizens, they're looking at the transactional capability to provide an improved user experience. Even local libraries are beginning to serve up their books and other materials directly to tablet devices. Education is also moving online, where certificates, college classes, and even home-schooling courses are available, taking advantage of bandwidth-intensive videoconferencing.

Cheap tickets may be the least of our concern, as cities work to bring smart technology approaches to healthcare by providing sensors that track their patients, and even diagnose illnesses and medical conditions based on puffs of breath and webcam consultations. And, of course, it cannot be overlooked that while information platforms may be expensive, the

[3] Organisation for Economic Co-operation and Development (2014), "OECD Broadband Portal." Retrieved February 14, 2015, from http://www.oecd.org/sti/broadband/oecdbroadbandportal.htm.

savings from reduced staff time—such as lower wages and the absence of benefits, human resource issues, and pensions—can considerably cut costs. It seems, then, that high efficiency is always deemed to be better, even at the cost of human interaction.

Consider the statement from a city leader interviewed for his role in an emerging smart city: "Technology can be massively useful, but what is more interesting is thinking about how people use services or use the city—that's what will bring the answers. . . . We have to remember: thinking about how humans act is where we are going to find the real solutions."[4] This is a common perspective. But really, if the provision and application of technology to our problems were just about how we use the city and then looking for better ways to use it, we're missing the most exciting opportunities—such as making things simpler and more efficient—but also correcting for failings we might never have noticed and fundamentally changing the way we produce, consume, interact, and build communities.

In fact, sometimes designing for problems that people don't know they have can bring profound changes and improvements; this doesn't necessarily require a revolution in design when an evolution might bring high rewards. Recall that "market surveys famously said the ultimate demand for computers was five units. That people didn't need Xeroxes because they would never need more than three copies of anything and carbon paper could handle it. That cellular phone demand was limited. That the Sony Walkman would be a flop."[5] Hardly anyone could say that they wanted these products, but there was obviously a latent need. And once adopted, they opened up their own flow of new ideas.

Arguably, we haven't gotten much better at zeroing in on "inside-the-box" thinking, and we may have become much worse. This is not surprising. Access to capital for new software ventures no longer requires a business plan, just a video on a crowdfunding website like Kickstarter or

---

[4] Cooper, Glenda (2010), "Using Technology to Improve Society," *The Guardian*. Retrieved February 14, 2015, from http://www.theguardian.com/smarter-cities/smarter-cities-new-technology-social-improvements.

[5] Coyne, Kevin; Gorman Clifford, Patrician; Dye, Renée (2007), "Breakthrough Thinking from Inside the Box," *Harvard Business Review*. Retrieved February 15, 2015, from https://hbr.org/2007/12/breakthrough-thinking-from-inside-the-box.

GoFundMe. Virtual work communities and the low barrier to entry into digital technology and distribution allow us to try things to see if they go viral and experience significant uptake among some cohort. This can result in marvelous services for people, but those services are going to be geared one way or another toward those who can pay for them directly or who are willing to trade their usage data to be targeted for advertising. This leaves some of the most important corners of exploration in our cities, those that could benefit the most from improvements, untouched. And thus, as argued in previous chapters, the propensity for city governments to want to steer clear of the technology applications and service business, other than to leverage tools from outside solutions providers, may ultimately fail for those who rely on city services the most.

10.3 People as Sensors

Reflexively, when we think of ICT, most of us think of digital communication devices and networking applications. But ICT comprehends radio, television, and cellular phones; it also includes the services and applications that are delivered across the enabling infrastructure. Every one of these channels has a role to play in the smart city, though over time, they will continue to converge and synchronize across devices. As we work to dispel the technocentricity that dominates smart city thinking, we can more fully realize the concomitant importance of connecting humans through technology to build stronger and healthier communities.

As discussed in earlier chapters, one of the most compelling use cases for the smart city is found at the nexus of the smartphone and people as sensors. The idea of people as sensors is somewhat ambiguous, mostly because people are nontechnical sensors but provide both knowledge and context-pensive intelligence to their phone's technical measurement. This is an incredibly powerful advantage to this "free" sensor deployment, as a mobile device collects absolute, calibrated data complemented by impressions, descriptions, and pictures.

Related to people as sensors is the notion of "collective sensing." In this case, analytics can explore data from a variety of networks—including Facebook, Twitter, and Foursquare—and gain an impression of a situation in an environment without any personally identifiable information factored into the mix. Other measurements made in the aggregate are those that include indications of crowd density or the dynamics of movement through a city square; this information can then be fused with other data sources to help place streetlights or even alter the flow of pedestrian traffic to encourage the improved use of spaces for public enjoyment. In discussing collective information sources, scientist Bernd Resch, in his 2013 work exploring the concept of contextual observations, explains the power of this emerging phenomenon, stating that "citizens augment their role, becoming agents of change by uncovering, visualizing, and sharing real-time measurements from their own everyday environment by exploiting and elevating their expertise and their personal, local experiences."[6]

As more people achieve connectivity through smartphones and less through wireline broadband and computers, the smartphone and any other sensors such as watches, glasses, and haptic devices, will help create a new narrative among connected communities both far and wide. But, in the context of the smart city, people as sensors will soon play a vital role in augmenting the relationships within communities—and connecting them with the larger world.

10.3.1 Convergence

Convergence used to mean that all devices would ultimately collapse into one nebulous black box into which all of our data feeds would flow. Then, the concept changed as we started to acquire many devices, each with their own connection to the Internet. Now convergence isn't related to hardware at all; it's related to content. It seems clear that with the advent of content synchronization through the cloud, user-generated content, and new media seamlessly flowing across many platforms, content does indeed seem to be converging. But the notion does not go far enough, most especially in the urban environment. Despite a plethora of sensors, smart devices, and intelligent systems emerging at a rapid clip (so rapid, recall, that futurist Kurzweil thinks we are quickly approaching the time where artificial intelligence is hitting its stride and will soon exceed our

---

[6] Resch, Bernd (2013), "People as Sensors and Collective Sensing—Contextual Observations Complementing Geo-Sensor Network Measurements." Retrieved February 16, 2015, from http://www.berndresch.com/download/work/publications/resch_people_as_sensors_lbs2012.pdf.

human cognitive capabilities), many of our most pressing urban challenges are not advanced at all, and relate primarily to basic services, such as waste management and clean water. Thus, in the city, we must think about convergence only as a matter of bringing digital capability to our analog world in a manner where our relationships with our urban infrastructure are enhanced and not subsumed by technology.

Henry Jenkins, the provost professor of communication, journalism, and cinematic arts at the University of Southern California, has written prolifically on the topic of new media and popular culture. In the introduction to his prescient 2006 book *Convergence Culture: Where Old and New Media Collide*, he suggests that although many of our systems are interconnected, there is simply no way to understand various media as self-contained. He says, "Convergence is taking place within the same appliances . . . within the same franchise . . . within the same company . . . within the brain of the consumer . . . and within the same fandom. Convergence involves both a change in the way media is produced and a change in the way media is consumed."[7] Written nearly a decade ago, the book frequently refers to system interdependence, where devices are pushed further and further to the edge of our networks and lives. But perhaps what is most important about his work is his convincing vision of a growing dynamism in the manner of our information flows that can often result in an entirely surprising effect. This has proved to be especially true when it comes to massive forms of participation, collaboration, and coordination—community efforts that are growing evermore dependent on technology.

10.3.2 From Access to Coordination

In Figure 10.1, we can see how connected people can rise up through the layers of capability by mastering new digital skills, ranging from simple access to the Internet to the ability to use connected devices for coordinating their personal lives and activities within the context of their community. First explored and referenced extensively by various

[7] Jenkins, Henry (2006), "Convergence and Divergence: Two Parts of the Same Process." Retrieved February 20, 2015, from http://henryjenkins. org/2006/06/convergence_and_divergence_two.html#more-1115.

Figure 10.1 People as sensors begins with access but results in community.

researchers as a concept called "The Three C's," this approach to social inclusion plays an important role in digital literacy, but as any practitioner of pedagogy will remind us, it is not enough to hand someone a book or a computer or a mobile phone and expect anything to happen. If we want to effectively integrate technology into our urban communities, then we must first have devices that provide us access, and then have a way to use these technologies to engage meaningfully with others.

Access. Significant investments in broadband technologies, coupled with open standards, have increased access to high-speed wireline and wireless broadband. The cycle of access is self-perpetuating, as the high penetrations of broadband have driven the "app economy" (the range of economic activity surrounding mobile applications), which in return drives the demand for higher-speed service. Billions of downloads are made each month globally on each major platform: Android via Google Play and the iPhone via the App Store.

Communication. Once people can connect to the Internet through the capacities of their mobile device, they are able to harness social media tools that hold communicative powers. Short of the wishes and dreams of some social media investors, the media does not create sociality, but it is a conveyance. It's true that a smartphone is a deeply personal convenience, but it may even be a reflection of our personality, since we're using it to create a new relationship with our environment. We pump all kinds of new information into our public network, to the level that it has the power to change what happens in those public spaces, as we will discuss shortly.

Collaboration. Software companies are in a race to make their apps more "sticky"—that is, they need you to use them over and over again. One way to accomplish this is to find ways to increase participation, enable people to share personal things, or encourage them to interact with an online community or in an online activity. We don't want to miss out; we want to know what's happening, and some of us want to participate. Many people call it the network effect, but frankly, that's a lot more complicated than it has to be. We engage in social networks, sometimes to astonishing levels, because other people are doing the same thing. Ever tried to get 200 of your friends to move from one place to another in a coordinated fashion? And then expect them to move 200 of their friends to a different location? And so on, and so on ad nauseum? No? That's because it doesn't work, especially online. We go where the people are.

The techniques that keep us engaged online are appealing to a very basic human instinct: personal efficacy. Designers in the field use techniques to exploit our need for personal power through gamification. This is the use of game mechanics (points, leveling up, leaderboards) to motivate people who are inspired by rewards, status levels, or self-promotion (selfies, status posts) to engage with others online. Gamification is now being used in businesses as a way to influence and motivate employee behavior, or even to increase return on investment (ROI) through improved customer engagement.

Coordination. In business, the common definition of coordination applies to efforts to link people's skills and activities to achieve a common goal. In social media, coordination does not always have to be entirely goal-directed; it can be much more ad hoc or spontaneous. Digitally enhanced communication leads to coordination in a very precise way: it allows common knowledge to emerge about the social activities and roles of the individuals participating in those activities in real time. This communication flow is usually initiated in a fairly limited manner, but as it grows, there is a level of observation that can strengthen even weak links between individuals and groups. Social network theory is actually quite complex and worthy of further exploration for any team of designers that wishes to drive a higher order of connectivity in the urban environment. There are actually rather compelling examples of how the phenomenon of impulsive coordination can occur even when a goal is only loosely defined and even nondeterministic (such as Occupy Wall Street versus "Log all your sales leads on this spreadsheet so the project manager can keep track and we don't have any overlap of effort"). More simply, coordination does not have to be a deliberate function of a group of managers, though some level of social identity linkage must emerge across various social media platforms in order for the effort to have a large-scale impact.

10.4 From Social Inclusion to Social Influence

There has yet to be a more profound demonstration of social coordination than the Arab Spring. While history has not yet helped us fully contextualize the role of social media in the Arab Spring movement, there are important harbingers that can help describe the role of technology in our future smart communities. Before delving into the Arab Spring case, let's look at two important aspects of a digitally literate community:

- *Presence.* A community's electronic presence is comprised of content generation and consumption, but it's only truly meaningful if the community creates it itself. If a community depends on outside sources to define its online presence, it will surely be lacking in accuracy and will likely do little to engage its intended audience.
- *Vitality.* A community's vitality is inextricably linked to its economic capacity and the strength of its local economy. This implies that even when forces may be beyond the immediate control of a community, the ability to leverage technology will increase not only the ability to find, get, and keep a job but also the ability to use technology applications and services to help local businesses be found and recognized, bringing in more money to the community and essentially placing it on the online map.

    Both of these efforts require not only access but also education to help people learn how to use social media and how to engage with customers online. They also require an ability to write and communicate in ways that can make a substantive difference in the daily lives of urban communities, help neighbors find neighbors, and allow technology to increase positive human interaction rather than separate and break down relationships.

The Arab Spring is the name for a wave of revolutionary protests and uprisings in the Arab world that began in late 2010 and that impacted the countries of the Arab league and surrounding areas. At the broadest level, the protest movement stemmed from a resentment of longtime Arab dictatorships and other forms of insecurity, including police brutality, inflation, and corruption. Many will argue that the Arab Spring was a failure because democracy has not been able to take hold in the region. However, what is remarkable about the Arab Spring is that it demonstrates the willingness of Arab people to rise up against the ruling elites under the witness of the entire world—in real time, thanks to the ubiquitous social networks of Facebook and Twitter.

Clearly, neither social networking platform was responsible for the revolution, but the technologies did have an unprecedented level of autonomous influence. Indeed, though, tech-savvy political activists used both of these communication channels to engineer the uprisings to create community presence. Twitter, especially, allowed a level of organization and coordination, coupled with the ability to broadcast tactical information that accelerated the conflagration. Because assembly was deemed unlawful by the authorities, the virtual spaces of Twitter and Facebook allowed unity and connection to flourish. But in the end, in the spirit of profound irony, when the Egyptian government physically shut down these communication channels, people flooded into the street, instigating the final collapse of the government.

This was the world's first new media revolution, and it was indisputably a function the modern-day reality of technology ubiquity that played a crucial role in the ongoing and difficult process that we call the #ArabSpring. Lord Guy Black, renowned free-speech expert and conservative member of the UK House of Lords since 2010 goes further to argue that social media "was one element of much more complex and much broader communications networks that fanned the flames of revolution. It helped shaped the environment but at the end of the day it would have been of no use without the courage of individuals who lit the sparks."

The Arab Spring movement is an example of nothing else if not the desire to revitalize the lives of the people. Representing loosely coordinated

uprisings that had been occurring independently for months, the movement quickly spread to Egypt, Libya, Syria, Yemen, Bahrain, Saudi
Arabia, and Jordan. Today, many will argue that the Arab Spring has
frozen and died, but the transition to change after decades of repression
is certainly not going to happen instantly. The message shouldn't be lost
in the world of politics: technology and connectedness allowed spotty
coalitions of women, artists, soccer fans, teachers, and insurgents to work
together toward a common goal, at least in the moment.

10.5 Crowdsourcing for a Smarter City

In Beijing, China, citizens can log on to a transport research center
website to help identify problems in the infrastructure of the city that
are causing issues for bicyclists and pedestrians. In the US, you can use
SeeClickFix to report neighborhood problems, and in the UK, just log on
to FillThatHole to report road wear and tear. If you have a special-needs
child, there are only certain playgrounds where the child can play safely.
Find it based on Playground for Everyone. Road kill? There's an app for
that. While cities have long known that outreach and communication are
key, even in the era of the Internet, it's largely been a one-way conversation, where every functional area of the city has at least a list of information and a place to download forms. But now, through technology, the
city is rapidly turning to open-source technology to improve the democratic process and to create a rich and full dialogue between the government and its citizens, and among the citizens themselves. Even large-scale
design can be enhanced by crowdsourcing, where cities can use the data
collected about behaviors and residents' answers to simple questions about
how they want to use their public spaces or acquire services to bring innovation and unconventional thinking to bear for powerful results.

   One might be tempted to access Wikipedia (www.wikipedia.org) to
see what it says about crowdsourcing; after all, Wikipedia could arguably be considered the most comprehensive encyclopedia the world has
ever known. And in a recursive moment, you might also realize that
Wikipedia is itself crowdsourced. Instead of a bevy of writers and edi-
tors, the world crowd is creating information on its own, and as such,
the quality of the content Wikipedia has improved. As we discussed earlier, the term "crowdsourcing" itself is believed to be a blending of the
words "crowd" and "outsourcing," where we call on participants to work

together to create content in a dramatic display of two heads being better than one. (Though, determining the origin of a word is dangerous business. Maybe the crowd will tell us for sure.)

10.5.1 Hacking the City

The concept of crowdsourcing and its related implementation through what has been called an "IdeaJam" provide a digital venue for feedback and suggestions. The approach has been leveraged by some of the world's most powerful and innovative companies, including IBM, Starbucks, Dell, and others, because it's an inexpensive way to get new product ideas while empowering customers. It's also dangerous. Why? Because crowdsourcing and ideajams are completely unpredictable. We all have heard of "trolls" (meaning, nasty individuals who are usually cruel and thrive on upsetting people online) who would like to distract the process, but listening to outliers is what is promised and where the gold nuggets can often be mined. Instructive ways of dealing with such people have emerged, but by far the most credible approach is to ignore the troll and simultaneously take the issue up with the group in a decent way. Then move on with the discussion. This may mean collapsing many related threads into one to drown out the troll or providing a constant and powerful opportunity for the crowd to edit and mark up itself, as in Wikipedia. It requires constant moderation and attention just to keep the cycle moving forward. But, when well tended, these ideajams and crowdsourced initiatives can help drive important initiatives that certainly shouldn't die on the vine because of an agitating force.

Crowdsourcing has evolved over the past few years and is more than just an easy way to hit up a large group of people for some feedback. There are three major areas of crowdsourcing (though new forms will certainly emerge the moment this book is completed) that can be leveraged by our urban citizens:

- *Innovation.* Cities need ideas to solve their problems—old problems and emerging ones. Crowdsourced innovation has been used quite successfully in business and is credited, for example, for encouraging Dell to roll out its Linux-based computers to heralded success. Forums for innovation give many interested parties a way to share ideas that can be made into a reality in the city. Government stakeholders, citizens, investors, and designers can benefit from these online discussions. Another important aspect of a crowdsourcing platform designed to enhance opportunities innovation is that people who do not normally have a voice can provide their ideas and knowledge. Further, an extension of innovation is crowdfunding (popularized by Kickstarter and GoFundMe), which allows people to back a project that they want to see come to fruition. Some investments in the city may be too small, too niche, or too uncertain. But crowdfunding can help artists, charities, and others raise money to prove out their ideas with a shared risk model.

- *Designing.* Some companies have used crowdsourcing to solve all sorts of design problems. And most of us have a friend or two who have posted a iteration of logos for their new company on Facebook and asked their friends to vote for their favorite. You never know: the furniture you sit in at the airport tomorrow or the T-shirt you're wearing right now may be products of crowdsourcing.

- *Microwork.* Sometimes called microtasks or microjobs, microworks result when someone uses a crowdsourcing platform to break up work into many tiny tasks and sends it out to the community for completion. Sometimes this approach can deliver near-immediate results. The closed-circuit TV (CCTV) crime-stopper sites we discussed earlier, where neighbors identify neighbors who are committing a crime, are examples microwork, but there are other, more-interesting examples. Seen by some as a way to exploit workers, microworks are often viewed negatively. But sites like IfWeRantheWorld (ifwerantheworld. com) and Crowdcrafting.org (crowdcrafting.org) are additive to taking good intentions and putting them to work. Some ideas are bold, such as giving all your excess money to the poor or committing to sharing with your children the issues of bullying. Other sites are more nuanced and provide a way to volunteer support across a variety of disciplines, from art and the humanities to biology and data analytics. One project on Crowdcrafting.org contained 1,800,000 images stored at the Johnson Space Center database, where volunteers signed up to help distinguish between stars, cities, and other objects as a way of addressing the problem of light pollution.

Taking all of these together, we can find some almost bewildering applications of crowdsourcing in the city. In 2012, the city of Calgary in

Canada (www.calgary.ca) ran a program called "Our City. Our Budget. Our Future," which allowed citizens to participate in drafting the budget to help inform the city on citizen priorities. This initiative still continues in the form of ongoing engagement opportunities.

10.5.2 How the Crowd Revitalized an Urban Neighborhood

The Kentlands Initiative in Salt Lake City, Utah, is a nonprofit development company that was looking for ways to deal with the political blowback and financing difficulties associated with launching new development projects. The group's first effort involved reclaiming a troubled rail and warehouse district in Salt Lake City called the Granary District. Although it's connected to downtown, the district fell into disrepair when the railroad moved on, leaving an area that showed all the usual signs of blight.

The first goal of the Kentlands Initiative was to help it be seen by district residents as a neighborhood. Funded partially through Kickstarter, the organization threw a block party where over 1,000 people showed up. The group sponsored movies, BBQs, and coffee parties to provide a space for the community to voice their concerns. The initiative worked to allow the neighborhood to reinvent itself, including developing a visual brand, a story, and a 20-year business plan with prioritized projects.

Journalist Tim Halbur—in describing the remaking of the Granary District, where businesses and residents live and work in the warehouse and industrial spaces—interviewed the Kentlands Initiative executive director James Alfandre about how he tapped into neighborhood engagement. Alfandre said, "We believe the best development starts there—with a project's prospective tenants and neighbors. . . . Energize this nexus and you awaken something powerful. When development is done poorly— when it's top-down . . . when development is done well—when it's crowd-sourced—these folks are your inspiration and your allies."[8] Alfandre taps into a broader point: that technology has the potential to support

[8] Halbur, Tim (2013), "Development Done Well Is a Community Affair," Planetizen. Retrieved February 20, 2015, from http://www.planetizen.com/node/63112.

urban life from the perspectives of planning, design, and development. Ideology and politics are really just an excuse to ignore the wisdom of the urban dweller. Positive debate can help improve the treatment of myriad urban concerns from transportation and climate mitigation to health and human services.

Chapter Eleven

Information Security and Privacy

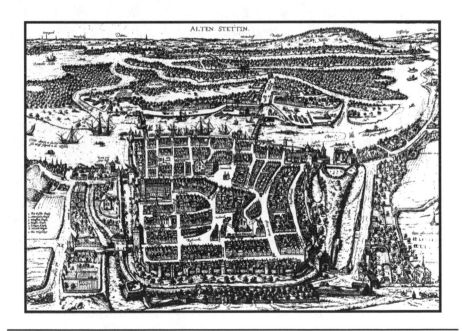

Map of Old Szczecin (Alten Stettin), Poland, created by topo-geographers Georg Bruin and Franz Hogenberg in England around 1575.[1]

---

[1] Image retrieved from the public domain at http://en.wikipedia.org/wiki/ Szczecin#/media/File:Store_Szteteno_(1575)A.png.

11.1 Chapter Goal

The objective of this chapter is to introduce the very complex conditions of creating a secure and private smart city where so many of the benefits are entangled with highly granular and frequently collected data from both the private and public domains. We explore the boundaries of our expectations about privacy and suggest that while it is a difficult problem, simplicity may be in order. We also discuss the role of open data and the value of the foundational principles of the widely accepted Privacy by Design framework.

11.2 Drawing the Lines

We are digital citizens now, and no more so than in the smart city. But with the growing collection of instrumented data from our natural and built environments, buildings, transportation systems, and other aspects of our broader infrastructure—and even the devices in our pockets and on our bodies—how and when we exert our preferences over the way data is gathered and analyzed has become overwhelmingly complicated. When we use new applications or websites, the terms and conditions that are presented to us (or implied by our use of some digital service) to help us understand our privacy protections are so obfuscated in legalese and jargon that most of us are willing to shunt off our reading of this important information and instead search for the "accept" button so that we can carry on with our task. We'll accept free access to nearly any service—like Wi-Fi at Starbucks—if we perceive that we need it. When we get a letter that a system was breached and our private information flowed out, we'll accept terms in the course of our jobs only with a second thought. As to the data we're generating—where it's going and how it's getting there—very few are really clear on that. We give away our security and privacy in dramatic ways in order to gain access to low-cost cloud infrastructure to run our lives and our businesses.

Our confusion belies many of the challenges of the data security and data privacy conversation, and it starts with the terminology. "Data security" and "data privacy" are often conflated into a single conversation, but while they may maintain a symbiotic relationship, they are in no way synonymous. It's commonly accepted that data security is about maintaining the confidentiality, integrity, and availability (and, yes, with the acronym "CIA") of data in every state, from its collection, transmission, and processing to its analysis and storage. It is data security that ensures that unauthorized systems or parties don't access our data and that it stays in an accurate and reliable state. Data privacy, on the other hand, is all about how the data is used. When trusted parties acquire data for their operations, are they using it in the way they said they'd use it? Do you even know where your vital data is and what's being done with it? Popular media focuses mostly on data security because it's simpler to understand and feels more tangible and controllable. It's also more closely associated with technology. A hacker violated the database and stole credit card data from Target. The hacktivist group Anonymous broke into Twitter and posted inappropriate slogans. In both those cases, it's the defenses that failed at least that's the perception. Privacy is much more troublesome because it's about the law, policy, and governance. Privacy only gets more nuanced and complex as we merge our everyday lives into the networked system.

In the smart cities, our relationships are magnified, and the security and integrity of these relationships are frequently digitally mediated, not just between people but also between servers and the Internet of Things (IoT). The real rub is that if we want to benefit from the promises of advanced technology in our cities and elsewhere, we need the data that's collected from the various interconnected systems—and not just from our public sources but from all of us. Without it, the ability to fully realize systems that not only can improve our lives but also can help address the existential threats from anthropogenic climate change and respond in emergency situations simply cannot occur. And those companies that seem so trusting with their company information? If they can't fully manage all levels of security, including malware protection, backups, and governance, they may be better off handing over these efforts to a centralized service. Central management of data saves time in IT provisioning and deployment processes, and it reduces the downtime caused by intrusive cybersecurity. It also eases the breadth and depth of a hacker attack once penetration is made at a single site, and it greatly simplifies the ability to monitor online activity. Over and over, security breaches from centralized locations result in sensitive information like Social Security numbers, national identification, and credit card numbers being lost to criminals. And these crimes then lead to extortion, stalking, harassing, and demands

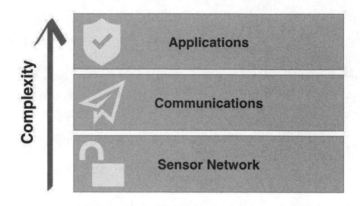

Figure 11.1   Security vulnerabilities increase as the digital infrastructure becomes more complex.

for ransoms for stolen information from computers acquired through property crime, social media accounts, e-mail, and hijacked web cams.

As described in Figure 11.1, the smart city digital infrastructure adds layers of technology as it moves from sensing and actuating tasks—where data is generated—through the communications infrastructure, to the applications that are used by city operations, analytical tools, and citizens. Indeed, complexity increases at every point where an application requests data and that data is served. These multiple touch points result in the fractional addition of data generation in a recursive system where information that's generated is information that's consumed, which generates data that may be used by many other applications. Vulnerability increases with the number of potential touch points in the system and in the data stream. Thus, wherever the collection of data requires authentication, the sophistication and complexity of the system naturally increase, as does the system's vulnerability to attack.

11.3 Security Deserves an Important Place in Design

At first, this may seem contrary to common sense, but complexity relates to the factors and characteristics of a system that has many parts, and when those parts interact with others in multiple ways, things get complicated. So really, the vulnerabilities in our smart city increase when our linkages between things (nodes) become more intricate and extensive. Further, despite the deterministic nature of the Internet, it's still difficult to predict with any sense of accuracy the interactions between nodes. If we cannot predict the behavior of a system that appears to be random, then the complexity itself is nondeterministic. But here's what a designer should keep in mind before becoming frustrated and lost in complex systems theory: even complicated systems generate simple patterns and can be considered coherent no matter how the parts interact. More simply, to make coherent designs, we must create systems based on our current assumptions of how things work. This has an odd side effect of creating a security stance that is reactive in nature instead of proactive, because we are engineering our systems to treat threat vectors that reflect how the system will be deployed and used. Once behavioral and unexpected deviations occur, the whole thing falls down. What we really need are ways to design security so that it can both adapt and respond to unexpected attacks.

Cybersecurity approaches in the smart city need to provide real predictive value to the city that more closely resemble models of complex systems. By viewing all the machine and human nodes of the network as a system of relationships, we can see that the couplings within the city are more similar to the human brain than to an engineered system of brittle rules that show little resilience. Complex systems theory shows how these system relationships give rise to a form of collective behavior that is called emergent behavior.

Nicholas Perony, an animal scientist, hypothesized that animals follow very simple rules that together can create larger patterns of behavior, underscoring how complexity is born of simplicity to help animals adapt to new circumstances. He tells of his study of meerkats. These mongooses tend to follow a dominant meerkat until the mob reaches some barrier, such as a road. What happens then? Nearly every time, a nondominant meerkat will cross the road first. The submissive animal wasn't instructed to channel its latent bravery; it just followed the rules. This is socially complex, but it helps ensure the survivability of the meerkats as a whole.[2]

Making predictions about the behavior of the city under attack is what we need to understand in order to move from a reactive to a proactive posture. Nobel Prize–winning economist and philosopher Friedrich

[2] Nicolas Perony (2013), "Puppies! Now That I've Got Your Attention, Complexity Theory." Retrieved February 22, 2015, from http://www.ted.com/talks/nicolas_perony_puppies_now_that_i_ve_got_your_attention_complexity_theory.

Hayek observed that complex systems' behavior is best predicted through modeling and an understanding of the systems' patterns rather than precise predictions.[3]

11.3.1 Evaluating Requirements

How do we begin to evaluate the requirements of security when we are designing for the smart city? It depends on whether you believe that security problems can be solved primarily through technology or primarily through the process we use to secure our systems and the people who use them. We can suggest two ways that smart city security topics can be categorized: by collection modality (for example, smart meters, social media, or transportation data) or by nominating the activity that created the data as the key identifier, regardless of the actual generating node. These might include activities such as consuming energy at home, searching on Twitter, or riding the subway. And why does it even matter when we have a dizzying array of attack vectors to deal with, from a door left ajar to a digital worm that can bring down a nuclear centrifuge? The answer depends on how we manage security incidents, become better at building in design from the beginning of the project, and take on a strategic perspective that actually helps us shift as a culture to take responsibility for not only our own role in security but also our neighbors' and our society's.

If we believe that security is both a responsibility and a requirement, and if we are to maintain an open and free society, then as our cities become more widely instrumented and deeply interconnected, it makes sense to protect our activities rather than just our nodes. Of course, device-level security is key, but it's simply not subject to the type of subversive abuse that higher-order data is.

11.3.2 Even Security Techniques Must Be Smart

The complexity of the cybersecurity threat has left innovators searching for ways that are less reactive (thus, "active") and have the potential

---

[3] Modified from *Big Data Analytics Strategies for the Smart Grid* by Carol L. Stimmel, with permission. ISBN: ISBN 9781482218282. © 2014 Taylor & Francis.

to directly deter the movements of attackers before they launch. Passive security models continually drive up costs without a coincident level of effectiveness, especially as they create overflow from event monitoring system that can create so much meaningless data that it is nearly impossible to detect meaningful events. Turning the tables on the adversary, an active defense drive up risks associated with a hacker's activities. Instead of tracking a discrete attack, the active defender focuses on identifying the mission of the attack and the tradecraft employed by the intruder. This can be achieved by linking events that in solitary seem unrelated, but that in context provide key clues as to what the next step might be instead of what the last step just was.

Once the mission of an attack is understood, passive defense strategies are implemented to confuse the attacker and continue to collect intelligence. Using the same principles that many hackers and social engineers have brought to bear, defenders will use deception to ultimately contain the attacker. The more information that can be collected in this process, the better policing agencies can be at creating an attack fingerprint, which can allow cities and government agencies to prosecute threat actors. This approach amplifies the efforts of cybersecurity to exclusively identify and predict patterns based on attack vectors, and it exploits characteristics to greatly improve the forward-looking stance of the city's cybersecurity model.

11.4 Privacy Begins in the Home

Authors Adel S. Elmaghraby and Michael M. Losavio in their original article "Cyber Security Challenges in Smart Cities: Safety, Security and Privacy" published in the *Cairo University Journal of Advanced Research* in 2014, present a model representing the interactions in persons, servers, and things in the smart city. In their discussion, they identify several core principles relating to privacy in US society, which can be extended to many democratic jurisdictions. Table 11.1 is informed by some of the key concepts that Elmaghraby and Losavio delineate in their works.[4]

---

[4] Elmaghraby, Adel S. and Losavio, Michael M. (2014), "Cyber Security Challenges in Smart Cities: Safety, Security and Privacy." *Journal of Advanced Research*, vol. 5, issue 4, pp. 491–497. Retrieved April 25, 2015, from http://www.sciencedirect.com/science/article/pii/S2090123214000290.

Table 11.1 General Expectations of Privacy in Democratic Societies

Place of Activity	Expectation of Privacy
At home	Highest level without a legal order to intrude
Areas that extend beyond the home	Variable, depending on how the space is construed by legal principles
In public with other people	Little to no protection
Publicly regulated activities	Little to no privacy protection
Online activity data	Based on consent, absent legal prohibition to use the data

Most of our legal and social constructs about privacy emerge from these basic generalizations. But when it comes to protecting these civil liberties, the smart city tangles all of them up—from data collection to analysis and even to the delivery of those benefits to citizens. Typically, we expect a life free of unwarranted interference, but we also want vehicle traffic to remain unsnarled, trains to run on time, and forewarning when construction zones are going to impede our progress (and then we certainly want a suggestion for an alternate route). None of this could be accomplished without locational data and other information, such as where you are, how fast you're going in your car, how fast everyone else is going in their cars, and even where they are going. (Have you stored a location for "home" in your GPS? Most users have.) Onboard systems that are designed to keep insurance rates low and drunk drivers off the highway can measure blood alcohol levels via breathalyzer, gauge car acceleration, monitor vehicle braking, and extrapolate emissions from your vehicle based on your driving habits as well as your propensity to be in an accident. Hardening this network of sensors from attack is important, but so are the transmission, storage, analysis, reuse, and republication of data through the service of applications.

Our common sense of privacy protection is obviously insufficient in how it relates to the collection of data. Supreme Court Justice Sonia Sotomayor wrote an opinion in *United States v. Jones* (2012) regarding global positioning system (GPS) data collection on a vehicle. She concluded that using this information amounts to a "search" under the US Fourth Amendment, which is an important reflection for those concerned about privacy and security in the smart city. She wrote:

Awareness that the Government may be watching chills associational and expressive freedoms. And the Government's unrestrained power to assemble data that reveal private aspects of identity is susceptible to abuse. The net result is that GPS monitoring—by making available at a relatively low cost such a substantial quantum of intimate information about any person whom the Government, in its unfettered discretion, chooses to track—may "alter the relationship between citizen and government in a way that is inimical to democratic society."[5]

She goes even further in her opinion, suggesting that the voluntarily disclosure of information to third parties precludes a reasonable expectation of privacy; she additionally notes that such a position is "ill suited to the digital age." This implies that the handing-over of privacy rights is required to carry out even the mundane tasks of living, including sending and receiving e-mail, visiting a city website to find out when garbage collection is scheduled, and dialing a phone number that is stored in an electronic contact manager on a phone (which is, of course, accompanied by a picture grabbed from LinkedIn, a list of all your last e-mails, personal details, and networking potential, all sourced by your mail application and augmented via the Facebook application programming interface [API]).

The Fourth Amendment, which is part of the Bill of Rights of the US Constitution, reads:

The right of the people to be secure in their persons, houses, papers, and effects, against unreasonable searches and seizures, shall not be violated, and no Warrants shall issue, but upon probable cause, supported by Oath or affirmation, and particularly describing the place to be searched, and the persons or things to be seized.

Many think that this mandate is purely US-centric, but it closely reflects the United Nation's Universal Declaration of Human Rights, Article 12, which states:

[5] Sullum, Jacob (2015), "Sonia Sotomayor's Heartening Defense of Privacy." Retrieved February 22, 2015, from http://reason.com/blog/2012/01/24/sonia-sotomayors-heartening-defense-of-p.

> No one shall be subjected to arbitrary interference with his
> privacy, family, home or correspondence, nor to attacks upon his
> honour and reputation. Everyone has the right to the protection
> of the law against such interference or attacks.[6]

This is clearly not just a Western concern. There are constitutional statements found in diverse countries across the globe that are written to protect privacy rights, though there are indeed those that do not provide any specific mention of privacy. And, of course, how these constitutional rights are actually regarded and enforced varies widely. It's clear, however, that privacy is accepted as a human rights issue where it is accepted at all, and it is a key part of providing dignity and freedom for all citizens. It is a strange hubris that some would assume that human rights and developing economies must somehow be mutually exclusive, and frankly it is only recently that serious debates have occurred in the United States, Canada, and Europe regarding surveillance policies. These discussions have been driven in part by the revelations of Edward Snowden, the American technology professional who leaked details of highly classified US National Security Agency (NSA) surveillance programs to the mainstream media beginning in June 2013.

Glenn Greenwald, American lawyer, journalist, author, and one of the recipients of confidential NSA documents from Snowden, gave an extremely popular and widely viewed Technology, Entertainment and Design (TED) talk on the topic called "Why Privacy Matters." In it, he discusses why even those among us who disclaim the need for our own privacy (with arguments that we are uninteresting) assume that those who are concerned about it are either doing something bad or allowing something bad to happen, such as terrorism or violent crime. This position makes no sense, and those who take it still password-protect their e-mail accounts, put locks on their bathroom doors, or—like Mark Zuckerberg, the founder and CEO of Facebook—buy land lots around their homes to keep away prying eyes.

Yes, Greenwald notes, we are social beings who will voluntarily publish information about ourselves, but we also have the right to *not* publish

---

[6] United Nations (n.d.), "The Universal Declaration of Human Rights." Retrieved April 25, 2015, from http://www.un.org/en/documents/udhr/index.shtml#a12.

information about ourselves. He says, "There are all sorts of things that we do and think that we're willing to tell our physician or our lawyer or our psychologist or our spouse or our best friend that we would be mortified for the rest of the world to learn."[7] Indeed, those teens who make us cringe when they seemingly post anything and everything on social media are the same young adults who are capable of actively managing their online privacy to conceal information from all sorts of people, like their parents and teachers. But even teens can't hold back technology advancements that have clearly overtaken our legal frameworks, which are designed to guard citizens and consumers from the inadequate protection of their personally identifying details.

Greenwald also points out that if we don't care about our privacy today, we just might tomorrow. In 2008, Jeroen van den Hoven, professor of ethics and technology at Delft University of Technology in the Netherlands, enumerated the reasons why we might change our minds. Table 11.2 interprets and adapts his work.[8]

Table 11.2 Van den Hoven's Moral Arguments
for the Provision of Data Privacy

Reason for Protection	Why It Matters
Prevention of harm	Personal information can be used in a variety of ways to hurt someone, especially locational data, private photos, or other guarded information.
Information inequality	Access to personal data can create an unfair advantage in contract negotiations or other partner relationships.
Informational injustice and discrimination	Personal information in one context can be used to discriminate against an individual in another context, especially in matters of healthcare.
Encroachment on moral autonomy	The exposure of private information can lead to a vulnerability of outside forces that can unfairly influence a person's decision-making capacity.

[7] Greenwald, Glenn (2014), "Why Privacy Matters." Retrieved February 23, 2015, from http://www.ted.com/talks/glenn_greenwald_why_privacy_matters/tran script?language=en.

[8] Van den Hoven, Jeroen; Blaauw, Martijn; Pieters, Wolter; and Warnier, Martijn (2014), "Privacy and Information Technology," *Stanford Encyclopedia of Philosophy*. Retrieved April 25, 2015, from http://plato.stanford.edu/entries/ it-privacy.

As we become evermore connected, access to information naturally increases (notice the plethora of background-check websites that scour free information and then charge a premium for it). This accessibility also increases the likelihood that someone will act on the data in deeply undesirable ways that a fair society will reject, including discrimination and other forms of harm. While we give up our privacy more and more often for the perceived benefits of a "free" online experience, systems and their algorithms become more and more influential in our experience. Major search engines produce content that it thinks we might like first (opinions that don't diverge from those it thinks we already have), or they only deliver us updates from friends it thinks we should be most interested in. On Facebook, depending on the state of your wall service, you may be punished for not generating enough likes fast enough or not posting a picture, effectively burying your voice deep in Facebook's edited news stream. At first, these activities seem like ancillary concerns to privacy, but these freedoms extend beyond hiding our credit card numbers from hackers or our home addresses from stalkers.

11.4.1 We Can, but Will We?

In 2013, an advertising firm in London was directed to halt its activities in the Square Mile (the original City of London). What was the company doing? The Renew ad firm had embedded smart technology in trash bins that measured the Wi-Fi signals from smartphones, capturing serial numbers and signal strength data to follow people up and down the street.[9] But now, New York City is counting and tracking all of its pedestrians with video. A start-up named Placemeter (placemeter.com) is using video feeds to gather and analyze information about vehicles and pedestrians on public streets. With a different approach, it achieves exactly the same end as the smart waste bins in London, since it recognizes a single individual as she walks from one building to the next with reportedly astounding accuracy. The company identifies all sorts of uses, including business marketing strategies, police handling of crowd situations along parade routes or

---

[9] "City of London Corporation Wants 'Spy Bins' Ditched" (2013), *The Guardian*. Retrieved February 23, 2015, from http://www.theguardian.com/world/2013/aug/12/city-london-corporation-spy-bins.

demonstrations, and even time management strategies for New Yorkers. As is the case with all data projects, data fusion and crowdsourcing enhance their capabilities. The company already has developed a sensing app for the phone that not only generates data but also receives information about crowds at a local grocery. Placemeter states that privacy isn't an issue because the company has made it a policy not to use facial recognition software, though it admits that it's not a technological limitation.[10]

Clearly, many innovators and their investors, as well as technology-focused users, worry that regulation and policy on privacy might hold back their work. And given the growing preponderance of business models that depend on data, this is not a concern that is just going to subside. However, every one of these companies and the individuals who lead them know that if they disregard the issues of privacy in a manner that exceeds social expectations or that erodes trust for their product or service, they will encounter terrible stumbling blocks, if not utter failure. There are myriad examples that show a positive correlation between poor data management policies and market share.

But this problem is not new. It's typical that we are forced to catch up in terms of building social consensus that can that become legislation or commonly accepted policies and procedures. Gemma Galdon Clavell, a society and privacy consultant, notes, "In the world of innovation, it is quite common for technical solutions to emerge before the social, political and legal consensus that can minimize their potential negative effects. When this happens, innovative solutions face an extra challenge: to propose acceptable consensus."[11]

Every city government that collects, retains, uses, and shares data must have established protocols and programs of governance for securing personal information. But what those policies should be and how such a system of protection is accomplished in a world where data can come from any source, be collected with ease, and travel in seconds across the

---

[10] Leber, Jessica (2014), "One Company Is Trying to Count and Track All of New York City's Pedestrians," Fast Company & Inc. Retrieved February 23, 2015, from http://www.fastcoexist.com/3025926/one-company-is-trying-to-count-and-track-all-of-new-york-citys-pedestrians.

[11] Galdon, Gemma (2014), "Privacy and Innovation: An Impossible Equation?" CCCBLAB. Retrieved February 23, 2015, from http://blogs.cccb.org/lab/en/article_privacitat-i-innovacio-una-suma-impossible.

ubiquitous Internet to anywhere on the earth (and into space, for that matter) may already be dangerously academic. When Bruce Schneier, chief technology officer of cybersecurity firm C03 Systems Inc. says, "A sufficiently skilled, motivated and funded attacker will get in, period." Then it should be clear that security as an afterthought is not going to scale in the world of IoT.[12]

11.5 The Role of Open Data in the Privacy Discussion

When we talk about open data and privacy, it is difficult to see how there is any common ground. We can all recognize the irony that there are significant benefits to be gained from opening up our data, but without some expectation of privacy, we will give up freedoms that will be difficult to restore. The idea behind the open data movement is that certain data should be free to anyone and everyone, reusable, modifiable, and totally without any mechanism of control (even if attribution is requested), such as a copyright, patent, or digital rights management scheme. There are many reasons for this, and there is significant traction for it even at the government level, as found in both the US (data.gov) and the UK (data.gov.uk). But Canada, Ghana, Japan, the EU, and many other countries, agencies, and states also maintain data catalogs.

Governments with open-data initiatives believe that making data accessible and discoverable carries benefits that far outweigh the risks, including improved policies, services, planning, research, transparency, and an increased ability to participate in the important dialogue of democracy. But who has leveraged open data? The data.gov websites list beneficiaries, including LinkedIn (which uses data from the Department of Labor and the Department of Education), the Climate Corp. (which uses National Weather Service and geological survey data, and National Aeronautics and Space Administration [NASA] imagery), several real estate search sites (which use National Oceanic and Atmospheric Administration

---

[12] Boulton, Clint (2014), "'Sony Is Snowden' for Corporations, Cybersecurity Expert Says," *The Wall Street Journal*. Retrieved February 23, 2015, from http://blogs.wsj.com/cio/2014/12/17/sony-is-snowden-for-corporations-cybersecurity-expert-says.

[NOAA], earthquake, survey, Federal Bureau of Investigation [FBI], Health and Human Services [HHS], and US Environmental Protection Agency [EPA] data; Federal Emergency Management Agency [FEMA] information; and labor statistics), travel sites (which use Federal Aviation Administration [FAA] data), energy-efficiency companies (which use census, energy-efficiency, and solar photovoltaic data), healthcare (which use HHS data and the National Drug Code Directory) and of course social media destinations (which use GPS and census data).

The arguments for open data range from the arcane (restrictions on data can create anticommons of fragmented and incomprehensible usage rights) to the near-spiritual (data belongs to the human race). Equally, the arguments against open data, which relate to the use of public funds (government money shouldn't be used to challenge the private sector) and to privacy concerns related to data ownership. Assuming that many of these arguments will be resolved through the traditional policy and regulatory channels over time, the real question is, if open data is required to empower citizens and solve real-world problems, then what, if any, are the moral reasons for privacy protection at any level?

In the belief that "sunlight is the best disinfectant," most openness advocates believe that transparency will actually reduce the unacceptable use of our personal data rather than push our private lives out to the world. Jeni Tennison, the technical director at the Open Data Institute puts it this way, "Openness about what data is shared, with whom, and for what purpose, could be used to provide a natural limitation on that sharing. Transparency about access to data could disincentivise unnecessary access as well as [provide] a justification and rationale for the sharing that does go on."[13]

At a gut level, this is a hard argument to make, but it has its merits. Open data is about data-use transparency, and with transparency comes accountability. After all, anyone who has gotten a strange series of advertisements on Facebook will admit to their curiosity about what Facebook thinks it knows about them and what it got wrong.

---

[13] Tennison, Jeni (2014), "How Can Openness Help to Protect Our Privacy?" Retrieved February 24, 2015, from https://www.omidyar.com/blog/how-can-openness-help-protect-our-privacy.

11.6 Putting This into Practice

Designing new products and services in an information and communications technology (ICT)-powered smart city must begin with a realization that people need to be able to identify and exercise their rights to privacy as they see fit. What this means is still of great debate, but overlooking or not taking into account the fact that every design can have a social impact ought to be turning heads. It's actually quite disgraceful for not only companies but also governments to be deploying advanced technologies that use surveillance techniques, whether those techniques are physical, online, or some hybrid of the two, without building in anonymization, encryption, and mechanisms that allow a person to not only find out what information is being collected but also access it or rectify it.

Some also argue for the right to be forgotten and to self-exclude their data, though that is difficult given the anonymized, generalized, and randomized nature of data collection, analysis, and reuse. Your fingerprint may always be in the system, but it may be impossible to be located on demand. The point is that when smart cities invest in designing new solutions for the community, they must also invest in protecting privacy. All applications in the smart city must comprehend privacy and trust from the level of the data that a device collects to how that data is secured and kept private. For example, do we want to trust that a company will adhere to a policy to not use facial recognition software in its video technology, or do we actually want to technologically inhibit the ability to perform such recognitions?

The relationship between design and information security is not new to the seasoned discipline of human-computer interaction (HCI). Yet, security concepts as they relate to HCI (or HCISec) are a new concern due to issues created by designers who completely disregarded concerns of security, and then—when an issue occurred or someone had an afterthought—a security bolt-on or patch emerged to fix the security hole. This occurs most often because either the designers lack a deep understanding of security or engineering-focused designers who have a poor grasp of usability principles introduce security flaws. They then create difficult interfaces that are intended to be rock-solid fortresses, but they're really headaches that cause users to work around security walls just to use the system with a minimum amount of friction.

Ann Cavoukian, the former information and privacy commissioner of Ontario, Canada, and progenitor of the Privacy by Design (PbD) framework included seven foundational principles in her work:

1. Proactive not reactive; preventive not remedial
2. Privacy as the default setting
3. Privacy embedded into design
4. Full functionality—positive-sum, not zero-sum
5. End-to-end security—full lifecycle protection
6. Visibility and transparency—keep it open
7. Respect for user privacy—keep it user-centric[14]

PbD can be applied in many areas of design and should be considered in scope with regard to surveillance, biometrics, the smart grid, near field communications (NFC), sensing devices, remote services, big-data analytics, and location services. PbD has been widely accepted and provides one of the most specific and actionable approaches to treating the exponentially growing privacy challenges. As Cavoukian reminds us, privacy is always about control, the essence of which is specifying and limiting the uses of one's personal information. There is nothing about these principles that would undermine a designer's vision and creativity, and should always be fostered as part of creating worthy human-centric solutions for the smart city.

[14] Cavoukian, Ann (2012), "Operationalizing *Privacy by Design*: A Guide to Implementing Strong Privacy Practices." Retrieved February 24, 2015, from https://www.privacybydesign.ca/content/uploads/2013/01/operationalizing-pbd-guide.pdf.

Section Three

Key Points

A city planning map for Hamar, Norway, first drafted by planning engineer Røyen in 1848.*

---

* Image retrieved from the public domain at http://en.wikipedia.org/wiki/File:Original_city_map_for_Hamar_Norway_1848.png.

Section Three

Key Points

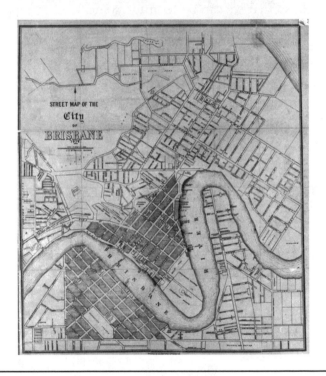

A street map of the city of Brisbane, Queensland, Australia, in 1878.[1]

[1] Image retrieved from the public domain at http://upload.wikimedia.org/
wikipedia/commons/b/be/StateLibQld_2_202047_Street_map_of_the_
city_of_Brisbane%2C_Queensland%2C_1878.jpg.

Chapter Nine

The Vocabulary of Analytics

×××××××××××××××××××××××××××××××××××××××

To make understanding analytics simpler, we organize the main approaches into categories. For the purposes of smart city data analytics, there are four model categories: descriptive, diagnostic, predictive, and prescriptive.

×××××××××××××××××××××××××××××××××××××××

- Models are symbolic representations of relationships, systems, and structures that we find in the urban environment. They simplify the real world so that we can better understand what is happening now and predict what might happen in the future.
- Analytics systems use a variety of approaches to produce results; thus, there is no progression in terms of value from one category to the next as they fulfill specific needs for particular kinds of problems.
- A variety of approaches and applications may be used to help solve a particular operational or business challenge.

Various Analytics Models Can Be Applied Together to Create Value

×××××××××××××××××××××××××××××××××××××××

While predictive and prescriptive analytics tend to be more complex in nature, descriptive and diagnostic analytics are required as part of the overall structure of analytic-driven problem-solving.

×××××××××××××××××××××××××××××××××××××××

As described in the following table, the basic analytical approaches help drive insights and can turn these fundamental insights into actionable information.

Analytic Approach	Function
Descriptive	What happened or what is happening now?
Diagnostic	Why did it happen or why is it happening now?
Predictive	What will happen next? What will happen under various conditions?
Prescriptive	What are the options to create the most optimal or high-value outcome?

As insights are turned into action, these actions will change how the business operates (sometimes unexpectedly), and filter back through the analytical process in a cycle of continuous change and improvement. This process is called generativity and is described in the following image.

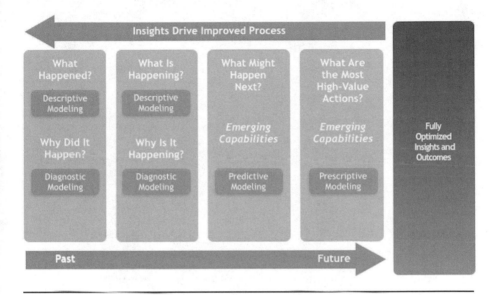

Analytic models use the past to prescribe the best business actions.

The Analytics of Things

It is becoming increasingly important to understand that without analytics as the motivating force behind widespread data collection initiatives, very little stands to be achieved from Internet-of-Things (IoT) deployments.

- The use of advanced algorithms is the intelligence that provides the ability to predict and prescribe future actions—such as forecasting crime outbreaks, planning better transportation solutions, or using facial recognition software to help police find a face in a wave of people.
- Given the ubiquity of the smartphone and its increasingly advanced capabilities, it is quickly becoming the most compelling sensor available in the urban environment.

- Almost every technological application in the smart city will find its way into the nexus of IoT and analytics, where human behavior is of immediate interest; the role of human-generated data is growing in availability and importance.

Chapter Ten

The Role of Technology in the Urban Community

Technology and mobile connectedness are creating an unprecedented opportunity to include people directly in helping to define and solve urban issues at a very personal level while also improving social inclusion and community connectedness.

- The digital divide—a defining line between people who can use new technologies and those who can't—has long been a problem. Yet in many ways, the digital divide is quickly being bridged and a different dynamic is emerging, relating to engagement among technologically disenfranchised groups.
- It is not the preponderance of sensors, their type, or even the massive volumes of data they collect. Instead, it's how we use the information we collect to provide opportunities for engagement.
- New technologies are exciting and have proved their importance and usefulness. Plus, technology capability is now fundamentally changing the way we live our lives at the levels of production and consumption, not to mention human interaction and community building. Designing with this shift in mind will produce the most rewarding smart city solutions.

The Nature of Convergence Is Changing in Our Cities

Convergence is no longer just about content synchronization, data feeds, and hardware. It is a concept that is quickly growing to mean the seamless relationship between a person, her devices, and her preferred content.

- Our growing technology dependence forces us to think about how our digital capabilities and analog world collide, raising concerns for how we live in a digital urban infrastructure that enhances and does not subsume our sense of humanity.

- Connected people progress through a process of improved capability by mastering new digital skills, ranging from simple access to the Internet to the ability to use connected devices for coordinating their personal lives and activities within the context of their community:
  - *Access.* The ability to connect to broadband connectivity and mobile devices.
  - *Communication.* Channels such as social media, e-mail, and web.
  - *Collaboration.* The repeated use of an Internet space to participate in work or personal relationships.
  - *Coordination.* Engagement in goal-directed collaboration activities.

From Social Inclusion to Social Influence

The digitally enabled social sphere not only allows communities of interest to be formed and coordinated but also enables change in our urban communities—or, more dramatically, revolution.

- Information and imagery related to insurgency, revolution, demonstrations, and riots are being transmitted in real time via social media channels. The ubiquity of Facebook and Twitter create opportunities for user-generated content to accelerate influence.
- Technology brings new levels of connectedness that allow spotty coalitions of people with a common goal to work together spontaneously in the moment.
- Technology has the potential to support urban life from the perspectives of planning, design, and development. Ideology and politics are quickly becoming more difficult as debate increasingly occurs in the digital social sphere. Conversations are touching on myriad urban concerns, from transportation and climate mitigation to health and human services.

Chapter Eleven

The Lines of Data Privacy and Security Are Blurry

Extremely complex conditions emerge in the smart city when it comes to creating a secure and private environment where so many of the benefits are entangled with highly granular and frequently collected data from both the private and public domains.

- With the growing collection of instrumented data from our natural and built environments, buildings, transportation systems, and other aspects of our broader infrastructure—and even the devices in our pockets and on our bodies—how and when we exert our preferences over the way data is gathered and analyzed has become confusing.
- More and more, urban dwellers are giving away security and privacy in dramatic ways in order to gain access to low-cost cloud infrastructure to run the business of our personal and professional lives.
- In the smart city, our relationships are magnified, and the security and integrity of these relationships are frequently digitally mediated, not just between people but also between servers and the IoT.

The Smart City Creates Layers of Confusion

The smart city digital infrastructure adds layers of technology as it moves from sensing and actuating tasks—where data is generated—through the communications infrastructure to the applications that are used by the city and its citizens.

- Data security and data privacy are often conflated into a single conversation, but while they may maintain a symbiotic relationship, they are in no way synonymous.
- Data security relates to the confidentiality, integrity, and availability of our data, whereas data privacy is all about how, when, and by whom our data is used and for what purpose.
- It's challenging to maintain the principles of security and privacy as data is analyzed and deployed for further consumption by other systems and applications.

Both Security and Privacy Must Be Designed in from the Beginning

◇◇◇◇◇◇◇◇◇◇◇◇◇◇◇◇◇◇◇◇◇◇◇◇◇◇◇◇◇◇◇◇◇◇◇◇◇◇◇

Privacy is always about control, the essence of which is specifying and limiting the uses of one's personal information. There is nothing about these principles that would undermine a designer's vision and creativity, and should always be fostered as part of creating worthy human-centric solutions for the smart city.

◇◇◇◇◇◇◇◇◇◇◇◇◇◇◇◇◇◇◇◇◇◇◇◇◇◇◇◇◇◇◇◇◇◇◇◇◇◇◇

- Companies and governments are deploying advanced technologies that use surveillance techniques—whether those techniques are physical, online, or some hybrid of the two—and neglecting to actively build in anonymization, encryption, and mechanisms that allow a person not only to find out what information is being collected but also to access it or rectify it.
- Every application deployed in the smart city must thoroughly comprehend privacy and trust from the level of data collection to how that data is secured and used.
- Ann Cavoukian, the former information and privacy commissioner of Ontario, Canada, and progenitor of the Privacy by Design (PbD) framework, included seven foundational principles in her work:

  1. Proactive not reactive; preventive not remedial
  2. Privacy as the default setting
  3. Privacy embedded into design
  4. Full functionality—positive-sum, not zero-sum
  5. End-to-end security—full lifecycle protection
  6. Visibility and transparency—keep it open
  7. Respect for user privacy—keep it user-centric[2]

---

[2] Cavoukian, Ann (2012), "Operationalizing *Privacy by Design*: A Guide to Implementing Strong Privacy Practices." Retrieved February 24, 2015, from https://www.privacybydesign.ca/content/uploads/2013/01/operationalizing-pbd-guide.pdf.

Section Four

Designing Innovation

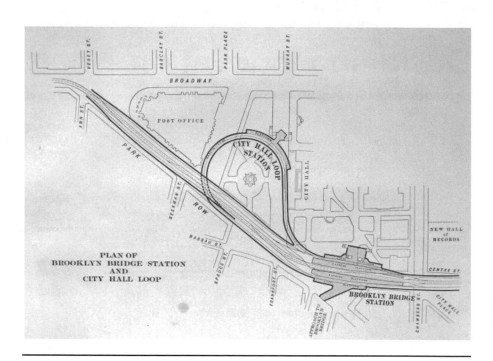

Schematic of the New York City City Hall Loop, designed by Rafael Guastavino in 1904.[*]

[*] Image retrieved from the public domain at http://upload.wikimedia.org/wikipedia/commons/7/79/City_Hall_station_plan.jpg.

Chapter Twelve

Hacking the City

An 1819 map of Neustadt an der Donau, a town in Lower Bavaria on the Danube River in Germany.[1]

---

[1] Image retrieved from the public domain at http://upload.wikimedia.org/wikipedia/commons/c/c3/StadtplanNeustadt_Do_1819.jpg.

12.1 Chapter Goal

This chapter seeks to highlight the importance of bringing together the disparate approaches to "hacking the city." We'll look at social network analysis, spatial arrangements, and the need to understand the more subjective components of place and what happens in certain spaces. We discuss the foundations of the graph and the ways of valuing the network and incorporating that knowledge into the creation, measurement, and validation phases of smart city design.

12.2 Designing Inspiration

A story requires an interaction; it requires a teller and a listener. And the way that a listener reacts to the story can change and influence the trajectory of the tale. It's a coordinated and interactive effort. Effective storytelling requires artful word shaping, the ability to capture the imagination with compelling narrative elements, and the skill to create an immediate bond between the storyteller and audience. But this bond is not gratuitous, and it's not empty inspiration. When designing for the urban environment, planners should elicit stories from the people they're designing for in order to participate in an act of cocreation. More importantly, designers can then gain an appropriate and useful point of view on the problem they're addressing.

Antoine de Saint-Exupéry said, "If you want to build a ship, don't drum up people to collect wood and don't assign them tasks and work, but rather teach them to long for the endless immensity of the sea."[2] Obviously, the French writer and aristocrat didn't mean that building a good ship isn't an important step in taking on a venture of ocean exploration. But he reminds us that no matter how awesome in magnitude and prowess our flotilla may be, if we have no reason for building it and we can't convince others that we have a reason, then in the end we have wasted our time. Instead, we begin with understanding. We need to understand people's stories so that we can infuse our designs with knowledge of how they will serve their goals. As discussed previously, the process depends on

[2] De Saint-Exupéry, Antoine (n.d.), Brainy Quote. Retrieved May 14, 2015, at http://www.brainyquote.com/quotes/quotes/a/MlBmTKrc0vawLPfH.99.

a structure of constraints, but organizational impatience and intolerance too often push product designers to rush to construction without reason or clear direction.

It is an unfortunate fact that designers and technology-oriented solutions providers rarely collaborate. Cities have complexities and challenges that can be treated with disruptive technologies, but nontechnological strategies must also be considered in order to build sustainable, purposeful solutions. Design thinking can bring these solutions to the fore. By reframing urban challenges in a way that improves the value of what we learn from analytics, design-thinking practices can dramatically improve the way that data drives new insights. On the flip side, analytics can help validate the value of human-centric innovation. As much as technologists need to think about the people that their applications both serve and impact, designers must gain inspiration and validation from data-driven information.

12.2.1 Civic Hacking

Many people think that hacking is a term that describes an effort to disrupt the normal operating behavior of a computer or a network of computers. It's a terribly misused term, and if we want to be precise, we must separate the malfeasant system crackers from the better-intentioned hackers. When we speak of hackers here, we're focusing on constructive and clever actions that may be technical or social in nature. In fact, some of the first so-called hackers were Massachusetts Institute of Technology (MIT) engineers who have a long tradition of carrying out technical experiments that are simply for fun, sometimes hilarious, and always designed to be learning activities. In the 1930s, Ken Wadleigh, a later dean at MIT, and his cohorts used a combination of social and technical engineering to distract a streetcar conductor while placing thermite bombs that welded the car to its metal rails. Surely, someone learned something invaluable. Civic hackers may be technologists, but they're also designers, entrepreneurs, artists, data scientists, city planners, urban dwellers, or anyone who wants to collaboratively address challenges in our cities in new and inventive ways.

In 2014, Chris Whong—a civic hacker, urbanist, and author—called New York's Freedom of Information Law (FOIL) the "computer-illiterate grandmother of Open Data." He took steps to obtain New York City taxi trip-sheet data to discover whether there were new ways that the data could be used by the BetaNYC project (BetaNYC.us), a self-described "network of civic-minded volunteers who contribute their skills toward digital platforms for local government and community service."[3] Under the auspices of FOIL, Whong obtained New York City taxi trip data for January through December 2013, corresponding to 174 million individual trips. It was a treasure trove and included data such as hackney license, pickup and time drop-off date and time, passenger count, trip time in seconds, trip distance, and latitude and longitude coordinates for pickup and drop-off locations.

Since then, the data has been served up from a torrent server to anyone who wants it, and it's now possible to acquire the visualization for Whong's "NYC Taxis: A Day in the Life," which visualizes the movements and earnings of a single taxi over the course of a day. Whong set out to show how we have data all around us that can be used to make decisions and build compelling cases to improve aspects of our urban life, even the highly regulated taxicab system, which is currently being sucker-punched by the likes of Uber and Lyft. His visualization illustrates not only the paths the cabs are taking but also when they disappear from the transportation grid, and how much they earn in a day, down to their reported tips.[4]

BetaNYC is a powerful example of the kinds of projects and tools that can emerge from civic hacking communities. Some of its projects have included Citygram NYC, which provides geographically centered notifications, and Heat Seek NYC, which focuses on the city's heating issues by bringing tenants, landlords, and justice organizations together. The project also collects data related to transportation, including crashes, injuries, and fatality information. But city hacking isn't new, despite the level of empowerment that digital capability and fluid and far-reaching sources of data bring. Indeed, folklore tells us that civic hacking has been happening for decades, and can very often begin in a bar or a pub, among friends who are entertaining riddles and conundrums.

[3] BetaNYC Facebook page. Retrieved March 7, 2015, from https://www.facebook.com/groups/betanyc.

[4] Whong uncovered another important reason for the standardization and security of city data: privacy. While searching for the source of some anomalous data, he was able to de-anonymize the taxicab data. The effort took just a few minutes of machine time once the security flaw was understood.

Other smaller-scale experiments across the globe continue to under-score the importance of balancing the mechanisms of technology for the smart city with an understanding of the usefulness of our interactions within the city. Tom Armitage, one of the collaborators behind the 2013 Hello Lamp Post (www.hellolamppost.co.uk) project that was staged in Bristol, England, and involved a playful way of engaging urbanites with actual city systems, describes how adapting our existing systems to new goals with existing technologies creates a layer of new opportunity for people in the city. He notes that "things like smart bus scheduling and smart bicycle hiring systems will prove a greater contribution than expensive, personal objects or smart thermostats for pricey houses. Again, the connected environment is at its most powerful, most transformative, when the technology and the connections are widely shared."[5]

12.2.2 Hacking Königsberg

As the story goes, there was a puzzle the townsfolk of Königsberg, Prussia (now part of Russia), entertained: Was it possible to walk through town and visit each part of the village, but cross each bridge only once? This is now called the "problem of seven bridges." As you can see in the map shown in Figure 12.1, Königsberg spanned both sides of the Pregel River (the town was decimated by bombs in World War II) and included two large islands; seven bridges crisscrossed the city. At the time, a Swiss mathematician named Leonhard Euler (1707–1783) was working at the Berlin Academy in Germany where he was presented with this very prob-lem in 1736. The rules were that each bridge could be crossed only once completely (no retracing and no halfway crossings), but it was not neces-sary to start and end the walk at the same spot.

Euler realized that attempting to list all the possible pathways would be way too exhausting and maybe impossible, so he abstracted the problem to consider only the landmasses and the bridges. Today, we would call the landmasses "nodes" (or vertices) and the bridges "edges," and the result is the basic vocabulary of graph theory. The problem could be solved on this new topological structure by taking a Eulerian walk—a trip around

---

[5] Martin, Glen (2014), "Most of What We Need for Smart Cities Already Exists," O'Reilly Radar. Retrieved March 4, 2015, from http://radar.oreilly. com/2014/05/most-of-what-we-need-for-smart-cities-already-exists.html.

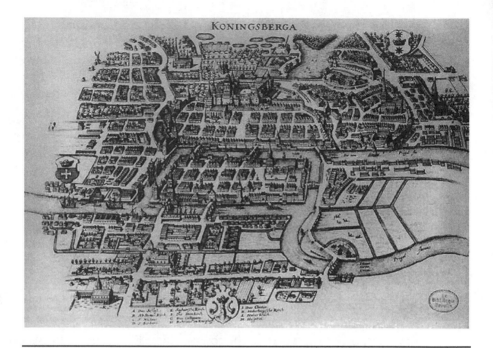

Figure 12.1   The map that spawned the problem of seven bridges of Königsberg.[6]

the map of nodes and edges where the connection information is the only relevant aspect to the problem. Thus, with the help of the graph, for every node entered on an edge, it would have to be left by another edge. So, to solve the Königsberg issue, the number of times one enters a nonterminal landmass must equal the number of times one leaves it to cross a different bridge. If every bridge has been crossed exactly once, then each one of those landmasses must have an even number of bridges (for coming and going). They didn't. So the disappointing answer to the bridge problem? It can't be done.

Euler helps us understand that no matter how complex the combinatorial problem at hand may be, it can be abstracted so that extremely hard data problems can be solved based on how nodes are connected to one another—the very foundation of network science. By observing nodal relationships spatially, in a manner that is unaffected by the shapes

[6] Image retrieved from the public domain at http://commons.wikimedia.org/wiki/File:Image-Koenigsberg,_Map_by_Merian-Erben_1652.jpg.

or sizes of the nodes themselves, we filter out irrelevant information that gives human cognition a boost. Based on a question of modest beginnings, Euler's approach to solving the problem now allows us to develop very powerful models that enable the facility to predict and optimize all varieties of networked systems, including the Internet, telecommunications networks, the electricity grid, and psychosocial systems.[7]

Today, Euler's contributions to graph theory strengthen our understanding of the way a more human network is represented in terms of connections and the strength of those connections (called ties). As shown in Figure 12.2, our network ties take on many dimensions, from the companionship and comfort of our strong ties, the weak ties that may be more casual and discrete, and of course, all those in the middle. One important thing we can learn from using a social graph to study urban networks is the structural indicators for how to navigate the social landscape of the city or community. Additionally, these ties show us friendly relationships, but they also show us sources of conflict such as indicators of group splintering and other symptoms of antagonism.

Based on the fundamentals of the graph, we can begin to study people in situations where they interact and affect one another. For our purposes, the graphs can reveal specifically which influences cause people to commit certain actions based on their desired outcome. Using game theory as an adjunct is one way to predict how decisions are made at both a local and community level. The ability to analyze both individual choices and those in aggregate are key to the efficient use of our resources; they're also critical to understanding how the choices of people change as their social graph evolves. When the phrase "rule of unintended consequences" is used to describe a surprising result from the application of some lever or design, it is often because the new system created some set of incentives that undermined the sought-after result.

Together, these theories are crucial to designing new practices, tools, and incentives that take into account the patterns in our evolving social connections and the role that various practices have in influencing the aggregate behavior of the city system being considered.

---

[7] Modified from *Big Data Analytics Strategies for the Smart Grid* by Carol L. Stimmel, with permission. ISBN: ISBN 9781482218282. © 2014 Taylor & Francis.

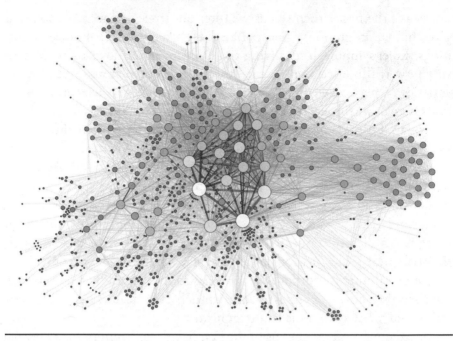

Figure 12.2   Visual graph representing the social network of hundreds of actors of the League of Nations.[8]

12.2.3 We're Still Walking the Edges

Euler may have brought us to the edge, but designers who are working within the context of a digital world should maintain basic knowledge, beyond the intuitive, as to how to value the communication network. Designers should be able to envision how network connections actually work, how a specific design might be implemented or scaled, and how these designs might impact strategic plans to provide value to urban dwellers. It is not always straightforward because there are many kinds of value that may be created within networks, and new devices and new ways of using those devices will continue to create as-of-yet unconceived or unidentified forms of value.

[8] Image retrieved from the public domain at https://fr.wikipedia.org/wiki/Représentation_graphique_de_données_statistiques#mediaviewer/File:Social_Network_Analysis_Visualization.png.

12.2.4 The Laws

At some point in the early 1980s, Robert Metcalfe described a perceived law of the telecommunications network that its value is proportional to the square of the number of connected users of the system (n^2). This is nominally called Metcalfe's Law. His law is derived from Euler's work and is, perhaps selfishly, an attempt to help accelerate networking (he is also called the father of Ethernet). Very simply, Metcalfe's Law expresses the value of a particular network of nodes mathematically, saying that the value of a network is based on the total number of potential connections. Naturally, this argument assumes that every connection is equally valuable. Thus, the value of a network is proportional to the square of the number of connected users of the system, or n^2. This seems hard to argue with, especially in the context of social networks, where it seems obvious to assume that the greater the number of users, the greater the value of the service (think "going viral"). Figure 12.3 shows this effect; the lines

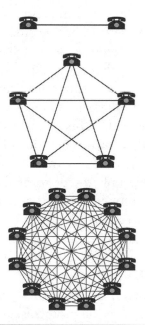

Figure 12.3 Diagram showing the network effect in simple phone networks.[9]

---

[9] Image retrieved from the public domain at http://commons.wikimedia.org/wiki/File:Metcalfe-Network-Effect.svg.

represent potential calls (interactions) between phones. Two telephones make only a single connection and a single opportunity to create a connection, 5 phones make 10, and 12 make 66.

As obvious as this law seems, there are problems. This observation has shortcomings in providing more than a utilitarian quantification for the value of a network. Specifically, it is overly simplistic to believe that the absolute number of nodes is all that's interesting. Instead, it's more likely that the nodes that are actively and frequently connected and contacted are the ones that drive value (where there is some benefit being generated by the nodes that are being connected). And thus, many designers are wise to understand when parts of a network are not in contact with the others. They then work to design around or address those forces—be they language, geography, lurking users, or the land-grabber phenomenon exerted by those who wish to dominate a social space for reasons of personal or economic efficacy. But how do we determine the value of the nodes, devices, and people that constitute the most active and frequent connections?

There are at least two ways to think about the question of node-level value. David Sarnoff, an American businessman and pioneer of radio and television at Radio Corporation of America (RCA), argues that a network is better valued by thinking about it as a broadcast medium with many receivers (users or devices), where the transmitters are scant and receivers are many. Sarnoff's Law says that the "value of the network is proportional to the n, the number of devices." This is most useful when thinking about events, but it doesn't really capture the value of social networks, because it doesn't account for interactions. Sarnoff's Law is certainly nontrivial, as the Internet is driving people to cut cords from traditional sources of information in growing numbers. For the first time in 2015, it was easy to watch the US National Football League (NFL) Super Bowl simply by streaming it from the broadcaster. But Sarnoff seems to leave the value of interaction out in the cold. What about all our friends? Reed's Law describes yet another path to value.

David P. Reed, an American computer scientist and designer of fundamental network communication protocols, asserts that the value of the network is related to its group-forming potential (he calls these group-forming networks, or GFNs), specifically where it is proportional to $2n$. Meaning, the network represents some exponent of interest group affiliation. Reed quantifies the fact that many groups arise from a single network, which creates value for participants. In short, this is a value-creation effect that shows how to boost returns as scale increases. Think about an online auction site like eBay. eBay surpassed 140 million active users in 2013—users who represent a powerful number of potential connections. Let's say I want to sell my cowboy boots on eBay. Do I think I have 140 million people who will want to buy my secondhand saddle straddlers? Not unless I'm a fool. I want to pitch them to cowgirls, a subset of eBay users called an affinity group. As eBay eases my ability to find those people, value potentially increases more rapidly at scale by focusing on transactions between communities rather than on anyone who just shows up on the network.

Finally, there is one law on network valuation that takes a very different approach. Instead of looking at the size of the network, or even the value of the interactions, it looks at the value of the transactions within the network. This is Beckstrom's Law as formulated by Rod Beckstrom, the former director of the US National Cybersecurity Center and president and CEO of the Internet Corporation for Assigned Names and Numbers (ICANN), stating, "The value of a network equals the net value added to each user's transactions (t) conducted through that network, summed over all users." The math is different because it's t that matters, not n. Beckstrom's own example can give some insight: "If it costs $26 to buy the book in a store or $16 to buy it over the Internet, including shipping, the net value is $10."[10] Sum up all those values for all the users, and you have Beckstrom's network value, which could be massive.

But, massive is not always better, as even a network can break down rapidly under excess strain. In a social construct, if you have a high number of Facebook friends because you're a bit of a popular guy, like Bill Gates, the value of the network will diminish quickly with an overwhelming number of notifications and requests. When that happens, the page will likely be ignored or deleted. Indeed, this happened to Bill Gates in 2009. His personal page generated so much activity that the site couldn't keep up with the maintenance. He now uses a Facebook Page (facebook.com/BillGates) and has over 14 million likes. Understandable response.

---

[10] Beckstrom, Rod (2009), "Beckstrom's Law & the Economics of Networks." Retrieved March 7, 2015, from http://www.slideshare.net/RodBeckstrom/beckstroms-law-the-economics-of-networks-icann.

Based on these four major schools of thought, designers can consider a variety of ways to think about the power of networks:

1. Sheer number of communication connections (Metcalfe's Law)
2. Reach as a medium of broadcast (Sarnoff's Law)
3. Ability to enable affinity groups (Reed's Law)
4. Optimization of the connections in the network (Beckstrom's Law)

How a designer chooses to assess network value is really up to the sponsor, the project constraints, and the best fit for the goals. Depending on the context, the appropriate use of any of these models can help unlock the value of design on the network in a more general capacity. What these laws lend to our understanding about our beliefs about how the smart city works, should work, and actually works from a network perspective will demonstrate one or all of these ideas. Most importantly, if designers believe that success just means scaling up to massive numbers of users, then they are in danger of losing focus on the value and benefit of those connections. In fact, they may make life worse for existing users of the network or system.

12.3 Sociospatial Perspectives

This book has attempted to challenge how we think about smart city design, advocating for a more human perspective and for using empathetic design processes to help direct innovation to move that point of view forward. At the same time, if we think about the city as a network of nodes—both of the hardware and human varieties—then we must seek the quantitative value derived by the use of network analytics to help us accelerate our efforts, measure the impacts of our designs, and quickly respond and rework them when necessary. Two forms of analysis are immediately helpful, including social and spatial analysis. While both spatial and social network analysis techniques are tools that use various graph-based analysis to shed light on our virtual and physical environments, they are less often employed together. As we have discussed at great length, social space generates change in our urban environment. But social space is more than a producer; it's also a product of the interactions between our built environment and our social actions. And most critically, social processes are no longer influenced by just our behaviors in space; they're also affected by our behaviors in place (more on this in a bit).

The bottom line is that our urban world is now both virtual and physical, and our analysis of both social and spatial network behaviors can help us design and measure the effectiveness of our plans as they relate to life in the urban space. The way we utilize space in our cities directly informs our social relationships. Spatial and social network analysis tools are not well integrated to comprehend people within the spaces they inhabit (especially in the context of digital relationships) such that one can draw meaningful conclusions about how our converged world will evolve.

12.3.1 People in Space, Before Place

Advancing the study of people's social relationships through the discipline of human geography may be key to fully realizing a deep and useful understanding of people in the digital communications network, especially in the smart city. Such studies find that particular communities and cultures place boundaries around their relationships, in both space and place. Like many academic disciplines, human geography is a domain that contains a variety of influential theories, philosophical systems, and political persuasions; however, it is also very diverse. Thus, this pursuit of human geography has been home to feminists, Marxists, and nearly every cultural model from which a methodology or system of measurement can be extracted. It is nowhere more pointed than in the urban environment. Truly, every historian who tells a complete story of people must describe the inhabitants of their world within their geographic space, knowing that whenever someone desires to describe a connection between physical and human properties, they are foraging into both physical and social arrangements. Human geographers have taken on animals, economics, population, politics, and, of course, rural and urban settlements. This is not a new field of study, but digital social networks have evolved quite quickly and their forces are creating new contexts that have not been well addressed, especially the collapse of virtual interactions on our physical spaces and places.

There is a difference between space and place, and it will increasingly become more than an academic concern for urban designers working with people in the context of the Internet of Things. April McCabe, an expert in the field of placemaking processes, managed to very simply state what can become a mind-bending conundrum. She says, "Space is one-dimensional and is only a physical location. Place, however is multi-layered and subjective. It is created when the physical attributes, emotional connections, and psychological perceptions are combined to impart individual meaning and value."[11] Thus, it is understood that a single space may be a setting for a multitude of places, in much the same way that a gallery can be used for a book club, an art show, or a cocktail party. Are we designing for spaces, places, or both? Many urban designers and technology solutions providers conflate the two, and it is part of the reason we fall into the trap of settling on designs that capture efficiencies of scale instead of flow.

12.3.2 Patient Zero

Epidemiology is a familiar and important use of spatial analysis, as described in Figure 12.4, where Dr. John Snow tracked an outbreak of cholera that spurred important new techniques for mapping the spread of disease and developing strategies to improve healthcare delivery. In London's Soho district, there was a terrible outbreak of cholera in 1854. At the time, the transmission of infection was not well understood and the outbreak was blamed on miasma theory (bad air). Since Louis Pasteur had not yet posited germ theory (that wasn't until 1861), Snow and Reverend Henry Whitehead talked to residents to help identify a centrally located water pump as the source of infection. The pump was built within feet of a leaking cesspool, causing fecal contamination of the water. Snow and Whitehead used their interview results to establish an understanding of the distribution of the infected cases that caused the authorities to finally remove the pump handle and end the outbreak.

Snow went on to create a map that showed this distribution, revealing that the most cases of cholera occurred where the closest available water source was the Broad Street pump. Interestingly, there was one

---

[11] McCabe, April (n.d.), "Space vs. Place: Defining the Difference." Retrieved March 6, 2015, from http://www.placepartners.com.au/blog/space-vs-place-defining-difference.

Figure 12.4 Dr. John Snow's map of cholera cases in the 1854 Broad Street cholera outbreak.[12]

confounding anomaly in the map, which was the monastery where none of the monks fell ill. Later, it was noted that the monks drank only beer, and likely the fermentation of the water for the brew made the beer far safer to drink than the supposedly fresh water from the pump. It should also be noted that Snow's theory was debunked and rejected by government officials as being far too unpleasant to be true.

The evolution of the field of epidemiology also provides a good case study for us to understand how a variety of fields will contribute to the overall usefulness of a particular form of analysis. Thus, to understand

[12] Image retrieved from the public domain at http://en.wikipedia.org/wiki/ Spatial_analysis#mediaviewer/File:Snow-cholera-map.jpg.

the conditions of disease and how it transmits, we consult the fields of biology, ecology, economics, and, of course, advanced techniques such as remote sensing and computational advancements such as fractals and scale invariance.

Our capacity to study vector-borne diseases in the city is just one important example of how we must accommodate the movement of human beings in continuous space, not between a single point or two, such as home or work, but at every point in between. If we want to understand human activity in the city, then we won't just study data at one sensor; we'll draw from myriad sensors and many other datasets. Further, if we only analyze people in the city based on the realities of physical space and not a deeper understanding of place, we immediately lose the importance of other connections within the system. Instead, we are opening the door to seeing our social relationships in new ways that free us to design in a manner that no longer views social proximity and physical proximity as one and the same. By exploring social phenomena in a way that comprehends both space and place, the depth of our study and potential impact of our designs grows.

Chapter Thirteen

Smart Cities: Problem or Promise?

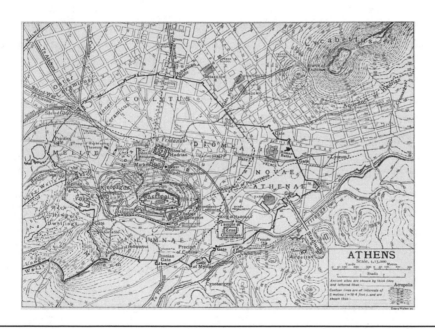

The Acropolis in ancient Athens, as shown in the 1911 *Encyclopædia Britannica*.[1]

[1] Image retrieved from the public domain at http://en.wikisource.org/wiki/1911_Encyclopædia_Britannica/Athens_(Greece).

13.1 Chapter Goal

In this final chapter of the book, we explore concluding thoughts about the tension between technology and design, and discuss the ways in which tension between private and public enterprise can be resolved for the intelligent management of our cities. Further, we explore the case study of Apple and how its commitment to human-centric design drove one of the most successful companies across the globe, and how we can tap into its principles in creating successful and innovative technology-enabled urban environments that consider the goals of people first, and technology second.

13.2 Forging a Partnership

In the first chapter of the book, we defined the term "smart city" as the new urban environment, one that's designed for performance through information and communications technologies (ICTs) and other forms of physical capital. Intelligent management of resources in the smart city is intended to drive a higher quality of life for citizens, drive down waste, and improve economic conditions. Yet, the ICT-enabled infrastructure of the smart city is often the focus of intelligent city design, while the important role of people has been denied, overlooked, or simply forgotten. It is undeniable that when the technology of the smart city is considered alone—without thought for the people who live in the environment—missteps of terrific scale have occurred, including failed showcase ecocities and one-size-fits-all approaches to creating sustainable living environments.

We have also discussed new ways of thinking about people in urban environments, as well as new ways to address their challenges and build technologically advanced smart cities that fully comprehend human living. Using design thinking, a human-centered approach to innovation, urban designers can create new products and processes that are well grounded in empathy. In fact, design thinking is really a cocreation process that is inspired by and also embraces rationality. The goal is that we will spend our precious resources—economic, human, and natural—on not just solving problems but on solving the right problems. Problems that matter. Because, if it's not clear yet to even the most humble reader of history, technical innovation—no matter how profound—will not in and of itself bring an end to scarcity or suffering. Still, technologically based tools, when directed in the service of shared cultural values, can help drive forward an urban agenda where the physical objects we have and hold—from the smallest sensor to the tallest skyscraper—are extended to improve the lives of people and communities.

Thus, if in reading this book, you were seeking an inventory of smart technologies, sensor types, and protocols and were hoping to learn how to place and position them in the smart city for maximum efficiency and analytical possibilities, you are surely disappointed. A catalog of technologies will never fulfill the promise of the smart city, in that engineering is almost always a reaction to a problem that involves hypothesis and logic. But that's not a sustainable strategy over the long term; people change, as do their circumstances, and more and more often, it's technology that is the seed of those changes. A design perspective provides a better path forward toward the goals that the smart city vision promises.

13.2.1 Human-Centered Design Is More Than Post-It Notes

Wireframes, agile, scrum, and the river of discarded Post-it Notes sacrificed in the name of "iterative" development can quickly become gimmicky implementations of design thinking used to justify high consulting chargebacks and company valuations. Extreme implementation practices are the bane of many great ideas, and design thinking isn't immune. The design-thinking process is much more complex than an expression of causal interest in human behavior. Design thinkers are relentlessly obsessed and curious about why things happen the way the do. They observe people, talk to them, hear their stories, and look at their adaptations to gain insights about how they can design a product that helps people reach their goals, often unspoken. It can be an intensely uncomfortable, creative, and profound process.

This messiness is a terrible and frightening prospect to traditional companies, which are accustomed to a nice, linear, and rational process from go to launch. Design-thinking projects may start with an idea for a product, but an overly codified process from there will be rejected by most participants. Even with the prospect of possible chaos, frustration, the creative process really must break from the formulaic. However, it is still vitally important that for ideas to become anything, proper constraints, solution refinement, and execution are key.

13.3 Create an Ecosystem

If we strive to codify design thinking in our product organizations or government processes like a Six Sigma or agile approach, we will undoubtedly fail to meet expectations. Continuing to attack problems in the smart city with technology-centric project management approaches will surely result in short-lived success. Design thinking does deliver, but so does business thinking. We say we want more innovation, but we don't want the big mess. We don't want prototypes; we want products. Here's the truth: design thinking does not deliver anywhere close to what the realities of business demand, especially in the context of city governments, but without new ways of thinking, business quickly becomes stagnant. Still, there is a way to implement design thinking with accessible positive impact to the business, and it has been done to the level of profound success. The creativity afforded by the design-thinking process must also respect the context of business, financial, and marketing constraints. Design thinking can bring breakthrough concepts to our cities, and those solutions will come from business leaders who champion a culture of innovation and want to deliver that innovation to their customers.

13.3.1 Thirty-Four Thousand Apples an Hour Keeps the Doctor Away

In 1999, as Apple skirted the edges of implosion, Microsoft was at a record high. In 2015, Apple is now twice as big as Microsoft. Many say it's because Steve Jobs was more visionary, that he was able to better predict the impact of mobility—a computer in every pocket. This is in part correct, but Jobs was also an unabashed lover of craft and believed that beautiful design mattered, because things should not only work, they should be desired. His strategy flew in the face of the prevailing wisdom for most software companies: to get out of the hardware business. But, he didn't and Apple won't. They still own their products (and thus, the product experience) end to end, because Jobs wanted everything about his company's devices to be perfect.

Early Macintosh users embraced this philosophy, despite the jokes about the expensive, bulbous, childlike devices with the "happy Mac" face. But now it seems that the human-centric approach has paid off. Apple has not only found its stride, it has also crushed every expectation that the public markets held for it. Many PC users have fled Microsoft, and despite the fact that Bill Gates and the now-deceased Steve Jobs—and by proxy their companies—shared both an intense rivalry and affection, even Gates the Engineer still seems surprised. While they have copied each other, sued each other, yet purportedly maintained a friendship that began in the 1970s, it wasn't until quite recently that Gates said, "[Jobs'] sense of design, that everything had to fit a certain aesthetic, the fact that he, with as little engineering background as he had—it shows that design can lead you in a certain direction so that phenomenal products came out of it."[2] Even that statement seems to miss the mark slightly, as Jobs himself said in 2003, "Design is not just what it looks like and feels like. Design is how it works."[3]

It's impossible to argue with 34,000 iPhone sales an hour and a market capitalization of nearly US$700 billion as reported by the *New York Times* in January 2015.[4] The facts of Apple's success are very clear, yet the lessons of how the company got there are sometimes muddled. Firstly, there were many committed players behind the scenes, from investors to employees, and there was and continues to be a remarkable level of passion. But why? Perhaps it was because Apple was never about producing computers; it was always about designing them.

Mark Markkula, a name heard much less often than Steve Jobs', was one of the first investors in Apple. He wrote a memo known as "The Apple Marketing Philosophy," which describes approaches and principles that every designer must, at the very least, know about, if not suck deep into her marrow. Not because iPhones, despite their cost, sell at an inordinate

---

[2] Kiss, Jemima (2013), "Bill Gates: Steve Jobs and I Grew Up Together," *The Guardian*. Retrieved March 13, 2015, from http://www.theguardian.com/technology/2013/may/13/bill-gates-steve-jobs-apple-microsoft.

[3] Steve Jobs (n.d.), Wikiquote. Retrieved March 13, 2015, from http://en.wikiquote.org/wiki/Steve_Jobs.

[4] Stewart, James B. (2015), "How, and Why, Apple Overtook Microsoft," *The New York Times*. Retrieved March 13, 2015, from http://www.nytimes.com/2015/01/30/business/how-and-why-apple-overtook-microsoft.html?_r=0.

rate worldwide, but because people covet them, to the extent that in 2010, a man lost one of his fingers when a thief tore an iPad out of his hands as he was leaving an Apple Store in Denver, Colorado. Tarps, tents, and lawn chairs litter the streets for days as consumers line up for the newest iPhone release. Windows 95 surely never acquired gawking media attention, but Apple does it over and over again. And it is because from its very inception, Apple brought an attitude that it could and should understand what consumers needed before they actually knew they had the need. The company knew that if it did its job right, people would more than want its products; they would crave them.

Markkula captured the functions of this desire when he wrote (somewhat awkwardly) a one-page paper that contained three principles that have come to define the Apple Computer experience. They are interpreted here as the following:

- *Empathy.* Apple must create an "intimate connection" with the feelings of its customers.
- *Focus.* To do that, Apple must "eliminate unimportant opportunities."
- *Impute* (a strange but effective way to describe how detailed attention to an experience can make a lifetime customer). A great product isn't enough; everything must be presented in a "creative and professional manner, [to] impute the desired qualities."[5]

13.3.2 Putting a Philosophy to Work

Clearly, Jobs had a natural inclination toward the principles of design thinking way before it became a process that many would seek to adopt, and Markkula had a way of expressing that fact in a manner that would carry Jobs' vision to the market. It was a potent combination. Today, the idea of empathizing with people should no longer be a conceptual leap, but it is. Not because we don't get it, but because it is not easy to quantify. That makes adopting the principles of design thinking a difficulty in the context of traditional product development techniques (where economies of scale come into play), where we are attempting to bring

[5] Kuang, Cliff (2011), "The 6 Pillars of Steve Jobs's Design Philosophy," Fast Co. Design. Retrieved March 14, 2015, from http://www.fastcodesign. com/1665375/the-6-pillars-of-steve-jobss-design-philosophy.

together advanced technologies and human forces. The end result is that for many companies, product managers, designers, and city planners, we tend toward the ease of doing *for* people instead of doing *with* people. We resolve to accept the inevitable resistance that bubbles up even for the most innocuous technological innovations (for example, smart meters). We become our own worst enemies, and a fertile breeding ground for the dystopian visions that pit man against machine at the expense of improving our daily urban lives with the benefit of technology.

But Apple's vision (clearly a successful one from the perspective of both shareholders and design aficionados) was remarkably simple; it only had three steps. Step 1, develop an intimate understanding of how people are; what they're doing, feeling, and coping with; and how you can serve them in their lives. Step 2, focus on designing something that provides that service. Step 3, respect the people you are serving and care about them, and whenever your work jeopardizes your ability to maintain that intimacy (see step 1), stop it. Figure 13.1 illustrates the virtuous cycle.

It is the principle of intimacy that first drew Apple to its use of physical metaphor on Apple interfaces (where we interpret the data through our five senses), especially the iPhone and iPad. Over time, the Apple

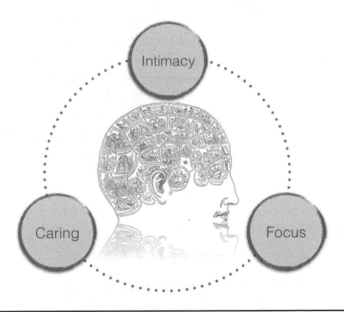

Figure 13.1 The Apple marketing philosophy. [Wells, Samuel (1870), "Symbolical Head, Illustrating the Natural Language of the Faculties," How to Read Character, p. 36, Wells Publishing, New York.]

vision has helped the company's devices meet us halfway, closer to the way we actually move through the world. Apple's designs reduce the friction between us and our technologies; they even allow us to explore our real world through with a very high level of fidelity. And in this way, our smart devices seem to fully comprehend our actual lives (even if not always perfectly).

But why the treatise on Apple? Because there is a reason this book has not been filled with case studies or positive examples of how to apply design thinking to the problems of our cities: there are very few such examples. Even massive investment in ecocities has done little to motivate people's interest in improving their lives, certainly not in the way that global positioning system (GPS) and map applications on our phones have. Or an app that allows me to buy train tickets from the cab on the way to Gare du Nord for a last-minute meeting in Amsterdam. Yet, it isn't because as a world of concerned people we don't have a vision for smart cities. We do. But except for rare exceptions, it's just a bag of loosely coupled ideals at this point, and where it is not ideals, it is ideas about how to extend an existing product line. And our own governments are not even sure how to engage.

Unfortunately, we just have not defined well or fully what the problems are in each of our unique cities (that is, when we even recognize them) and worse, we do not express succinct goals. Apple showed us how a willingness and commitment to people first, then technology, can bring unprecedented success. But we continue to take the opposite tack. We don't have a coherent or cohesive vision yet about how technology will serve the people of the city because we haven't developed enough breadth or depth of understanding about what the goals are for people living in an urban environment. That understanding will help translate the high-level vision of efficiency and optimization in transportation, or in improved systems for reaching the poor; better access to food and healthcare; and more-efficient use of our natural resources in communities, public places, and buildings that promote productivity and joy.

13.4 Crossing the Chasm of Fear

Our lack of desire to tackle human problems in design isn't the sole fault of a cabal of engineers who are afflicted somehow and can only make high-tech products that are kludgy. That's certainly true for the dominant subculture of Nerd, but it's much deeper than that. It is because our history and culture have driven a wedge between art and technology. The idea that technology is dangerous is not new. It is a persistent part of the global psyche that has dominated literature and movies for hundreds of years, beginning with myths like the fall from Eden, where a different sort of apple represents the temptation of knowledge and its role in isolating us from our loved ones. Films like *Robocop*, *The Matrix*, *Terminator*, *Avatar*, and *The Hunger Games* teach us to intensely fear technological progress. We fear oppression, technological dependence, and technological singularity. And we're always on guard against the unfathomable loss of intellectual capacity and control to artificial intelligence.

At the root of it, perhaps many of us fear the loss of our humanity, and our cultural artifacts seem to underscore that truth. Psychologists, philosophers, economists, conspiracy theorists, and the news media all weigh in on this topic with little coherent impact, yet we barely understand the terms-of-use policies we click "agree" to every time we access a new Internet property or purchase a digital product. We don't know where our personal information is going; how it's being accessed, used, analyzed, or repackaged; who's getting it; or how it's getting there. So we certainly can't understand our personal relationship to advanced technologies. Instead, we get black and white thinking. Our smart cities are either going to be all good or all bad, depending on who you ask, yet we lack dialogue on the important issues raised or a willingness to develop a framework that will help attenuate some of the more dramatic, fear-driven concerns that provoke an equally shrill technophiliac response. This is the reason that developers have chosen to build smart cities from scratch, bottom up, and hope that people will adapt. Alternatively, they try to sneak in technological systems through the "social good" meme.

These cultural tendencies will not be easily buried, and perhaps rightly so, as our systems of policy and governance are so far behind the forward pace of our technological capabilities. We persist in reinforcing our fears at the movies, in the books we read, the media we consume, the music we play, and the documentaries we watch about how our food is killing us, the government is spying on us, and the electric company can extract our most private habits by watching our consumption behaviors. While we, like Theodore in the 2013 movie *Her*, fall in love with our operating systems, we struggle against our proclivity to outright reject technological advancements because they're an existential threat to our very survival, an affront to the biological imperative.

And yet we are terribly inconsistent. Although we worry that one day we will be less than human at the hands of IBM Watson, we can't tear our ears away from Stephen Hawking's squawk box, and we dab tears from our eyes when we watch YouTube videos of people with cochlear implants who hear their child's voice for the first time. We applaud Olympic athletes with prosthetic limbs or listen slack-jawed to a colorblind man tell his story about what it's like to see blue for the first time through specially designed lenses. We do not deride people who install insulin pumps or heart stents as less than human for the technological reparations; we are fascinated; we are grateful; we are excited about how future cures will save our own bodies and those of our loved ones. We marvel at how technology enriches our lives and how it can even make us more than who we would be without it. We reminisce with every elementary school friend we find on Facebook. But in the back of our minds, we wonder when the next Edward Snowden will emerge with a nightmare story of how we are nothing more than floating specks in some National Security Agency (NSA) crucible. And then, we click "like."

What does all this have to do with human-centered design thinking? It reminds us that human beings are messy and fickle, and when it comes to technology, we can become supremely conflicted and confused. Every day, we fall further out of touch with advanced technologies and how they work and what they're doing. Even software engineers and app designers don't know anymore. As software has become more open and layered, we've stopped writing our own routines and use other people's work. We don't want to know how something works if all we want is to extract some interesting content from it. And when there are bugs, we hope someone in the "community" will fix it. This allows us to bring new ideas to fruition more quickly, incrementally, and show progress where we must to our financial investors, Wall Street, our managers, and our customers. But beneath this reality is a paradox: that technology takes away from our experience of living as much as it adds to it.

13.5 How Design Thinking Can Work for the Smart City

Jesper Christiansen, research manager at MindLab, works on themes related to transforming policy development and public service. At a talk at New York University's Governance Lab (GovLab), he spoke about the value of human-centered design and its role in promoting citizen relationships with the government. He commented that the design process "helps public servants understand the needs of the people and communities they are designing for, create innovative approaches to respond to these needs and deliver solutions and services designed to address the specific contexts of users."[6] When faced with a looming gap between what the urban citizen wants and needs and the ability of the public system to deliver it, any opportunity to reconnect people with their community and their government is an advantage.

But, in a world where every product strategy is tied to corporate growth and city governments are more inclined to hire consultants and solutions providers to smarten the city, we are building a world that cannibalizes its own efforts and products. It is, in fact, a habit for many companies to eat their own young—even Apple has shown an appetite to drive its designs into a shallow grave (consider the iPod-to-iPhone transition for music storage and play) when they no longer serve the corporate strategy. In this environment, genuine opportunity for innovation becomes difficult. While it is a fair and reasonable strategy to seek the low-hanging fruit in testing out the impact of technology, cities are expensive and extensive operations. We can't walk in one day with a technology solution that might work and then rip it out the next day when it fails to meet our expectations. With design thinking, every problem in the smart city becomes a solutions-oriented approach to solving customer problems, even if the answer is to put sensors on every underground train that no human traveler will ever notice.

It is not useful to assume that design thinking is contrary to engineer-driven approaches, because the failure of a poorly conceived project is substantial. And when spending taxpayer dollars, it is never more important to recognize that design thinking helps mitigate risks through rapid, iterative improvements. Pivoting before the big bets get made requires that local government play a role in their development of new applications and services, especially because private consumer product companies are necessarily motivated by revenue, not public policy goals. Michael Hanlon,

---

[6] Longo, Justin (2014), "Jesper Christiansen: Applying Human-Centered Design to Public Problems," blog post, GovLab, New York University. Retrieved March 15, 2015, from http://thegovlab.org/jesper-christiansen-govlab-luncheon.

a science journalist and coauthor of *In the Interests of Safety: The Absurd Rules that Blight Our Lives and How We Can Change Them*, says it most succinctly: "When wealth accumulates so spectacularly by doing nothing, there is less impetus to invest in genuine innovation."[7]

When corporate growth becomes the sole progenitor of innovation—which requires rapid obsolescence to move a consumer through new product releases—then the opportunity for truly revolutionary design becomes lost to the pump-and-dump development cycle of profiteering. Human-centered design frustrates this model because it requires designers to reflect on a situation, conduct research that is often quite in-depth, and be comfortable with the fact the early iterations of the design will be wrong and often may do more to cull out what isn't working than what is. Bluntly, it takes resolve. And if you have it in your cities or in the bowels of your product company, you open yourself up to the extraordinary. But if it's done halfway, with a small appetite for experimentation, multiple perspectives, and teamwork, "ineffective" only mildly captures the debased use of this powerful tool.

13.6 So, You Want to Design a Smarter City?

There is a Talmudic saying that goes something like this: "We do not see things as they are, we see things as we are." Unfortunately, many technology-oriented designers seem to chant this as their mantra. If we want to design vibrant urban environments that serve all people in their purview, we must see things as they are and not as we want them to be. With design thinking, we are enabled to take a new stance, one that represents behaviors and attitudes that are often very different from our own. Design thinking allows us to improve ideas and designs over and over until they work, which means they serve some need. To some, this feels like a wildly optimistic approach, and it is, because it allows us to see potential. Design thinking opposes the development of a hypothesis because that approach depends on diluting down very complex realities to something flat and featureless that can be easily stated and framed.

[7] Hanlon, Michael (2014), "Why Has Human Progress Ground to a Halt?" Aeon. Retrieved March 15, 2015, from http://aeon.co/magazine/science/why-has-human-progress-ground-to-a-halt.

In 1969, Herbert A. Simon wrote *The Sciences of the Artificial*, where he shared his thoughts about design thinking. He described the approach as a way of transforming the current state into a preferred one, specifically one that could create an improved future. He wrote, "Design thinking is a creative process based around the 'building up' of ideas. There are no judgments in design thinking. This eliminates the fear of failure and encourages maximum input and participation. Wild ideas are welcome, since these often lead to the most creative solutions. Everyone is a designer, and design thinking is a way to apply design methodologies to any of life's situations."[8]

So you want to design a smart city. If you are an engineer, planner, or simply a rational person and you picked up this book asking, "How do I do this?," then you are surely disappointed. Of course we want our cities to be efficient and resource-savvy, we want good transportation systems, we want everyone to have easy access to food and healthcare. Hardly anyone would disagree with these general principles. It's only when we start proposing ideas that many points of view will emerge. First, we must think about why. Why is it important that our cities are healthy, operate energy efficiently, provide good food to their people, and offer safe ways for inhabitants to travel to and from work? Because globalization has brought economic changes and the city dwellers are coming. They need homes, jobs, community, culture, and positive environmental conditions.

In every possible application of technology in the smart city, the goal must be to create a place where decisions are easier to make, potential problems are proactively managed, and our resources are carefully allocated. In our cities, we live, work, learn, eat, socialize, exercise, take the train, and depend on a cohesive system of public safety that includes everything from traffic lights to law enforcement. Many people will be born and die in our cities. We must consider the revolutionary impact of technology and the data that we both generate and consume in the urban form. How we build our smart cities are best borne of our conclusions for how we can most fortuitously link people with the natural and built environments. These decisions will inalterably and dramatically shape the lives of the majority of our global citizens.

[8] Verity, Julie (2012), *The New Strategic Landscape: Innovative Perspectives on Strategy*, p. 53, Palgrave Macmillan, London. Retrieved May 20, 2015, from https://books.google.com/books?id=-sgs4sCIt_0C&pgis=1.

Section Four

Key Points

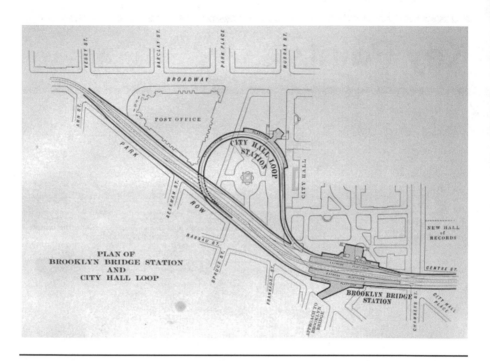

Schematic of the New York City City Hall Loop, designed by Rafael Guastavino in 1904.[*]

Section Four

Key Points

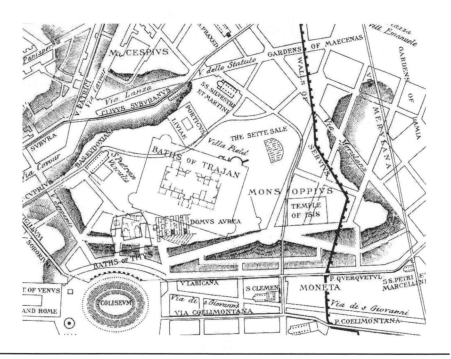

Pianta della Regio III, Isis et Serapis, da Rodolfo Lanciani; the ruins and excavations of ancient Rome, 1897.[1]

---

[1] Image retrieved from the public domain at http://commons.wikimedia.org/wiki/File:Pianta_regio_III_da_Lanciani.jpg

Chapter Twelve

<hr>

When designing for the urban environment, planners must elicit stories from the people they're designing for in order to participate in an act of cocreation. Only then can designers gain an appropriate and useful point of view on the problem they're addressing.

<hr>

Designing for Inspiration

- Designers and technology-oriented solutions providers rarely collaborate. Cities have complexities and challenges that can be treated with disruptive technologies, but nontechnological strategies must also be considered in order to build sustainable, purposeful solutions.
- By reframing urban challenges in a way that improves the value of what we learn from analytics, design-thinking practices can dramatically improve the way that data drives new insights. Equally, analytics validate the value of human-centric innovation.
- As much as technologists need to think about the people whom their applications both serve and impact, designers can gain inspiration and validation from data-driven information.

Understanding Networks

<hr>

Network theory helps us understand evolving patterns and connections in the city. The ability to analyze both individual choices and those in aggregate is key to the efficient use of our resources; it's also critical to understanding how the choices of people change as their social graph evolves.

<hr>

- Based on the work of Leonhard Euler (1707–1783) and his solution to the problem of seven bridges, we have learned to abstract very hard data problems and solve them based on these early foundations for network theory.
- By observing nodal relationships spatially, in a manner that is unaffected by the shapes or sizes of the nodes themselves, we filter out irrelevant information that gives human cognition a boost.

- Considering the fundamentals of the network graph, we can begin to study people in situations where they interact and affect one another. In the smart city, our graphs can reveal specifically which influences cause people to commit certain actions based on their desired outcome.

We Are People in Space and Place

Designers who understand how network connections actually work, how a specific design might be implemented or scaled, and how these designs might impact the city will create as-of-yet unconceived or unidentified forms of value.

- Based on four major schools of thought about valuing a network, city planners and product designers can consider a variety of ways to think about the power of connection within their designs:
  - Sheer number of communication connections (Metcalfe's Law)
  - Reach as a medium of broadcast (Sarnoff's Law)
  - Ability to enable affinity groups (Reed's Law)
  - Optimization of the connections in the network (Beckstrom's Law)

- How a designer chooses to assess network value is really up to the sponsor, the project constraints, and the best fit for the goals. Depending on the context, the appropriate use of any of these models can help unlock design potential.

Chapter Thirteen

Forging a Partnership

>◇◇◇◇◇◇◇◇◇◇◇◇◇◇◇◇◇◇◇◇◇◇◇◇◇◇◇◇◇◇◇◇
>
> *The tension between technology and design must be resolved if we are going to create successful collaborations between private and public enterprise that improve the outcomes of our urban environments.*
>
> ◇◇◇◇◇◇◇◇◇◇◇◇◇◇◇◇◇◇◇◇◇◇◇◇◇◇◇◇◇◇◇◇

- Enabled by information and communications technologies, the smart city infrastructure is often the focus of intelligent city design, while the important role of people has been denied, overlooked, or simply forgotten. When the technology of the smart city is considered alone—without thought for the people who live in the environment—missteps of terrific scale will occur.
- Technical innovation—no matter how profound—will not in and of itself bring an end to scarcity or suffering. Instead, technologically based tools, directed in the service of shared cultural values, can improve the lives of people and communities.
- Technology alone will never fulfill the promise of the smart city, as engineering is almost always a reaction to a problem that involves applying hypothesis and logic to human problems. But people change, as do their circumstances, and more and more often, it's technology that is the seed of those changes.

Human-Centered Design Is a Little Messy

> ◇◇◇◇◇◇◇◇◇◇◇◇◇◇◇◇◇◇◇◇◇◇◇◇◇◇◇◇◇◇◇◇
>
> *Designers observe people, talk to them, hear their stories, and examine their adaptations to gain insight into how they can design a product that helps people reach their goals, often unspoken. It can be an intensely uncomfortable, creative, and profound process.*
>
> ◇◇◇◇◇◇◇◇◇◇◇◇◇◇◇◇◇◇◇◇◇◇◇◇◇◇◇◇◇◇◇◇

- Project messiness is a terrible and frightening prospect to traditional companies, which are accustomed to a nice, linear, and rational process from go to launch. Design-thinking projects may start with an idea for a product, but an overly codified process from there will be rejected by most participants.

- If we strive to codify design thinking in the product organization or in government processes, we will undoubtedly fail to meet expectations. Yet, if we continue to attack problems in the smart city with technology-centric approaches, success will be short-lived.
- The creativity afforded by the design-thinking process must also respect the context of business, financial, and marketing constraints.

Rising Above Fear for the Benefit of the People

Our lack of desire to tackle human problems can't be blamed solely on engineering philosophy. We must also realize that our history and culture have driven a wedge between art and technology. We need to reframe this perspective to move forward.

- The idea that technology is dangerous is not new. It is a persistent part of the global psyche that has dominated literature and movies for hundreds of years, beginning with myths like the fall from Eden, where we find the temptation of knowledge as the key factor that isolates us from our loved ones.
- We tend toward black and white thinking, where smart cities are either going to be all good or all bad, depending on who you ask. Yet, we lack dialogue on the important issues raised or a willingness to develop a framework that will help attenuate some of the more dramatic, fear-driven concerns that provoke us.
- While we may have differences in approach, we can converge in our solutions if we consider that every possible application of technology in the smart city must be focused on the goal of creating a place where decisions are easier to make, potential problems are proactively managed, and our resources are carefully allocated.

Glossary

Chapter 1

GDP   gross domestic product
ICT   information and communication technologies
NSA   National Security Administration
US   United States

Chapter 2

6LowPAN   IPv6 over Low power Wireless Personal Area Networks
CCTV   closed-circuit television
CO_2 carbon dioxide
GPS   global positioning system
IBM   International Business Machines
IoE   Internet of Everything
IoT   Internet of Things
IP   Internet Protocol
RFID   Radio Frequency Identification
US   United States

Chapter 3

CRC   Community Research Connections
DoD   Department of Defense

EU	European Union
GPS	global positioning system
KAL	Korean Airlines
LED	light-emitting diode
NASA	National Aeronautics and Space Administration
NAVSTAR	Navigation Satellite Timing & Ranging
US	United States
USSR	Union of Soviet Socialist Republics

Chapter 4

ESPN	Entertainment and Sports Programming Network
IM	Impossible Mission
MBA	Master of Business Administration
MFA	Master of Fine Arts
VHS	Video Home System

Chapter 5

CPTED	crime prevention through environmental design
DOC	Designing Out Crime
GDP	gross domestic product
GPS	global positioning system
ICT	information and communications technology
SMS	Short Message Service
WSN	wireless sensor network

Chapter 6

DSM	demand-side management
GDP	gross domestic product
GPS	global positioning system
ICT	information and communications technology
IoT	Internet of Things
LED	light-emitting diode
M2M	machine to machine

Chapter 7

BMS	building management system
CCTV	closed-circuit TV
CO_2	carbon dioxide
GDP	gross domestic product
HVAC	heating, ventilation, and air conditioning
ICT	information and communications technology
IHD	in-home display
IoT	Internet of Things
IP	Internet Protocol
IT-OT	information technology–operations technology convergence
MPG	miles per gallon
M2M	machine to machine
NGOs	nongovernment organizations
PHEV	plug-in hybrid electric vehicle
REAP	Renewable Energy Alaska Project
RMI	Rocky Mountain Institute

Chapter 8

API	application programming interface
CCTV	closed-circuit TV
EU	European Union
ICT	information communications technology
ITS	intelligent transport system
GPS	global positioning system
HTT	Hyperloop Transportation Technologies
LoDo	Lower Downtown
RFID	radio frequency identification
VMT	vehicle miles traveled

Chapter 9

API	application programming interface
CCTV	closed-circuit TV

COTS	commercial off-the-shelf
DHS	Department of Homeland Security
ICT	information and communications technology
IoT	Internet-of-Things
MMC	Media Monitoring Capability
NOC	National Operations Center
ROI	return on investment

Chapter 10

CCTV	closed-circuit TV
ICT	information and communications technology
OECD	Organisation for Economic Co-operation and Development

Chapter 11

CIA	confidentiality, integrity, and availability
EPA	Environmental Protection Agency
FAA	Federal Aviation Administration
FBI	Federal Bureau of Investigation
FEMA	Federal Emergency Management Agency
HCI	human–computer interaction
HHS	Health and Human Services
ICT	information and communications technology
IoT	Internet of Things
IT	information technology
NASA	National Aeronautics and Space Administration
NOAA	National Oceanic and Atmospheric Administration
NSA	National Security Agency
PbD	Privacy by Design
TED	Technology, Entertainment and Design

Chapter 12

FOIL	Freedom of Information Law
GFN	group-forming network

NYC	New York City
ICANN	Internet Corporation for Assigned Names and Numbers
RCA	Radio Corporation of America
SNA	social network analysis

Chapter 13

ICT	information and communications technologies
GovLab	Governance Lab
GPS	global positioning system
NSA	National Security Agency

Index